The
New
Apocrypha

John Sladek

The
New
Apocrypha

A Guide to Strange Science and Occult Beliefs

Hart-Davis, MacGibbon   London

Granada Publishing Limited
First published in Great Britain 1973 by Hart-Davis, MacGibbon Ltd,
Frogmore, St Albans, Hertfordshire AL2 2NF,
and
3 Upper James Street, London W1R 4BP

ISBN 0 246 10715 4
Printed in Great Britain by
Fletcher & Son Ltd, Norwich

ACKNOWLEDGEMENTS

First, I'd like to thank Michael Moorcock, who originated the idea of this book and gave it a title. In its present form, it may well be only an underwater distortion of his idea, but here it is, Mike, and thanks.

I'd also like to thank Bob Marsden, *Bookends*, Langdon Jones and others for lending me obscure pseudo-scientific texts. For any errors of taste or judgement, and for any wrong-headed opinions, I have only myself to thank.

'Einstein and people like Einstein said that the Earth was flat.'
Lobsang Rampa

'"You are under the Holy Spirit. Over and out..." The next night, as I was sitting in the front yard, having magnetized a hamburger and eaten same...'
Robert Alexander

Contents

List of Illustrations

List of Tables

Science came into the world a couple of centuries ago, with a twin, pseudo-science, gripping its heel. Ever since, both have been manoeuvring to get our blessing: Science, by giving us gifts, and its twin, by a sly imposture.

Like blind Isaac, we dither, trying to make up our minds. The newspaper that carries moonshot pictures on the front page also carries the daily horoscope inside. Heart transplants and faith-healing are treated with equal seriousness by all but the most responsible papers – and even these can seldom resist a hot Loch Ness story.

Other media manage no better. The sales of occult books have never been better. TV producers splice together film of serious brain research with film of amateurs playing with their brain waves. Following the underground press, slick middle-brow magazines feature frequent articles on ESP, fad diets and spiritualism.

There are several reasons for dithering. First, anything that looks like science seems an impeccable source of truth. We invest the slightest hint from a laboratory with terrible signifi-cance. If a doctor indicates the possibility of a connection between cholesterol and heart disease, we rush out to buy corn-oil margarine. 'Any scientist will tell you ...' and 'science says' have become habitual ways of clinching any argu-ment.

Then there's the mystery of science. The entities of physics – quark, boson, maser – are as unknowable to most of us as anything produced in a spirit medium's cabinet, and the full name of Tobacco Mosaic Virus, Dahlemense Strain, which contains 1,185 letters ('Acetylseryltyrosylserylisoleucyl ...') might as well be glossolalia.

Galloping science fiction contributes its droppings to ferti-lizing our fantasies. Space travel, death rays and machine brains were once mere science fiction props. Now we can see similar inventions on television, itself a science fiction dream. Why then shouldn't the rest of the SF paraphernalia become real?

Why not time travel, parallel universes, gravity shields, bug-eyed monsters, invisibility and communication with the dead? Our imaginations are drunk with Future Now, and – unlike scientists – we see no obstacles.

Finally, all is not well with science. It is under attack for not having solved all our problems, for not having even attempted to solve many of them. It is called a tool of techno-cratic domination:

> The technocracy [is] that society in which those who govern justify themselves by appeal to technical experts who, in turn, justify themselves by appeal to scientific forms of knowledge. And beyond the authority of science, there is no appeal.[1]

It is said to be soulless – or rather, indifferent to the needs of the psyche. If a man has a job, a car, a house, a wife and a statistical number of children, if he has comforts like psycho-analysis, insurance and an electronic cigarette lighter, what more (asks the technocracy) can he need?

Well, science may yet develop a conscience, and scientists may yet come to realize that their final allegiance must be, not to company X or government Y, but to everyone. The indict-ment may yet have its effect.

Outside science, the message that science is unwell has filtered down to the ignorant as a garbled rumour: Science is dead. Some welcome the news as justification for the pseudo-science they've always believed in anyway. Others, led by Colin Wilson, find it an excuse for a wholehearted plunge into the occult.

So science ignores the spiritual man? Very well, turn to Theosophy, with its evolution of the soul. Science can't weigh and measure love? Very well, try Wilhelm Reich, with his careful measurements of the blue rays emitted during orgasm. Science says we can't go faster than light? Lobsang Rampa does it all the time. Science can't cure cancer? A thousand quick cures appear. If the modern Scripture seems to give as scientific law 'thou shalt not', a new Apocrypha says 'thou shalt and must'.

The chapters that follow are meant to show a representative sample of these new apocrypha. I try to describe them with a minimum of 'debunking', although I must confess in advance my own bias against many occult and pseudo-scientific claims. Nevertheless, the effort is made to distinguish between ideas which are off the beaten track and those which are simply off the rails.

I try to include a sample of just about everything. To name a few highlights: Atlantis, Bacon's ciphers in Shakespeare's plays, circle-squaring, dowsing, ESP, flat earth, the Great Pyramid, homeopathy, *I Ching*, junk myths, Koreshanity, Loch Ness, mediums, Nostradamus, organic food, perpetual motion, quasar codes, radiesthesia, Scientology, Ted Serios, UFOs, Velikovsky, Wilhelm Reich, X-ray vision, yeti and Zen macrobiotics.

Not included are witchcraft, satanism and some religious or philosophical systems, such as those of P. D. Ouspensky and Aleister Crowley, having little to do with physical causality. For different reasons I omit everyday superstitions about black cats and lucky 7; Martingales and other betting systems; and the private compulsive acts with which many people ornament their lives. These are too many and too dull to even list, outside a work on psychology.

Finally, I omit alchemy, which certainly qualifies as a pseudo-science. But most alchemical literature seems to be either historical (portraits of Paracelsus and Albertus Magnus) or else, well, like this:

> Here being the Thalamic giant icicles beginning to melt, but now the Prototyped Source of the Fiery Drip, of the New Virgin Sperming Atomic Grace. The unified Thalami now giving of a one-pointed vision, directing all Cranial nerves with its ever unfolding rebirth.
>
> Therefore the positive preambulance of the enciente aspiring compassion, is now born of reclassified Atomic preambulatory conscious conception.
>
> For by such mighty wealth having been taken through Time, and Merope's unification through molecularization in Relativity, the god had become a mighty Atom of Atomic fulness of Holy propensity.[2]

These samples are from an article in *Occult Gazette*, entitled 'The Focalization of the Yods as the Divine Stream of Tympanic Royalty'. I wish I could quote more of Gladys I. Spearman-Cook's splendid ultra-violet patches, but now it's time to descend from the Fiery Drip to good old flat terra firma.

Watch this Space

Flatland

Perhaps one day we'll colonize Mars. If so, one of the first signs that our colony is getting really civilized will be the formation of a Flat Mars Society. Indeed, the main purpose of our civilization may turn out to be just that: to spread flatness to the stars.

On our own planet, civilization is getting along nicely. Flat earthers are unperturbed by NASA's patent fakery, as they were never perturbed by ships that pretended to sink below the horizon.

About 1890, John Alexander Dowie founded the flat earth community of Zion, Illinois. He declared himself Elijah III and financed his Christian Catholic Apostolic Church by stock swindles. Wilbur Glen Voliva succeeded him on his death in 1905, and ran Zion on the principles of flatness, faith-healing and fundamentalism until 1942.

It stood to reason that the Creator wouldn't put man on a ball whirling through black space. It was common sense that He made the world flat and solid, with Hell in the basement and Heaven upstairs. Voliva reasoned that, since the sun's only function was to give daylight, it must be close at hand, like a bedside lamp. He judged it to be about thirty-two miles in diameter and three thousand miles from the globe – oops, the map.

Voliva's notion of the map was a circle, with the North Pole at the centre and a wall of ice around the edge. When someone pointed out to him that this would make the coastline of Antarctica several times as long as it has been measured to be, he changed the subject.

Flat earth arguments usually evolve from literal, naïve readings of the Bible. There's a great Christian precedent for these. Though men of the fourth century BC understood that the earth was round, Augustine, seven centuries later, thought otherwise. There couldn't possibly be people on the bottom side of the earth, because they wouldn't be able to see Christ come down from Heaven on Judgement Day. St Lactantius reasoned that people can't walk around with their feet above their heads, and rain can't fall upwards. Recent members of the cult have added few new arguments, but much spirit, to the debate. Apparently Voliva circumnavigated the globe several times in the course of his lecture tours, without losing faith. He bet $5,000 that no one could ever prove to him that the earth was round, and no one ever did.

In Britain, John Hampden had made a similar offer in 1870: £500 said the earth was flat. Alfred Russel Wallace, the naturalist who shared in Darwin's discovery of evolution, took up the challenge. An experiment on a six-mile stretch of the Old Bedford Canal showed the surface of the water to be not a plane but a convex curve, and Wallace collected. Hampden and his friends disputed the decision. They repeated the experiment privately with more satisfying results, and they wrote a series of pamphlets, including 'The Bedford Canal Swindle detected and exposed. John Hampden, 1870', and 'John Hampden Triumphant! Always was and always will be. By Himself, 1871'.

There are two popular kinds of *hollow* earth theories. In the first, the earth is a hollow globe with access holes at the Poles. It contains another sun inside, evidently to provide daylight for the race of dwarfs, Atlanteans or other strangers dwelling within. In 1818 John Cleaves Symmes, a retired American army officer, tried to mount an expedition to the North Pole hole. Symmes decided that the earth contained a number of concentric hollow spheres, all habitable.

> He declared it to be a natural law that everything was hollow, as witness the bones of animals and birds, the hairs on our heads, the stalks of wheat and other grasses ... hence the planets must be hollow, too.[1]

His son, Americus Symmes, suspected that the Lost Tribes of Israel had simply slipped over the edge and were living on the inside.

According to another nineteenth-century American, Cyrus ('Koresh') Teed, *we* live on the inside. If there must be flat and convex theories, it seems logical to have a concave theory, and Koresh came up with it:

There isn't anything outside. The earth is just a kind of bubble of rock, containing us, the sun, moon and stars, and floating in a universe of nothing. Gravity is presumably nothing but centrifugal force.

The sun only appears to rise and set. It stays right in the middle, revolving to show us its bright face by day and its dark face by night. The rising and setting are caused by a set of special optical laws invented by Koresh. Other such laws account for the optical illusions we call the moon and stars, and still more laws explain how light curves so that we can't see over the evident horizon. All this came to Koresh one night in a vision, for which no special optics seem to account.

Teed's ideas drew a fair following. He formed the Koreshan Unity commune in Chicago. Koreshan Universologists went out to measure the curvature of the earth with T-squares, and found it concave, just as Hampden's friends had found it flat.

Rebuffed by scientists, Koresh compared himself to Harvey and Galileo. To deny the earth's concavity, he said, was to deny God. Opposition to Koreshanity was antichrist.

Such messianic notions transmitted well, over the years, to Nazi Germany, where they inspired the *Hohlweltlehre*, or Hollow World Theory. This theory also explained why it was that a Berliner couldn't look up in the sky and see Paris hanging there: Koreshan optics. Light travels in a tight curve, returning to the surface within a few miles – giving the impression of a horizon. But different wavelengths of light curve more or less sharply. This gave the German admiralty a swell idea. If these curious optical laws held, it should be possible, using infra-red light, to see over the horizon – to see the British fleet, in British ports!

> A party of about ten men was sent out from Berlin to the Isle of Rügen [in the Baltic] to photograph the British fleet with infrared equipment at an upward angle of some forty-five degrees.[2]

But Germany was also being swept by Hans Hörbiger's *Welteislehre*, or World Ice Theory, a far more ambitious scheme. Hörbiger believed that the moon was about to crash down on us. That is, it was not just orbiting the earth, but *spiralling in*.

Basic to the World Ice Theory is the notion that space isn't really empty, but filled with viscous fluid. Any body moving through this syrup is naturally losing energy through friction. Therefore any orbiting body is gradually spiralling in. The earth is slowly falling into the sun (as are all planets) and the moon is slowly falling earthward. The present moon was once wandering past, and syrup plus gravity captured it. Before that, we had another moon, but it crashed down, causing great earthquakes and the Deluge. Before that, we had another moon, and so on. In fact, it's the norm for Terra to be assaulted by its moons. Look out!

Now for the ice. Hörbiger claimed that all the bodies of the solar system, except the earth and sun, are thickly coated with ice. More ice is always dropping into the sun, causing sun-spots. Finally, the Milky Way is nothing but an enormous aggregate of ice cubes.

This theory has been taken most seriously in Britain and in Germany. The Nazis welcomed it an alternative to the conventional theories of 'Jewish science'. More of Nazi science later.

It's certainly possible that the earth did capture a wandering moon. But the most probable capture theory going requires that the moon approach the earth moving slower than it now moves, and that it be aimed very close to the earth – so close that it would almost certainly come within the earth's 'Roche limit'. Within the Roche limit distance, it would be torn apart by the earth's gravity.

Worse news for Hörbiger's disciples is the discovery that the moon is not spiralling in at all. In fact, it is spiralling *outward*, increasing its orbit by about an inch per year.[3]

These facts, plus the absence of ice in moon-landing areas, will probably cause crises in the Hörbiger cult, but they will almost certainly not end it. World Ice people will either deny the facts categorically, deny other physical principles, or else alter their theory just enough to keep going. They will never abandon it, however, because the *Götterdämmerung* aspect of crashing moons is just too good to give up.

Attack of the Vermin from Venus
The most popular theories in pseudo-astronomy predict catastrophes equivalent to Hörbiger's moon crashes. Some have

explained Old Testament wonders as comets plcughing into the earth, collisions with other planets or the sudden eruption of the moon from beneath the former continent of Atlantis.

Of these, Dr Immanuel Velikovsky is surely the catastrophe king. In his theory, the earth becomes the punching bag of the solar system, subject to mammoth quakes and tides, rains of fire and brimstone, meteorites, electrocution and a lot more. Even the titles of Velikovsky's three books partake of cosmic violence:

WORLDS IN COLLISION!
AGES IN CHAOS!
EARTH IN UPHEAVAL!

I have added exclamation points to these titles, which might be taken from science fiction films of the 1950s (compare *Invasion from Space* and *Panic in the Year Zero*).

Worlds in Collision explains that, between 1500 and 700 BC, the earth was visited by a series of comet-induced catastrophes, which Velikovsky has choreographed thus: Jupiter collides with Saturn, knocking a piece out of itself which becomes a comet. The comet collides with the earth several times (causing earthquakes, floods, meteor showers, etc.). It then collides with Mars, knocking it out of orbit. Mars bears down on us (more quakes, etc.). Finally, Mars and the comet collide again, very near the earth. Small comets are pulled off the comet's tail: they become the asteroid belt, while Mars is knocked back into orbit, and the comet settles down to become the planet Venus.

Here on earth these collisions seem to have caused all of the large miracles of the Old Testament. When, for example, Pharoah refused to let Moses' people go, comet Venus caused ten plagues to descend: Red dust fell from the comet's tail, turning the rivers blood-coloured (No. 1), causing boils in men (No. 2) and plague in cattle (No. 3). Frogs, lice, flies and locusts may also have fallen from its tail (Nos 4, 5, 6, 7). 'Hail' was really a fall of meteorites from the tail, accompanied by a rain of burning oil (No. 8), darkness (No. 9) was caused by effects of the comet's gravity and electromagnetism on our planet, causing it to either stop dead or tip over to a new axis. Finally, since Pharoah still wouldn't listen, the comet contrived to kill the Egyptian first-born with an earthquake.

As if it had not done enough already, the comet then parted the Red Sea for the Hebrews' crossing. The manna which sustained them in the desert is easily explained as a 'precipitate of carbohydrates' from our old friend, the comet's tail. Just why it happened to precipitate into clean, palatable junket, free of lice, frogs and dust, six days a week for forty years, Velikovsky does not explain.

Two months after parting the Red Sea, the comet was back, this time over Mount Sinai. Moses mistook the resulting earthquake for the voice of God.

> It appears that ... the sound that 'sounded long' rose ten times; in this roaring the Hebrews heard the Decalogue. 'Thou shalt not kill' (*Lo tirzah*); 'Thou shalt not commit adultery' (*Lo tin'af*) ...[4]

Velikovsky applies the same arguments to the destruction of Jericho, the sun's standing still upon Gibeon, the destruction of Sennacharib's army, and so on. In fact, he ranges over the mythologies of many nations, finding in their floods, fires, quakes and miracles evidence for Velikovsky's comet. Take his rain of oil, for example:

> A rain of fire-water contributed to the earth's supply of petroleum; rock oil in the ground appears to be, partly at least 'star oil' brought down at the close of world ages, notably the age that came to an end in the second millennium before our era.[5]

His evidence for this startling disclosure (Why should oil sink down thousands of feet under land and sea?) is found in Plutarch, St Augustine, Exodus, Siberian mythology, East Indian aborigine myths, the Norse Ragnarok, an Egyptian papyrus and several documents from Central America, all of which mention fire or rain. But all Plutarch said was that he wondered where oil came from, and Augustine merely opined that Prometheus and Moses were contemporaries. And at least one of the Central American documents is a spurious translation of a manuscript which actually says nothing of fire or rain.*

* The translator is the Abbé Brasseur (see page 66).

When it first appeared in 1950, and periodically since, *Worlds in Collision* has received a lot of serious attention from the public. Astronomers and physicists, enraged by its popularity, debated Velikovsky in public and in print. What ought to have been the unremarkable publication of a crank's speculations became instead a 'Velikovsky affair'; his detractors began to make fools of themselves over trying too hard to show him up. They fumed like the bishops at Joan of Arc's trial, while the good doctor, like that saint, remained calm and turned away all their objections.

Damon Knight[6] among others seems to find a kind of moral, if not scientific, justification for Velikovsky's theories in this heresy-trial picture. But it may be instructively compared to a scene described by the author of *Saint Joan*, in which a flatearther addressed a public meeting. Shaw says that the lecturer remained completely calm amid the 'spluttering fury' of his questioners and 'answered easily' their strongest objections. When someone asked if the lecturer had never watched through a telescope a ship sinking beneath the horizon, 'He blandly inquired whether the questioner had ever used a telescope in this manner.' He hadn't.

> The lecturer went on, 'I myself have witnessed this interesting illusion. My questioner ... has no doubt often stood on a railway bridge and seen the two parallel tracks converge and meet in the distance. May I ask whether he believes that the two lines do actually converge and meet as they seem to do?'[7]

No one should be too surprised at scientists' losing their tempers in debate with an amateur who proposes to overthrow all their theories of geology, astronomy, history and biological evolution with a wild-sounding notion of comet collisions. And no one should be surprised that Velikovsky kept his cool; for he is, after all, a psychiatrist.

Velikovsky sees his task as putting all mankind on the analytic couch, and digging out its buried traumatic experience (world-collision) by studying its dreams (myths). In so doing he ignores all problems of reading the myths of stranger cultures. He assumes all men everywhere to be psychologically equivalent (they all make myths that he can correctly interpret) yet they are never allowed to make equivalent leaps of imagination. If two myths speak of a flood, it must be one and the same real flood.

His theory is a Procrustean bed, which all mythologies are invited to try out for size. For example, comets can look hairy, feminine, serpentine, angelic, flaming, feathered or ox-like, so any myth referring to any of these conditions is taken and used. Mythologies which happen to lack any such references must have 'repressed' them; he speaks of 'collective amnesia'.

It isn't hard to see that anything at all can be made of such plastic data. What of Velikovsky's physical evidence? Damon Knight mentions the discovery (since 1950) that the sun and planets have electromagnetic fields. This, he says, is 'evidence confirming' the disaster theory. Unfortunately Knight thus confirms my suspicion that he doesn't know what evidence is. Electromagnetic fields are necessary to explain Velikovsky's theories, but they are not sufficient; we might as well say that the discovery that the earth is not a perfect sphere (but rather pear shaped) 'confirms' the theory that it is flat as a billiard table.

In a 1967 edition of his book, Velikovsky cites other presumed supporting evidence:

> a submarine gigantic canyon that runs almost twice around the globe – a sign of a global twist; a layer of ash of extra-terrestial origin underlying all oceans; paleomagnetic evidence that the magnetic poles were suddenly and repeatedly reversed, and, it is claimed, the terrestial axis with them.[8]

The submarine canyon is not a sign of a global twist, but part of a far more complicated situation. The entire globe is believed to be covered with large rigid plates which are gradually being pushed apart by lava flows in the ocean floor. The leading edge of each plate grinds into the next, either riding up over it or else plunging back down into the melting pot below. This process has been going on steadily for millions of years; it was not initiated by Moses' comet.[9]

The 'layer of ash' may refer to sediment of continental origin[10] or to cosmic dust, which the earth picks up at the rate of about two thousand tons per day. There have been reversals of the earth's magnetic poles, but they have never been 'sudden'. Each reversal takes several thousands of years, and the intervals between them have varied from fifty thousand to twenty million years.[11]

Some of these facts might seem to weigh against the notion that the earth has been stopped dead, twisted, burnt, flooded, tipped over and oiled by Venus; but Velikovsky's followers, accepting the *Gestalt* of his theory, probably find details unimportant. There is bound to remain a kernel of belief in his catastrophic theory, since it implies that another spectacular End may be At Hand. And that idea will flourish long after we have failed to find vermin on Venus[12] or manna on Mars.[13]

One Damned Thing after Another

Velikovsky, like so many cranks, considers himself every centimetre a scientist. He has sought scientific recognition of his genius as persistently as any circle-squarer.

Charles Fort, going one better, declared that science itself was defective, a 'mutilated octopus. If its tentacles were not clipped to stumps, it would feel its way into disturbing contacts.'[14] He had no wish to join the 'scientific priestcraft', and if he ever put forward a serious theory, it was that all theories were ridiculous.

It was his friend Theodore Dreiser who persuaded a publisher to take Fort's *The Book of the Damned* in 1919. The 'damned' were data that science had overlooked, ignored or otherwise excluded from science heaven: items carefully culled from newspapers and scientific periodicals: the unexplained. Stones floated in the air. Wheels of light were seen in the ocean depths. A man walked around his horse and disappeared. A horse was seen swimming in the sky. Lights appeared on the moon, and Saturn's rings (supposed to be whirling at high speed) developed fixed spots. Here and there, mysterious thumps, lights, explosions.

Things fell from the sky which, according to scientists, just couldn't be up there: blood, red snow, manna, autumn leaves in April, manure, butter, ashes, silk and sulphur (to name a few substances); bugs, frogs, snakes, fish, worms, lizards and turtles (to name a few species). Fort continued his Ripleyesque series in three later books. He died in 1932, having spent the previous twenty-six years collecting these embarrassments to science.

Collecting but not analysing, for that would be pretending that the collection made some kind of sense. Damon Knight, in his biography of Fort, says:

> He explicitly rejected statistical methods, probably because they were the tool of his enemy, organized science; he never drew up tables or made charts of his data.[15]

Wisely, I think. Later chapters will show what happens when data, collected at random and unsubstantiated, becomes the basis of a systematic theory.

At best, Fort considered scientists 'sleepwalkers', in Arthur Koestler's sense, hypnotized by their own deductions and calculations and oblivious to everything else; at worst, they were charlatans. Astronomers he compared to astrologers, who 'squirmed into prestige and emolument by shooting at marks, disregarding their misses, and recording their hits with unseemly advertisement'.[16] Astronomers predicted that there was one planet external to Uranus, or else two, or else none. Neptune was found. All bets having been covered, astronomy triumphed again.

Fort believed, or pretended to believe, that all scientific hypotheses were equally true, and all equally false. He opposed categorical thinking of any kind, and suggested compromises. Thus he allowed that the earth might rotate *a little* – say, only once a year. His disciples became fond of expressions like 'true/ false' and 'good/bad', indicating that they had done away with categorical thinking.

This is all wonderfully symmetrical and Hegelian in the abstract, but not always practical. We may safely ignore the 'good' effects of such 'good/bad' entities as concentration camps, and we generally choose to regard the moon as very largely stone and very little green cheese. Some truths/ falsehoods are plainly more probable than others.

Fort was cagey about proposing hypotheses himself. He seems to have coined them, like epigrams, for intellectual exercise only, renouncing in advance any commitment to them. He said, for instance, that:

1   The stars are holes in a gelatinous shell that rotates. As the jelly quivers, they twinkle.*

2   There are vast islands or ships drifting invisibly above us in some Super-Sargasso Sea, called Genesistrine, Azurian, Elvera or Monstrator. From them fall substances, animals, artifacts.

3   We're property.

4   Man did not evolve from lower animals, but appeared here on earth (from elsewhere) in the distant past. Various species used him for a model, evolving in imitation. 'Though the gorillas ... are only caricatures, some of the rest of us are passable imitations of human beings.'[17]

5   We're fished for.

6   An earlier Egypt was populated by sphinxes.

7   Falls of strange objects may be love poetry: 'Some other world, meeting this earth, ransacking his solid imagination and uttering her living metaphors: singing a flood of mastodons, purring her butterflies, bellowing an ardour of buffaloes ...'[18]

Fort believed no more in his own cosmologies than in those of other people. He delighted in finding tautologies in the statements of the mighty. Thus he pointed out that Darwin's notion of the survival of the fittest depended upon a definition of the fittest as those who survive; while Euclid's straight line, 'the shortest distance between two points', required that distance to be measured along a straight line. It seems unlikely that Fort seriously intended such 'discoveries' to disparage the work of Darwin or Euclid.

His followers, however, took Fort's epigrams far more seriously. The Fortean Society – which Fort characteristically refused to join – tried to carry on his work after his death. Its magazine *Doubt*, formed to print the master's unpublished notes, promptly headed off in all directions. It promoted the 'Cosmic Constant' (also known as the Golden Section, and

* In *The Sleepwalkers*, Arthur Koestler describes a comparable universe devised by Anaximander, about 580 BC. The earth is cylindrical, and the universe, which rotates around it, is made of layers of bark filled with fire. The stars are pinholes, and the fire twinkles through them. This seems to chime with 'Doc' Sam H. Smith's theory (unpublished) that what we believe to be common pins are really star-holes.

discussed in chapter 22), flat earth beliefs, theories of the moon as an expanding ice cube, down with fluoridation and vaccination, and a hundred other humourless crank schemes. While *Doubt* collected data on flying saucers, the editor concluded that they were an invention of the military, to take people's minds off their real problems (like vaccination).

What would Fort himself have made of flying saucers? Crockery slung in a titanic kitchen squabble? Uninflated planets? Gargantuan lost collar buttons? Scaled-up red corpuscles flowing along some arterial galaxy? Whatever wry hypotheses he might have shaped, we may be sure that Fort would have come to no final decision. Like a proper scientist, he was well able to content himself with chronicling uncertain events – mystery airships, flying jellyfish, airborne torpedoes, discs with tails and luminous circles – while suspending his judgement forever.

In the 1950s, Americans suddenly became obsessed with security. Whether the obsession was related to fears about the atomic bomb or to postwar prosperity and boredom is hard to say, but they became vigilant owners, insurers, defenders against some unspecified enemy. In 1948 Congress published *The Strategy and Tactics of World Communism*. In 1949 Americans could read *Nineteen Eighty Four*. Words like *invasion, infiltration, subversion* and *brain-washing* became part of even the lowest, or newspaper, vocabulary.

Officially the era began with Joe McCarthy waving his laundry list in the Senate ('I have here the names of eighty-seven card-carrying communists in the State Department'); it ended with Sputnik rising in the sky and Americans feverishly building fall-out shelters. In between, they were entertained by scores of paranoid science fiction films: Velikovskyan catastrophes and terrifying invasions. The first flying saucers appeared in 1947, and were immediately identified as invaders, from Mars or from Russia, but definitely *hostile*.

Unidentified flying objects, as the saucers came to be called, have been seen for centuries. In 1561 the residents of Nuremburg saw the sky fill up with blue, black and red balls, red crosses, a black sphere and several transparent tubes. These all began to fight one another, then fell down and vanished in steam. A broadsheet was published celebrating the event. Five years later, the people of Basle had a similar experience.[1]

In 1947, businessman Kenneth Arnold was flying his private plane over the Cascade Mountains, searching for the wreck of a missing plane. Near Mount Rainier he saw a string of bright metallic objects flying in single file. There were nine: eight discs and one crescent. He estimated their speed as 1,700 mph (later revised to 1,200 mph) and their size as equal to nine DC-4 airliners. They dodged around the mountain peaks with 'flipping, erratic movements'.

After landing at one airfield, Arnold told a few friends the story. He then took off for a second airfield, where he was met by excited reporters. He said that the objects flew like 'pie plates' or 'saucers being skipped over water'. *Flying Saucer* entered the language, and the nation was invaded by headlines.

The seeing of saucers spread like an epidemic of demon possession over the US, Canada, England and Australia, and later to all civilized parts. Reporters wanted sightings, verified or not, and the public obliged with flying discs, doughnuts, rings, flaming cigars, fireballs, fire eggs, humming orbs, dimes, teardrops and ice-cream cones.

Two classic cases will be discussed here; more appear in the next chapter. They are 'classic' in that they involve more than a simple sighting. Some additional effect seems to corroborate the story: a man is singed, a plane crashes, a car engine stops. Each classic remains unexplained for a time, during which it generates wild rumours. Often these persist long after the case has been explained and explained.

In January 1948, people in various parts of Kentucky reported a large, glowing object in the sky. Captain Thomas Mantell and two other pilots were already aloft in small planes when the tower ordered them to search for the object.

Soon Mantell reported: 'I've sighted the thing – it looks metallic and it's tremendous in size.'

The other two pilots either failed to see the object or lost sight of it, and returned to base. Mantell carried on, climbing through broken clouds to higher altitudes – about twenty thousand feet.

Hours later, search teams found his body and wrecked plane. One morbid rumour said that his corpse was cooked, as though by intense radiation. Another said that his skull was neatly sliced off just above the eyes.*

---

* As recent as 1970 we find the following version, in which I have italicized misinformation:

There was a tremendous explosion, and Captain Mantell's plane crashed ... Mantell, *who had sent no message through his radio, was killed instantly*. Was the UFO in this case a 'secret weapon' and did Mantell die because his plane ventured too close to the strange object? To this day, no one can answer that question.

(Dennis Barden, *Mysterious Worlds*, London: Fontana, 1972, p. 237.)

It now seems likely that what Mantell chased was a Navy 'skyhook' balloon. These huge balloons, used for high-altitude research, were a Navy secret at the time; neither Mantell nor the public could have known of them. They looked like huge, metallic objects. It also seems likely that Mantell, whose plane carried no oxygen equipment, simply flew too high, fainted and crashed.

The other classic is the Case of the Scorched Scoutmaster. In August 1952, Florida scoutmaster D. S. Desvergers was driving three boys home from a scout meeting when they noticed a peculiar light flashing from a nearby woods. Desvergers left the car and went alone to investigate. When he hadn't returned in twenty minutes, the boys went for help to a nearby farm. The scoutmaster was found in a slightly dazed condition, with faint burns on his forearms and face, and a scorch-mark on his cap. This was his story:

He walked in to a clearing fifty yards from the road, where he noticed a rise in temperature and an odd, pungent odour. Looking up, he saw a huge disc, metallic grey, hovering ten yards overhead. The edge was equipped with vanes and nozzles, and the top was domed. He heard a sound from the dome 'like the opening of a well-oiled safe door', then a fireball or red mist came down to engulf him, and he lost consciousness. He was conscious when found.

The boy scouts claimed that they had seen Desvergers from the car, shining his flashlight up at something, and being hit by a red fireball. The Air Force investigation showed that the boys could not have seen a light in the clearing, even by standing on the roof of the car. Desvergers' burns were very light, no worse than sunburn. A doctor, by way of demonstration, inflicted similar burns on himself with a cigarette lighter. The initial flashing light in the woods was caused by a nearby farmer doing arc-welding. The rest of the case depends on Desvergers' own testimony.

He was no model citizen, having both a criminal record and a local reputation for leg-pulling. Just after the incident, he hired a press agent and began releasing wild statements that 'he ... and the Air Force knew what he'd seen, but he couldn't tell – it would create a national panic'.[2]

One puzzling clue remains. The Air Force took grass samples from the clearing, and found them to have charred roots. This so impressed the investigating officer that he later wrote:

UFO propulsion comes into the picture when one remembers Dr Einstein's unified field theory, concerning the relationship between electromagnetism and gravity.[3]

But a 'gravity field' strong enough to heat the soil in the clearing would certainly have heated any coins or keys in the scoutmaster's pockets, charring them, and damaged the batteries in his flashlight. When we learn that the grass samples were mislaid by the investigating officer for several days – left behind at one Air Force base while he flew to another – the gravity wave explanation seems less certain. Even this officer was finally forced to conclude that the case was a hoax.

Calling All Angels, Robots, Dwarfs and Galactic Bees!
Donald E. Keyhoe, a retired Marine pilot, conducted his own UFO investigation.[4] He found that the Air Force's Project Bluebook, ostensibly set up to investigate reports, was really intended to hide some terrible truth from the public.

The truth as Keyhoe sees it is of course invasion from space. His books quote cases like the above as hard evidence, and, from a completely non-committal reply to his letter to the Air Force, he deduces 'an official Air Force admission that the saucers came from space!'[5] Elsewhere he quotes two paragraphs from an Air Force report, saying that chances are, eleven neighbouring stars have space-travelling creatures. These two paragraphs do not appear anywhere in the original report.[6]

Frank Scully's *Behind the Flying Saucers*, 1951, claimed that saucers used 'magnetic propulsion', came from Venus, could travel faster than light, and were manned by three-foot midgets. He had inside information that one of these craft had crashed, and that six tiny corpses were in the custody of the Air Force. The UFO was made of some new hard metal, impervious to diamond drills. When alive, the little 'Venusians' had written in picture symbols, dined on food wafers, and – wait for it – drank 'heavy water'. We all know *those* Venusians: Doing their hair in shock waves, smoking electrical coronas, wearing Van Allen belts and resting their tiny elbows on a Geiger counter ...

Raymond Palmer and Richard Shaver connected the saucers with Lemuria which they declared (at first in a science fiction story, but later as fact) to be inside our hollow earth. Lemuria is inhabited by a race of dwarfs know as the Abandondero, or 'dero' for short. Like the Nibelungen, they are evil, demented and degenerate. Besides piloting saucers, they cause wars, accidents, disappearances and even nightmares (using a special beam called 'dream mech'). They seem to have made a 'gas attack' on the home of one UFOlogist in 1967.[7] (For earlier, similar attacks, see chapter 26.)

Gerald Heard, a devotee of ESP, author of a dozen books on prayer, and translator of a book explaining how coloured light cures disease, believes the saucer occupants to be Martian bees, far superior in intelligence than mere *homo* so-called *sapiens*.[8]

In November 1952, George Adamski met and talked with a visitor from Venus in the Californian desert. He (the Venerean) was a slight gent, five foot six inches tall, with long, fair hair and grey eyes. He wore a brown jump-suit and oxblood fabric shoes. Like Adamski, he believed in telepathy, so no communication problem arose. He explained that all the solar planets are inhabited by men just like us, and that many Venereans are walking around here, disguised as humans. Like Heard's bees, he was worried about our nuclear experiments. His ship was powered by Scully-type magnetic forces.

The stranger seemed to know little about the planet Venus; nothing, in fact, that Adamski had not already guessed in a science fiction story. Adamski was allowed to take pictures of his saucer, but the cunning alien contrived to make them come out looking like cheap fabrications.[9]

George Hunt Williamson, a friend of Adamski's, later found that he could contact aliens in their saucers by means of a ouija board. Here speaks the planchette, passing on the wisdom of 'Regga of Masar':

> I must tell you a few things of interest. These true facts may even surprise you, but they are so. Many of your people on Earth know them to be true. Your Sun, which is our Sun also, is not a hot flaming body. It is a cool body ... You think your sun gives off great heat because you can 'feel' it. Certain forces come from the Sun and when they

enter the earth's magnetic field this resonating field causes friction. And from friction you get heat.[10]

'Masar' turns out to be a ouijagraphical error for 'Mars'. Regga next suggested that Williamson's seance group try to contact him by radio. They enlisted the aid of a sympathetic ham operator, who managed to hear some dots and dashes of what he took to be a strange Interplanetary Morse Code. Despite its unfamiliarity, he succeeded in cracking it in a few minutes, receiving the messages ZO and AFFA. Back to the old ouija board, where these turned out to be the names of a couple of Regga's pals.

Less friendly aliens contacted Albert K. Bender, if we are to believe his *Flying Saucers and the Three Men*, 1963. His plan was to get the entire membership of his flying saucer club to concentrate on sending a single message by telepathy to the skies. In a dry, office-memo style, filled with phrases like 'what we would term' and 'I proceeded to take part', the book explains how the experiment worked. Bender composed the psalmodic message to be sent:

> Calling all occupants of interplanetary craft! ... Please come in peace and help us with our EARTHLY problems. Give us some sign that you have received our message. Be responsible for creating a miracle here on our planet to wake up the ignorant ones to reality. Let us hear from you. We are your friends.[11]

The reply was a terrifying religious experience. After lying down, closing his eyes and repeating the messages three times, Bender got what I believe epileptics and migraine sufferers know as an aura: a powerful sulphurous odour and blue, flashing lights. Speaking in a dry, office-memo style, a voice warned him:

> We have been watching you and your activities. Please be advised to discontinue delving into the mysteries of the universe. We will make an appearance if you disobey.[12]

I believe that poor Mr Bender was so advised.

In *The Hollow Earth*, 1964, Raymond Bernard seems to have combined Palmer's dero theories, Atlantis stories, and the idea of a Brazilian Theosophist that there is a subterranean land called Agharta, to conclude that saucers are flown by Germans from the depths. But Gavin Gibbon, in *The Coming of the Space Ships*, 1956, placed the homeland of saucerites on a former 'tenth planet', now the asteroid belt. W. Gordon Allen, in *Spacecraft from Beyond Three Dimensions*, 1959, thought the fourth dimension a reasonable place to park UFOs when they weren't scaring pilots. The vanishing of saucers when chased, the lack of crashed specimens, the seeming non-existence of a home base – just about anything can be explained by the fourth dimension, alias oblivion.

It was Allen who published a picture of two men holding hands with a midget, captioned:

> A 'saucer crewman' very much like the moon man (or spirit) described by Swedenborg in his writings about the inhabitants of different planets ... This photograph is from Germany (note trench coats and North European types) but the 'saucer crewman' is from a UFO that crashed near Mexico City; the corpses were sent to Germany for study. Was he based on Luna?[13]

There has never been the slightest scrap of evidence of this crashed UFO except Allen's photo. Scientists working on the Condon Report asked him for more information about it, but he demanded an exorbitant price, and they lost interest. No one else in Germany or Mexico seems to have heard of it.

In *Flying Saucers through the Ages*, 1965, Paul Thomas suggested that the appearance of the Virgin Mary at Fatima may actually have been a UFO landing. He did not specify whether he meant the BVM to be a UFO, or merely to be a UFO pilot (Virgin on the ridiculous).

The profane side has also been covered, in Coral Lorenzen's *Flying Saucers: The Startling Evidence of the Invasion from Outer Space*, 1962, 1966. There we hear the one about the travelling UFO-woman and the farmer's son. It seems that a space egg landed on a Brazilian farm, and wee men emerged. The farmer knocked down the first one, but others subdued him and took him aboard. They conferred, talking about him in dog-howls. After a technical examination, he met his mate:

> The woman's purpose was immediately evident. She held

herself close to [the farmer] rubbing her head against his face. She did not attempt to communicate in any way except by the grunts and howling noises, like the 'men' had uttered. A very normal sex act took place, and after more pettings she responded again ...[14]

And so on, as in all such stories. Mrs Lorenzen also repeated other descriptions of aliens: little men in black, big men in plastic suits, gnomish bipeds with glowing eyes, and the robots who, belching sleep-inducing smoke, chased one man up a tree and kept him there all night. The sleepy smoke seems to have failed to knock him out. Maybe they should have given him readings from UFO literature, guaranteed to make anyone drop off.

So much for lone eyewitness accounts. Whether or not we accept any of them, it should be clear that UFOs cannot simultaneously be piloted by all these fantastic creatures. Even if we could reconcile the creature who speaks fluent Portuguese in Fatima with that which grunts and howls in Brazil, there are hundreds of other variants in the vast literature on UFOs.

Reports of more apparent substance, investigated by a team of scientists for the US Air Force, are discussed in the next chapter.

The Condon Report[1] took over thirty scientists and engineers two years to prepare. The Air Force had been collecting their data for the previous twenty years. If nothing else, the Condon Report should have convinced ufologists that saucers were being taken seriously.

It didn't. Scientists who worked on it, Dr Edward U. Condon in particular, were accused of being 'anti-UFO', and their 'professional bias' was often noted by amateurs who themselves showed little inclination to accept anything less than visitors from space. Leaders of two large amateur saucer groups, NICAP and APRO* lost faith in the project early on. Donald Keyhoe sent an angry telegram to President Johnson urging him to terminate the project. Richard Shaver found Condon a 'pedant' for not getting on with the real business of science, i.e. fighting the evil, telepathic dero. (Shaver referred to the dero by the Velikovskyan phrase 'vermin from space'.)

The work of the project was to investigate old reports from the Air Force and other sources; to analyse any UFO photographs; physical evidence and radar evidence; and as nearly as possible try 'on the spot' immediate investigation of new sightings. Contrary to accusations of the flying saucer clubs, the purpose of the project was not to lay the ghost of UFO, nor to find out what kind of nut believes in flying saucers. It was to find in any of the thousands of reports of UFO sightings *anything* of scientific value.

Amateur ufologists have made much of the accumulating Air Force statistics on sightings, and of the fact that a certain number of these resist all attempts at explanation. During the years 1953-65, sighting were classified as in Table 3-1. The 253 'unidentified' sightings, about $3\frac{1}{4}$ per cent of the total, are,

* National Investigations Committee for Aerial Research (run by James and Coral Lorenzen) and Aerial Phenomena Research Organization (run by Donald Keyhoe).

Table 3-1   UFO Cases Classified by Categories, by US Air Force
Project Bluebook, 1953-65

Astronomical (includes meteors, stars, planets, etc.)	2403
Aircraft - - - - - -	1367
Balloon - - - - - -	691
Insufficient data - - - - -	1313
Other* - - - - - -	1051
Satellite - - - - - -	563
Unidentified - - - - -	253
TOTAL	7641

* *Other* includes hoaxes, missiles, rockets, reflections, flares, fire-works, mirages, searchlight, clouds, contrails, chaff, birds, physical specimens, radar and photo analysis, satellite decay, etc.

to determined ufologists, hard evidence of Something Out There. But it would be unrealistic to expect scientists to explain every single sighting on whatever evidence happens to be available. At least some of the notorious $3\frac{1}{4}$ per cent might have explanations like these:

1 Mistakes in eye witnesses' stories. One man reported seeing a green light the size of a two-storey building which landed each night several miles from his home. Watching it through binoculars, he saw 'two rows of windows on a dome-shaped object that seemed to have jets firing from its bottom.'[2] An investigator visited him, and saw that it was a bright planet near the horizon.

2 Natural phenomena which are unknown to the investigators. One example, which could actually account for some cases, is ball lightning generated by peculiar weather conditions, power lines or supersonic aircraft. Ball lightning is far more common than was formerly supposed.

3 Undetected pranks. One incident, involving six witnesses who were hunting racoons on a ranch at night, produced varying but interesting accounts of an object that had flown over, shined a brilliant beam of light on them, and departed. It seem that most of them, at least for a time, considered it a flying saucer. Some reported that it hovered, and some that it made a sharp 90° turn when departing. One described it as an object fifty feet in diameter, and glowing. Investigators

found that 'a rather slow twin-engine Navy airplane equipped with a powerful searchlight had departed ... on a course ... that would have taken [it] almost directly over the location of the sighting', and that the man in it had discussed the possibility of just such a prank.[3] Had the plane been far off its flight path, this might be classified 'unidentified'.

4 Inaccurate data. One case, in which a police chief who was called out to look at a UFO, saw a large, silvery object drifting to the southwest, cannot be identified as a balloon because the prevailing winds were against it, or at least across its path. Still it is possible that the police chief, and some of his men, who also saw it, were mistaken about the object's motion (as others have been) or that freak local weather conditions moved it in an irregular path. Otherwise this 'unidentified' object looked and behaved like a balloon, e.g. it took ninety minutes to drift out of sight.[4]

5 Data difficult of interpretation. Such a case was the much-publicized Tremonton, Utah, motion picture of a cluster of bright objects milling about and fluctuating in brightness, at the limits of perception. The facts that the film was taken by an experienced Navy photographer, and that photographic experts were divided in their opinions, inclined amateur groups to make of this sighting 'hard evidence' of extraterrestial invaders.

The Air Force decided that the objects could not be airplanes (no engine noise) or balloons (one had reversed direction and departed from the others). The Navy decided that the objects could not be birds or airplanes (they seemed to give off light, not just reflect it).

Taking into account all analyses, the project investigator identified the objects as white birds, probably gulls. His identification is not conclusive, but the evidence in its favour is strong.[5]

In view of these, and perhaps other, possibilities, it's rash to call even unexplained UFOs space invaders.

Photographic Analysis
Of thirty-five photographic cases from the period 1966-8, all were identified after analysis. Of eighteen older cases also investigated, only two remained unidentified. Analysis showed most cases to be (probably):

1 Fabrication, including pictures of frisbees thrown in the air, the lens cap of a camera suspended on a thread, double exposures and photomontages (one of these, from Brazil, shows that the saucer is lit from the left, while trees and other foliage are lit from the right).

2 Natural or man-made phenomena: The Tremonton movie (above); one photo of a smoke ring from a simulated atomic bomb explosion; lenticular cloud formations; Venus.

3 Cases where data is insufficient or inconclusive: Photos of poor quality, damaged photos or film, etc.

4 Cases where testimony of witnesses conflicts with the photos, so that no conclusions can be reached.

The two cases left could be the 'hard evidence' that amateur ufologists are looking for. One took place on a farm near McMinnville, Oregon. Allegedly a woman saw a metal disc in the sky, called her husband, and he took two photographs of it. These, after analysis, show what is either a fabrication or a UFO. The object, which looks remarkably like a pot lid with a handle, could be suspended by fine wire or thread from overhead power or telephone lines which are invisible in the picture. Equally it might be an 'extraordinary flying object, silvery, metallic, disc-shaped, tens of metres in diameter, and evidently artificial'.[6]

The other case took place at Great Falls, Montana, where the manager of a baseball team and his secretary saw two white lights moving slowly across the sky, and took movies of them. The objects could be aircraft, but some factors make this extremely unlikely. Unfortunately, most analyses which rule out balloons and aircraft depend on the date being 15 August 1950, and this date is uncertain. The phenomena are unexplainable only if the date is 15 August 1950. The baseball manager claimed, however, that he was inspecting the stadium for a game that afternoon, and no game was played at the Great Falls stadium between 9 and 18 August.[7]

UFOs on Radar

Most of the radar cases investigated were those involving visual sightings also. Someone either saw a radar blip which was later located by sight, or else saw an object later picked up on radar. The majority of radar cases turned out to be 'radar mirage', easily-explained natural effects. Often an odd radar blip was searched for visually and finally sighted, but in many cases the visual object proved to be a star. We see what we're looking for, on and off radar screens.

Physical Evidence

The project looked at two kinds of physical evidence: direct (pieces of UFOs, burnt ground, etc.) and indirect (effects supposedly produced by UFOs, such as stalled car engines).

Many *saucer nests* were analysed. These are areas, usually circular or ring-shaped, where grass is burnt or broken or soil blown away. None was ever successfully connected with any UFO, none was found to be radioactive, and at least one was done with ordinary lighter fuel.

Angel hair, a filmy material, had often been reported. Like Fortean blobs and manna, it had the property of disintegrating soon after falling. Some was thought to be the webs of ballooning spiders. The project never received a sample of angel hair, though one man sent some white powder found on the eaves of his house. It turned out to be titanium oxide, the pigment of house paint.

Space grass was more substantial, consisting of threads of metal of varying lengths. This turned out to be aluminium 'chaff' dropped from planes or balloons to test radar. One sample was traced, through colour-coded markings, to a manufacturer who delivered the assurance that his space grass was made, not in some remote corner of the universe, but in Brooklyn.

Amateur ufologists tend to get carried away with reports of interesting cases and neglect to check them out. Frank Edwards, in *Flying Saucers, Serious Business,*[8] mentions three UFO artifacts: a flying disc said to have crashed in Norway in 1952, recovered by the Norwegian Air Force; a one-lb fragment of a glowing disc shot off by a Naval interceptor plane over Washington DC in 1952; and a 3,000-lb fragment of spaceship fished from the St Lawrence River in 1960.

The Norwegian saucer turned out to be the hoax of a West German journalist. The Navy had no record, even in Secret files, of any UFO-shooting incident, had no planes over the capital city anyway, and had never had a pilot of the name Edwards gave.

The 3,000-lb mass of metal was real enough, though it

proved identical in every respect to an ordinary chunk of foundry waste.

Jim and Coral Lorenzen submitted to the project a magnesium fragment with an unusual history. In 1957 a society columnist in Brazil printed a letter in his column, said to be from a man who obtained it while fishing near Ubatuba with friends. The man saw

> a flying disc. It approached the beach at an unbelievable speed and an accident, i.e. a crash into the sea seemed imminent. At the last moment, however, when it was almost striking the water, it made a sharp turn upward and climbed rapidly on a fantastic impulse. We followed the spectacle with our eyes, startled, when we saw the disc explode into flames. It disintegrated into thousands of fiery fragments, which fell.... Most of these fragments ... fell into the sea. But a number of small pieces fell close to the beach and we picked up a large amount of this material – which was as light as paper. I am enclosing a sample of it.[9]

A Brazilian ufologist contacted the columnist for more information. He was told that the letter's signature was illegible and that the columnist had thrown away the envelope with the return address. Hmm.

The ufologist sent part of the sample to the Brazilian government for analysis and the rest to the Lorenzens. They too had some of it tested. These tests showed, according to the Lorenzens, magnesium of a purity much greater than any that could be obtained by earthly technologies.

The project tested the sample and found that it was much less pure than a sample made by Dow Chemical (of this earth). Mr Illegible and his fishing pals were never located.

Far from being satisfied with these findings, Coral Lorenzen tried to maintain the air of mystery by changing her claim. In 1962 she wrote:

> The most advanced laboratory tests indicate the fragments recovered could not have been produced through the application of any known terrestial techniques.[10]

Later, after the Condon Report project had tested it and found otherwise, she wrote:

That the material was not 100 per cent magnesium does not lessen the impact of the case, for we still have to explain how that magnesium got to a remote beach at that time.[11]

But do we? Only the letter-writer knows where it came from. Mrs Lorenzen's statement indicates that she is willing to accept an anonymous tip to a gossip columnist as first-class evidence, without any corroboration.

Indirect Physical Evidence
Many UFOs have been reported manoeuvring at supersonic speeds. The absence of sonic booms in some cases – like Sherlock Holmes's dog that didn't bark – leads to interesting speculations. The Condon Report considers three possibilities: overestimated speeds, special weather conditions muffling booms, or suppression of booms by some technical means. The project generously ignores a fourth possibility: Most silent sightings occurred in the early days of supersonic flight, before most people were aware of sonic booms.

In 1965, reports of UFOs came from several stations at the South Pole, on the appropriately named Deception Island. Some at least turned out to be practical jokes by bored men. Checks for magnetic disturbances showed nothing unusual.

Now for the famous stalled-car cases, a favourite piece of UFO lore. Usually a UFO flies over a car, whose engine and sometimes lights fail. After the UFO passes, the car resumes normal operation. The theories are:

1 That the air around the car is ionized. But this would blister the paint, damage local vegetation and even local people.

2 That the car's electrical system is short-circuited. But then it would not operate later. This leaves only:

3 That a powerful electromagnetic field cuts out the car's electrical system. This theory was checked in two ways. First, various car electrical components were tested inside a high-intensity magnetic field. No component used on American cars was stopped by this field.

Second, though it's not commonly known, cars that have been magnetized show it. The body of every car has a 'magnetic signature'. That is, every body part stamped out on the same machine becomes slightly magnetized by the earth. It turns out that cars which are made in the same factory retain their peculiar pattern of magnetism for years.

The project mapped the magnetic signature of one car reportedly stalled by a UFO and compared it to three similar cars. It matched cars A and B. Car C had been wrecked and repaired, so that its signature was different from those of A, B and the UFO car. It was also shown that even a very weak magnetic field will alter the signature of a car – it can be done with a common permanent magnet.

Stopped car engines are by no means a new phenomenon. There were such rumours going the rounds in the 1930s:

> As I heard the story in 1938 it was that an English family on holiday in Germany would be travelling in a car when its engine would suddenly fail ... A German sentry would then step out of the trees and tell them that there were special tests in progress and that they would be unable to proceed. Some time later he would come back and tell them that it was all right for them to start the engine again and the engine would immediately fire and they were able to drive off.[12]

The stories, when traced down, always took place near the two places in Germany where there were television towers. As it turned out, car engines interfered with transmission tests, so the German authorities had posted sentries to stop cars and ask them *to switch off* their engines during brief tests.

Ufologist John G. Fuller has tried to link UFOs with the Great Northeastern Blackout of 1965, which cut the power in New York and other areas:

> Ostensibly, backup Relay #Q-29 ... was eventually pinpointed as the source of the massive failure. But ... nothing in the relay was broken when it was removed for inspection. In fact, it went back into operation when power was restored.[13]

Of course Q-29 was working; its working caused the power failure. The function of such a relay is to cut out when a line is dangerously overloaded (and cut back in when the load drops). Personnel at the power plant did not know the load limit of this relay, however. They allowed its line to overload under the rare conditions which produced the blackout. Relay Q-29 was the 'source' of the failure, but the cause was human error.

The project did check on 148 other power failures over a twelve-year period. Only three had been attributed to 'unknown' causes, and no UFOs had been reported in their vicinity.*

Awkward Questions
Under the pressure of objective investigation, UFOs have been retreating, like unicorns, deeper into the forests of fantasy. There is now no question but that the majority of UFO sightings are mistakes of one kind or another, built up by natural curiosity, a convenient myth, and the action of rumour. For most ufologists, the question 'Are there any real UFOs?' has hardened into a dogmatic 'There are!' In the next chapter, UFO myths are seen already well integrated into other myths.

Assuming for the moment that there are solid physical UFOs, ufologists still have not satisfactorily answered questions like these:

1 Why have no saucers crashed and been found?

2 Where are they, when they aren't thrilling or menacing anyone? How can thousands or even millions of them have gone and come from this planet without their traffic being detected?

3 What possible purpose can they serve? Not to contact us (they've thrown away thousands of chances). Not to avoid us (since they're noticed so often). Hardly to stop bomb tests in any conceivable way. Hardly to study human behaviour, since they ignore large population centres to pow-wow with Adamski behind a dune.

Ufologists have repeatedly answered such questions, but to no one's satisfaction – not even other ufologists'. It should be clear that UFOs, as they treat them, are like ghosts, fairies, demons, angels, Nibelungen, leprechauns, and of course, like gods of old.

* Any great crisis like the Blackout generates similar rumours. See page 301 for more examples.

Alien Corn

The production of UFO exposés has not diminished since the release of the Condon Report, nor their quality improved. If anything, ufologists have become more strident and less concerned with facts. Now more than ever, they aim to shed light, not upon the subject, but full into the eyes of their audience.

> We are suggesting that it would not have been impossible for certain intellectually gifted scientists (alchemists) to have mastered radio transmission, powered heavier-than-air flight, and many other discoveries about the time Columbus discovered America.[1]

Thus write Brad Steiger and Joan Whritenour, who also manage to get Wilhelm Reich, Shaver's dero, sea monsters and yeti into their saucer book, whose central legend concerns the 'Allende Letters'.

Two letters from a 'Carl Allen' alias 'Carlos Miguel Allende' to the late M. K. Jessup, a ufologist, describe an experiment performed by the US Navy in 1943, or so they say. Using Einstein's unified field theory, the Navy made a destroyer invisible while at sea. Then they shifted a ship from its berth in Philadelphia to another in Virginia, and back again, within a few minutes. Crewmen were said to have gone mad from the experience, and some of them suffered from other annoying after-effects, like freezing solid or suddenly going invisible.

The Allende letters are associated with a copy of Jessup's book, *The Case for the UFOs*, 1955, mailed to the Office of Naval Research. The book had been annotated in ink of three different colours, evidently by three people. The ONR showed it to Jessup, and photocopies were circulated among other interested ufologists.

Predictably, one of them suggested that the annotators were extraterrestials secretly living among men. A new and completely groundless legend was born.

The three annotators, known as Mr A, Mr B and 'Jemi', maintain a running commentary on the speculations in Jessup's book. They are inclined to gloat over the ignorance of mere Terrans:

> Jemi (on mysterious disappearances): Heh! If he only knew why, he'd die of shock! [2]
> Mr A (on man's refusal to admit his inferiority): Huh, he'll never admit it: pride! [3]
> Mr B (on being quick-frozen): Heh! If he only knew by experience, he'd keep silent and not write or speak of it ever again in his lifetime. He couldn't speak of it, for you see, Jemi, it paralyzes one's sense of time and nullifies mental cognition, functioning and memory. [4]

Apparently all three aliens have been reading the same space comics. Not only do they keep breaking out in Dr Sylvanus chortles, but their extraterrestial science borrows heavily from science fiction of previous eras. 'Telepathy', 'force-fields', 'scout ships', 'mother ship', antigravity, hydroponic farms and undersea exploration are clearly identified (omitting only death rays, time machines and robots), and these are combined with dark references to Fort, secret Gipsy tongues, Lemuria and of course the Navy's famous experiments.

At the same time, these aliens are alien indeed to conventional science. Mr B argues that a rather plain metal cross found in Georgia, which he calls 'Atruscan-Lemurian', could not have been made by primitive people because they would have required elaborate modern drawing instruments (a similar argument might be advanced regarding the architects of tepees). Jemi thinks 'quixotic' is synonymous with 'paradoxical', and Mr B uses 'telecontrol' when he clearly means 'control'. Many inferior earthly scientists may be puzzled by the term 'vortice', though some may be intelligent enough to understand 'a magnetic net ... one with a reverse "snap neutralizer" in it' and the like.

Steiger and Whritenour claim that

> either the book was annotated by three individuals who decided to attempt one of the most elaborate and pointless hoaxes in history ... or the notations were made by three

individuals who are members of an older Earth civilization with full knowledge of the origin of UFOs and a mental library of remarkable facts.[5]

But internal evidence suggests a hoax (or delusion) propagated by only one person, probably 'Carlos Miguel Allende', and not by three aliens crowding around a table with their three pens, heatedly debating Jessup's speculations.

It is in the interests of such as Steiger and Whritenour, however, to ignore the annotator's lack of credibility, and to pretend that the US Navy was vitally interested in the Allende letters. It all fits in with these ufologists' theory that Gipsies came from space.

The Ninth Dimension

T. Lobsang Rampa, who claims to be an Oriental mystic under the skin of a Westerner, has a different answer:

> There are certain unknown flying objects ... which come to this Earth actually from the world of antimatter. They cannot come too close or they would explode, but they are exploring just the same as we send a rocket to the Moon. ... People complain that if there were anything in this saucer business the people aboard would land or make contact with people upon this Earth. The whole truth of the matter is that they cannot, because if they touch down there is an explosion and no longer a flying saucer.[6]

Antimatter is an old favourite in science fiction, and also a hypothesis popular among physicists since the discovery of the positron, or positively-charged electron. The idea is that all the subatomic particles of ordinary matter have counterparts exactly like them, but with opposite electrical charges, somewhere in the universe. If so, such antiparticles might get together to form antimatter. It is quite imaginable that other galaxies in the universe could be composed of antimatter. And since matter and antimatter would annihilate each other on contact, we might expect craft from such a galaxy to be unable to land on the earth.

Rampa makes a naïve mistake, however, in quoting accounts of UFOs suddenly vanishing from radar screens as evidence of their antimatter composition. For UFOs have been sailing along through our atmosphere at great speed, for long periods, which antimatter ships could not do. Such ships would be quickly exploded by contact with our air, and the explosions would be of H-bomb proportions. This could hardly be missed, even on a radar screen. Since no such spectacular explosions have been detected, Rampa's hypothesis is disproved. Besides, it's hard to imagine an alien intelligence so dull as to keep sending out ships for twenty-five years continuously, to certain destruction.

Rampa's background may explain his lack of scientific sense. He claims to be an Englishman whose body has been taken over by a Tibetan lama. Besides *The Third Eye* and nine other books forming one enormous pep-talk on mysticism, Rampa's enterprises sell 'touch-stones' and meditation records of the master's voice. His main message seems to be that meditation can be fun. It is delivered through snippets of Oriental and Occidental philosophy, interlarded with Rampa's imagined adventures in Tibet, and with homely anecdotes. His books bear an uncanny resemblance to those energetic stories of Norman Vincent Peale (e.g., faith in God helps executive put through company merger; salesman is in despair until his eye falls on a passage in his Gideon Bible), except that Rampa's parables often show the Zen quality of pointlessness.

Rampa's scientific ideas seem to be culled from Allende's sources. He believes that the Chinese seized Tibet because the Himalayas, being higher, are the best places from which to launch rockets (they'll go farther before hitting the ground).[7] He thinks the Himalayas themselves are exinct volcanoes.[8] He relies heavily on arguments involving antimatter, parallel universes, the *ninth* dimension, telepathy, teleportation, reincarnation, and crystal-gazing. Faster-than-light travel? No problem:

> When people travel beyond the speed of light they will be able to see each other and see what lies ahead of them. The only difference is that the things they see will be of a different color ...[9]

Well, there is *one* other difference, Einstein aside. Anything less than 62,000 miles ahead would be invisible, since it would flash past in less than an eyeblink. Even if this were not so (and, again, Einstein aside) travel from one point to another on the earth's surface would involve accelerations of no less than 1,400 million g's, making the traveller weigh around 80 million tons.

Like other cranks, Rampa seems to have a love/hate relationship with science, on the one hand reviling it for short-sightedness:

> Einstein and people like Einstein said that the world was flat; Einstein and people like Einstein said Man would never travel faster than the speed of sound.[10]

On the other hand defending the Allende disappearing ship trick, ostensibly based on Einstein's unified field theory. Laugh if you will at Allende, he says, they laughed at lasers.[11] Funny, but I'd always imagined that it was orthodox science that took lasers seriously.

One final quotation before we leave Rampa to his lucrative meditations:

> It is always amazing that people can readily believe that the heart can pump ten tons of blood in an hour, or that there are 60,000 miles of capillary tubing in the body, and yet a simple thing like parallel worlds causes them to raise their eyebrows in disbelief.[12]

Space-Hopping with Captain God

Ufologists have become so numerous that they have all but used up their best data. New sightings are quickly snapped up, digested, tabulated and used to support going theories. In order to find fresh material, UFO men have been forced to graze in less likely fields.

Some chose distant lands. Obligingly there have been sudden upsurges of sightings in South America,* and a New Guinea missionary has successfully converted his flock to UFO belief.

Others turned to dim recent history. John A. Keel, an

---

* Like fashions in pop music or clothes, UFOs move rather slowly across cultural boundaries. They spread first from the US to Canada, Britain and Australia, later to the rest of Europe, and much later to South America and other remote parts.

ex-reporter, has examined old newspaper files on the subject of UFO sightings in California in 1896, while *Fate* magazine recently featured 'The Flying Cucumber of 1903'.[13] *Flying Saucer Review* carries articles like 'The Airship Wave of 1909' and John A. Keel's 'Mystery Airplanes of the 1930s'.[14] One obvious advantage of such material is that no one can dispute its accuracy. The press probably liked a rumour as much then as it does now, and mildewed rumours can never be verified.

However, Keel still feels the lack of usable stuff, for in an article on UFO 'flaps' (crises) he says:

> We must also take into account the apparent deceptions, diversions and 'hoaxes' which seem to be carefully engineered by some unknown group to lead us astray and keep us in confusion. Ufologists must study psychological warfare and police investigative methods so that they will be prepared to cope with such deceptions and recognize them for what they are. There is a tremendous amount of evidence that 'they' don't want us to know too much about their nature or origin.[15]

In other words, if data are scarce, someone is making them scarce! The naked paranoia of such a statement need not be taken to imply that ufologists are usually paranoid, but it does seem related to the abnormal fears with which UFOs have been invested from the beginning.

Statistical analysis provides a third field for UFO research. John Keel, Jaques Vallée, Aimé Michel, Damon Knight and others have moved into it. Sightings have been classified by area; date; age and sex of observer; day of week; colour; proximity, etc. They have been correlated with positions of the planets, sunspot activity, lunar and other cycles. None of these systems has so far yielded insights into UFO origins, for reasons which chapter 22 may help explain.

A fourth group of ufologists, following Velikovsky's lead, have begun delving into mythology. The most successful of these is Erich von Däniken, whose first book[16] (serialized in the London *Sunday Mirror* as 'Was God an Astronaut?') is a kind of crank compendium. Nearly every dubious theory of the past century is enlisted to prove that spacemen visited the earth at some time in the dim, dumb past. Von Däniken's index includes such hardy perennials as antimatter, Noah's Ark, Edgar Cayce, Easter Island, Ezekiel, etc. (Connoisseurs of Crank will miss Atlantis, the Cabala and Teilhard de Chardin; these are included in von Däniken's second book.)

Not only does this ufologist insist that aliens landed on earth in prehistoric times, he insists that they looked like men, acted like men, and used twentieth-century appliances to keep the natives awed. They planned the Deluge as part of a grand eugenics scheme, sired Noah on an earth-gal, and snatched Elijah into the clouds. They were worshipped by the Egyptians, Chinese, Hebrews, Mayans and others, to whom they gave token gifts: pyramids, written languages and modern gadgets.

Von Däniken's archaeology will be taken up in chapter 6, but this will introduce his methods of Scriptural exegesis:

> Moses relates the exact instructions which 'God' gave for building the Ark of the Covenant. The directions are given to the very inch and how and where staves and rings are to be fitted and from what alloy the metals are to be made.[17]

Anyone who doesn't know inches from cubits, or who thinks metals are made from alloys, has no business trying to interpret Exodus as a radio manual, but that's exactly what von Däniken intends. The Ark was nothing less than a radio receiver, designed to pick up messages from God in his saucer. Von Däniken supports this by the death of Uzzah (II Sam. 6), who put his hand to the Ark to keep it from falling over on him, and was struck dead for this reflex of little faith. Von Däniken's *post mortem*:

> Undoubtedly the Ark was electrically charged! If we construct it according to the instructions handed down by Moses, a voltage of several hundred volts is produced.[18]

There must be *some* room for doubt. The Ark was simply a box of gold-plated wood, very much like Egyptian sacred utensils of the day (Tutankhamun's viscera was contained in such a box). It isn't likely that it held a charge, but even if it had, it would have electrocuted those who lifted it on gold-plated wood staves thrust through its gold rings. If Uzzah

was 'undoubtedly' electrocuted, then Adam and Eve were undoubtedly barred from Eden by an angel with a soldering iron.
And why not gadget explanations for everything in the Bible?

Jonah's whale	=	A submarine
The three in the fiery furnace	=	Asbestos suits
Pillar of fire	=	A streetlamp
Loaves & fishes	=	Freeze-dried foods
Cures of deaf	=	Hearing aids
Raising Lazarus	=	Heart massage
Ezekiel's vision	=	Television commercial*

Von Däniken tackles Arabian myths in the same manner,
rubbing the lustre off each bright story:

> Where did the narrators of *The Thousand and one Nights*
> get their staggering wealth of ideas? How did anyone come
> to describe a lamp from which a magician spoke when the
> owner wished?[19]

So Aladdin's wonderful lamp was only a radio. Notice how
von Däniken changes a genii with fantastic mountain-moving
powers into a magician's voice – after making the original story
dull, he wonders how it got so interesting. He refuses to credit
the Arabs with any creativity, and he harps on the 'primitive
imagination' of the Mayans. Obviously the writers and painters
of the past cannot invent, only chronicle, and all the real
creative work is to be done by twentieth-century European
hack journalists.

Von Däniken's astronomy is as misshapen as his history. He
merely sets out any statistics that look good (there are likely
some life-bearing planets in our galaxy) and ignores those that
don't (our galaxy is very large). He tries to give the impression
that our galaxy is teeming with advanced civilizations, and
that it is very likely that one of these has visited us in mankind's past—an impression that is very probably false.

Our galaxy, the Milky Way, contains 10^{11} stars. As many

---

* My suggestions. But von Däniken does propose that Sindibad's
Roc is a helicopter, and Ali Baba's magic Sesame, a supermarket
door.

as 50 million of these could possibly support planets bearing
intelligent life. The problem is, the Milky Way is enormous.
Light takes 80,000 years to cross it. In order for a stellar ship
to find one other planet with life on it, it would have to explore
the planets, if any, of 100,000 stars. Moving at the speed of
light, this would probably take the stellar ship about 400,000
years, with no stops. As Dr Condon puts it:

> To gain a little perspective on the meaning of such dis-
> tances to human affairs, we may observe that the news of
> Christ's life on earth could not yet have reached as much
> as a tenth of the distance from the Earth to the centre of
> our galaxy.[20]

Suppose that a civilization at the centre of our galaxy invented
a powerful telescope that enabled them to see life on the earth.
Looking through it today, they would see woolly mammoths
trotting around in the snows of the last Ice Age. Suppose the
aliens at once set out for mammoth-land. They will not arrive
before the year 28,000 AD, nor carry the news home before
54,000 AD, that the mammoths are extinct.

Von Däniken, and his colleagues, Peter Kolosimo and
Andrew Tomas, like to pass up such items almost as much as
they like quoting from one another. The general tendency
among pseudo-scientists seems to be to cannibalize one another's books, without ever checking on the origin of information. In the Condon Report, Samuel Rosenberg mentions

> a 'UFO case history' given credence and attention in books
> by Vallee, Green, Trench, Desmond and Adamski, Jessup
> and Thomas. The report is an alleged 'observation made in
> 1290 at Byland Abbey, Yorkshire, of a large silvery disk
> flying slowly, a classical one and [one that] can be found in
> a number of books' (Vallee, 1965).[21]

He quotes the transcript of this remarkable incident, given in
Desmond and Adamski in Latin, and in a translation by
'A. X. Chumley':

> But when Henry the Abbot was about to say grace, John,
> one of the brethren, came in and said there was a great

portent outside. Then they all went out and LO! a large
round silver thing like a disk flew slowly over them, and
excited the greatest terror.[22]

Rosenberg, unlike the ufologists he mentions, actually checked
out the existence of this manuscript, said to be found in
Ampleforth Abbey in 1953. He found it to be a hoax per-
petrated by two schoolboys in a letter to the London *Times*.
At least one ufologist suspected a hoax in 1965, but, even after
Condon, it remains in ufological currency. In Peter Kolosimo's
book, published in 1969, here it is:

and also in England in Byland Abbey, Yorkshire, we have
that 'great portent' falling on October 20th 1290 when 'a
silver object like a ring was seen slowly flying.'[23]

Still, it's best to keep what ufologists, with characteristic
euphemism, call 'an open mind'. After all, those schoolboys
might be Masartians in cunning disguise, doing their best to
obscure the vital data and discredit ufology's vital researches.
Heh! If earthling scientists only knew ...

Lost and Profound

Atlantis

The bottom of the ocean has the same attraction for some of us as the Dark Side of the moon, or Planet X in Galaxy Y: It is inaccessible, hence completely at the command of our imaginations. For this reason, Atlantis has persisted, while so many other delightful lands – Cockaigne, El Dorado, Shangri-La – have evaporated.

Plato introduced Atlantis into two of his dialogues, *Timeaus* and *Critias*, using it to point a moral: Luxurious living leads to earthquakes which sink your island. His contemporaries seemed to doubt that Plato really had special knowledge of what happened centuries before in some real but far-off place. Aristotle treated Atlantis as a fable.

Not so later thinkers. Atlantis was variously identified with the Americas, the Canaries, the Caribbean, Sweden, South Africa and even Ceylon. Its location remained vague, until, in the nineteenth century, Ignatius Donnelly sank it firmly in the Atlantic.

Donnelly was a Minnesota politician and leader of the reform Populist party. He founded a love community. He wrote a comet catastrophe book, *Ragnarok*, anticipating Velikovsky by seventy years. He wrote books proving that Francis Bacon was the true author of Shakespeare's plays, by means of spurious ciphers which he found in them (see chapter 23). And he wrote the most popular book ever on the lost continent, *Atlantis*, in 1882. It has been translated into many languages, and new editions have appeared regularly up to 1970.

Atlantis evidently impressed most people. Prime Minister William Ewart Gladstone tried to organize an expedition to look for the vanished land (Donnelly achieved some political fame himself, becoming a US Congressman and the Populist candidate for Vice President).

The latest edition of *Atlantis*[1] is edited by Egerton Sykes, head of the Hörbiger Institute in Britain, who also has a keen interest in climbing Mount Ararat to find Noah's Ark. In his

Preface, Sykes admits that the Hörbiger World Ice Theory 'has fallen behind' recently, but he puts this down to its popularity among Nazis, and expects 'justice to be done' to the theory by the end of the century.

Atlantis explains that the gods of the Greeks, Phoenicians, Hindus, Scandinavians and practically everyone else were really kings, queens and heroes of the old continent. They colonized Egypt and Peru, founded most of the ancient civilizations of Europe, Africa and the Americas, introduced the Bronze and Iron Ages, invented alphabets for the Phoenicians and Mayans, and invented the calendar. Then a 'terrible convulsion of nature' sank this birthplace of civilization. Only a few escaped to tell others, who handed down the news to us in the form of Eden and Deluge myths.

To prove his theory, Donnelly compared remote cultures and found satisfying correspondences. Customs like marriage and divorce, embalming, skull surgery; beliefs in an afterlife; similarities in astronomy, architecture, agriculture; and linguistic connections seemed to turn up in places as remote as Peru and Egypt, or China and Mexico.

His erudition and patience were great, but his understanding small. Not only did he 'read' Mayan using the spurious alphabet of Diego de Landa (see page 65), but he obtained other correspondences by misreading Chinese. Since this, plus what Martin Gardner calls 'questionable geological, archaeological and legendary material', makes up his strongest 'evidence', Donnelly's Atlantis can hardly be expected to appeal to serious scholars.

Its appeal to cranks, on the other hand, has led to the publication of thousands of Atlantean books, moving further and further from any consideration of facts, books like Joseph B. Leslie's *Submerged Atlantis Restored*, Rochester NY, 1911, composed entirely of evidence from spirit mediums. The noted mystic Edgar Cayce similarly obtained his information about the sunken continent from the aether.

The one thing all believers in Atlantis agree on is the violence of the final dunking. Explanations offered have been volcanoes, underground steam, the collapse of hollow underground chambers, strange gases, Velikovsky's comet and Hörbiger's falling moon, the eruption of our present moon from beneath the sea, and recently, Atlantean nuclear bomb experiments. Egerton Sykes even seems to find meaning in one of the adventures of Sindibad the sailor, who landed on an island and built a fire, only to have the island turn out to be a whale which dived to the depths.[2]

Donnelly's notion that the sunken land was the original home of the Aryans, or 'Indo-European family of nations' naturally aroused the interest of Nazi pseudo-scientists. In 1922, Karl Georg Zschartzsch published *Atlantis, die Urheimat der Arien* (Atlantis, the Original Home of the Aryans) showing it to be a nature-loving commune of the master race, who owed much of their perfection to being vegetarians. But a non-Aryan woman invented or imported alcoholic drink (Eve and the forbidden cider) to cause their fall from grace. Atlantis promptly collided with the tail of a comet.* Only three persons escaped: an old man, a small girl and a pregnant woman.

Fleeing from the fire, they discovered a cold geyser which squirted its water into the boughs of a large tree. The old man noticed that a snake and a she-wolf disappeared among the roots of the tree and reasoned that there was a cave under the roots. Inside, the woman died and the old man went to get cold water; a small meteorite burned out one of his eyes; but the she-wolf suckled the child.[3]

Thus Atlantis was to account for a variety of myths, such as one-eyed Wotan and Romulus without Remus.

Of course many Atlantis believers discount such fictions as this, while still maintaining there must be some truth in the main story. I'm tempted to ask *which* truth? Is Atlantis sunken, but not a paradise? A sunken paradise, but not inhabited by Aryans? A sunken paradise inhabited by Aryans, but not destroyed by a comet? At each step the story turns upon a new and completely unfounded assertion, until the myth-maker has piled up a Pelion on an Ossa on an Olympus of absurdity, balanced precariously on flimsy evidence.

An example of such evidence is the owl-headed vase of Dr Paul Schliemann. Schliemann was the grandson of the archae-

* Comets' tails, though enormous, don't contain enough solid material to 'collide' with. The effect of such a collision would be about as noticeable as the collision of an airplane with airborne bacteria.

ologist Heinrich Schliemann, the discoverer of Troy. But while his grandfather was a reputable scientist, Dr Paul plunged into the headlines with 'How I Discovered Atlantis, the Source of All Civilization'. Therein he described a supposed inheritance from his grandfather of an owl-headed vase and some papers. Inside the vase were

> square coins of platinum-aluminium-silver alloy and a metal plate inscribed, in Phoenician: 'Issued in the Temple of Transparent Walls.' Among [the papers] he came across an account of finding at Troy a large bronze vase inscribed: FROM THE KING CRONOS OF ATLANTIS.[4]

The rest of the article was evidently a rehash of the arguments of previous Atlantologists and Lemuriologists, with little or nothing in the way of new ideas. Needless to say, the owl-headed vase and the square coins were never shown to archaeologists or the public.

Occultists haven't been slow in taking up Atlantological proofs like these, or in exploring their mythical land. Theosophists like Madame Blavatsky, Annie Besant and W. Scott-Elliott staked their claims early; they were followed by Rosicrucians like Wishar S. Cerve and anthroposophist Rudolf Steiner, and free-lancers Lewis Spence and James Churchward. It was Churchward who propagated the revealed truth about Mu.

Sacred Mu

Maybe the original sunken paradise was getting too crowded, but for some reason, the Theosophists decided to found a new one, Lemuria, in about 1860. The name came from a scientific theory then going the rounds. An Austrian geologist proposed that India and Africa were once linked by a land bridge. He estimated that the connection would have been broken some sixty million years ago and of course he said nothing at all about ancient civilizations. The land bridge idea was dropped by later geologists (the current theory being that India broke off from Africa and moved up via continental drift) but Lemuria had already infected Madame Blavatsky's crowd.

Helena Petrovna Blavatsky claimed Lemuria as the home of what she called the Third Root Race. Root Races are part of the Theosophical mechanism for evolution. There are seven consecutive Root Races in the scheme, and each develops seven sub-races (on the St Ives pattern) before it is wiped out by the sinking of a continent. The next Root Race arises from one of the sub-races of its predecessor, and so on.

The First Root Race was utterly aethereal (I'm not sure how they could drown); the Second had semi-substantial bodies. The Third, who lived on Lemuria, were ape-like giants, hermaphroditic, oviparous, four-armed and three-eyed. These gradually evolved into human types and their doom was caused by the discovery of normal sex. Lemuria sank.

The Fourth Root Race arose on Atlantis. W. Scott-Elliott's *The Story of Atlantis*, 1914, describes its seven sub-races, beginning with the Rmoahal, who were black and ten feet tall, through the Tlavatli; the Toltec (twenty-seven feet tall); the Turanians, the Semites (from which developed the Fifth Root Race); the Akkadians and the Mongolians. Atlantis sank.

The Fifth Root Race, the Aryans, went from Egypt to the Gobi Desert, where they developed their first five sub-races: the Indians, the Egyptians, the Persians, the Celts and finally the Germans. According to Annie Besant, the sixth sub-race is just now being born, in Southern California. Out of them will develop the Sixth Root Race, expected to inhabit a new continent which is just about to rise out of the Pacific.

The name 'Mu' is often taken to be short for 'Lemuria', but it has another history. It seems to have begun[5] with the pseudo-linguistics of Diego de Landa, an early bishop of Yucatan and self-appointed critic of Mayan culture.

Landa's first contribution to our understanding of the Mayans was to burn every scrap of their writing he could lay hands on. So successful was his purge that only three Mayan books remain: The Dresden Codex, which is damaged, the Codex Perezianus, and the Tro-Cortesianus Codex. Later, the bishop had second thoughts. It might not be such a bad thing to learn some of this Mayan stuff. He demanded of the natives the 'Mayan alphabet'.

Since Mayan is a pictographic language, it has no alphabet, but apparently the natives tried to oblige. For A, they showed him *aac* (turtle), a turtle's head. For B, they showed him *be* (road), a picture of a road with a footprint on it (Figure 5-1).

Naturally Landa's alphabet was useless. In 1864 the Abbé

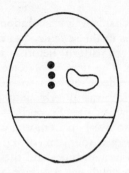

Fig. 5–1 Landa's 'Mayan B'

Brasseur de Bourbourg tried using it to translate the Troano Codex (half of the Tro-Cortesianus Codex) and came out with a garbled story about a volcanic explosion. He took a pair of recurring symbols, the M and U of Landa's alphabet, to be the name of the disaster area, and Mu was born.

The de Camps, quoting directly from Brasseur's study, give his translation as beginning:

> The master is he of the upheaved earth, the master of the calabash, the earth upheaved of the tawny beast (at the place engulfed beneath the floods); it is he, the master of the upheaved earth, of the swollen earth, beyond measure, he the master ... of the basin of water.[6]

H. S. Bellamy, in his English translation of Hörbiger, gives another version:

> In the sixth year of Kan, in the month of Sak, on the eleventh of Muluk, earthquakes began, of a violence not hitherto experienced. They continued without interruption until the thirteenth of Chuen. The island of Mu, the land of the mud-mountains ... met its end through them.[7]

The Troano Codex was actually translated later. It turned out to be a quite coherent astrological treatise, making no mention of earthquakes, volcanoes or Mu.

The most well-known champion of Mu has always been James Churchward, the retired British army colonel who wrote a series of pseudo-scholastic books on it: *The Lost Continent*

of Mu, The Children of Mu, The Sacred Symbols of Mu,
etc., etc. The essence of these is a set of 'Naacal tablets' which
he claims were shown to him in an Eastern monastery. The
monastery was located in India in one of his books, but shifted
to Tibet in another. Believers probably won't bother about
such details (Kolosimo quotes Churchward extensively). The
colonel translated these tablets to reveal the long and tedious
truth about Lemuria. That he was over seventy years of age
when he began them probably has something to do with their
rambling semi-coherence, their jumble of anti-evolution, reincarnation, anti-gravity (which Jesus used to walk on water),
hopeless geology and footnotes like '4. Greek record.' or '6.
Various records.' The frontispiece of *The Lost Continent of
Mu* is a dim picture of a vase with markings on it, some of
which can almost be distinguished. It is, he claims, Schliemann's vase.

Pseudo-archaic forgeries have lately attracted ufologists to
Theosophy. A key Theosophical work is the *Book* (or *Stanzas*)
of Dyzan, said to have been buried for aeons under one of the
Himalayas in a secret library, and then revealed in trances
to Mme Blavatsky in 1888. She promptly wrote it all down
in her six-volume *The Secret Doctrine.*[8] Now Erich von
Däniken has been digging into this and finding yet more
evidence of a visit from the stars.[9] Another ufologist, Frank
Edwards, claims that Dyzan tells how aliens arrived in a ship
that circled the earth before landing; how they settled here
but met hostility; and how they then went aloft in a metal
ship and

> while they were many leagues from the city of their enemies
> they launched a great shining lance that rode on a beam of
> light. It burst apart in the city of their enemies with a great
> ball of flame that shot up to the heavens.... All those in the
> city were horribly burned.[10]

Samuel Rosenberg investigated this astounding quotation. He
found that, first, the Book of Dyzan isn't extant outside the
Theosophical Society editions; and second, that none of these
contains the nuclear war passage above. Someone slipped
Edwards a forgery.

Von Däniken takes no chances, he quotes from the Blavatsky

version, which turns out to be fairly standard occult stuff:

> The root of life was in every drop of the ocean of immor-
> tality, and the ocean was radiant light.... Behold ... bright
> space, son of dark space ...[11]

and so on, to the seven breaths of the dragon of wisdom. When
this tedious document appeared, at least one scholar was able
to show that it wasn't any ancient Sanskrit work, but came
straight from the pen, and reading, of Madame B:

> He showed that her main sources were H. H. Wilson's
> translation of the ancient Indian *Vishnu Purana*; Alexander
> Winchell's *World Life; or Comparative Geology*; Donnelly's
> *Atlantis*; and other contemporary scientific, pseudo-scientific,
> and occult works, plagiarized without credit and used in a
> blundering manner that showed but skin-deep acquaintance
> with the matters discussed. Most of the *Stanzas of Dyzan*
> were cribbed from the *Hymn of Creation* in the ancient
> Sanskrit *Rig-Veda*, as a comparison of the two works readily
> shows.[12]

Clarion

Almost as appealing as the theory that Christ is awaiting the
Second Coming on Venus, or Godfried Bueren's theory that
the sun is hollow and has plants growing inside[13] is the idea of
a planet hiding behind the sun.

Clarion is such a planet. It's supposed to move in an orbit
which corresponds to the earth's, keeping it continuously out
of our sight. Like sunken lands, or regions on the inside of the
earth, it can be imaginatively populated with lost races, demons,
giants and so on.

At first the idea doesn't seem impossible. Even though the
earth's orbit is an ellipse, not a circle, it might still be possible
for Clarion to remain in permanent opposition. It could then
be a source for UFOs, or a duplicate Earth where Fate produces
doppelgängers for all of us ...

Alas, Clarion's strange orbit would only work if Clarion and
Earth were the sun's only children. As it is, the hidden planet's
orbit would be so perturbed by the attraction of Venus and
Mars that it would soon come creeping into view. Computations

carried out by the Nautical Almanac office of the US Naval Observatory showed that Clarion could not remain out of sight for more than about thirty years. Also, Clarion would itself perturb the orbits of other planets noticeably. Finally, even if Clarion had *zero mass*, the earth's orbit is perturbed by other planets, and it would, in less than a century, creep out of alignment with its twin enough to see it. The solar system stubbornly continues to behave as if Clarion were either weightless *and* invisible, or else non-existent.[14]

Impossible? Ridiculous? It is mostly those people who feel that they are absolutely bound by the laws of nature who make the most stupid objections.[1]

Objections, that is, to Erich von Däniken's theory concerning the Great Pyramid: that it was a freezing chamber, where the Egyptian dead were quick-frozen until astronaut Ra could come back to revive them. Why else embalm them? he asks. Why else entomb food and valuables with them? I can only stupidly object that Ra would have a truly god-like task in reviving a mummy from which the brain and viscera have been removed.

The Great Pyramid's awesome size, spooky function and exotic Egyptianness have commended it to generations of pseudo-scientists. Arabs thought it might be a waterproof library, protecting Egypt's wisdom from the Deluge. Early Christians thought it one of Joseph's granaries, built to tide folks over those seven lean years.

By the nineteenth century it was known to be a tomb[2] built for King Khufu (Greek: Cheops).[3] This didn't stop John Taylor from writing in 1859 that it was the work of Noah, architected by God.[4] He proved this by finding in its dimensions a number of mathematical truths and correspondences to nature, which he backed up with biblical evidence: 'In that day there shall be an altar to the Lord in the land of Egypt' (Isaiah 19:19). It's hard to resist objecting that 'Thou shalt not build it of hewn stone' (Exodus 20:25).

When Taylor's idea was taken up by Charles Piazzi Smyth in 1864, pyramidology caught the public's fancy.[5] Not only was Smyth highly respectable, being Astronomer Royal of Scotland, but he found even more mathematical curiosities in the Pyramid's dimensions, such as:

1 Dividing twice the length of one side of the Pyramid's base, b, by its height, h, gives the value of the circular ratio, pi ($=3.14159 \ldots$).

2 Multiplying *h* by 1000 million gives the distance from the earth to the sun.

3 Dividing *b* by the width of one of the Pyramid's casing stones gives 365, the approximate number of days in a year.

Smyth also thought Cheops' sarcophagous was a measure of volume. Many of his quantities depended on the width of a casing stone. For instance, he derived an original, or 'Pyramid' inch by dividing this width by twenty-five. The Pyramid inch was used, he said, in building the Ark, and our own inch had descended from it. Later it turned out that the Pyramid's casing stones were all of different widths.

The location and orientation of the Pyramid were also remarkable, according to Smyth. He found that it was placed at the apex of a triangle formed by the Nile delta, and

> that there is more land along the meridian of the Pyramid than on any other all the world around; that there is more land in the latitude of the Pyramid than on any other ...; that the Pyramid territory of Lower Egypt is at the centre of the dry land habitable by man all the world over ...[6]

Richard Proctor, writing in 1896, pointed out that there are too many facts here: any two of them must fix the location of the Pyramid absolutely.

Smyth – and many pyramidologists following him – have laboured long to produce calculations relating the dimensions of the Pyramid to natural quantities such as the circumference and mass of the earth. These calculations provide an object lesson in pseudo-mathematics, or tailoring reality to fit a pet theory. They 'work out' because of three kinds of errors:

1 The Great Pyramid's dimensions were uncertain when Smyth began his figuring. Not only had it been considerably mutilated (the outer casing and pyramidal capstone were gone) since building, but precise measurements weren't made until later in the nineteenth century. Estimates of its original height, for instance, varied by 40 feet. Pyramidologists may select whichever one of a dozen values that fits their theory.

2 Natural quantities are not always fixed. For instance, the earth is no *precise* number of miles from the sun. Its elliptical orbit carries it as close as 91,300,000 miles, as far as 94,452,000

miles, giving pyramidologists some 3 million miles to play around with.

3 Making such calculations is a game without rules. Given the large number of measurements obtainable from the Pyramid (height, weight, volume, base length, base area, lateral area, edge, base diagonal, slant height, etc., etc.) and an almost infinite number of natural quantities, only a moron could fail to find any correspondences. Is its height significant? Then so are the heights of Old St Paul's, London, and Rouen Cathedral. The height of the Eiffel Tower times 1,000 million equals the 'diameter' of the earth's orbit. My own height, times one million, gives the moon's radius.

One of Smyth's followers finds significance in the Pyramid's having five corners and five sides, since there are five books of Moses, five digits on each human limb, five senses and so on. But the paper I'm writing on has equally sacred significance in its four corners and four edges (corresponding to the number of human limbs, the number of evangelists, and the number of compass directions).[7] This is simple numerolatry of the Lucky 13 level.

The value of *pi* seems about the only figure obtainable from the Pyramid without fudging. According to Martin Gardner, Herodotus claimed the Pyramid was built so that the area of each triangular face was equal to the area of a square whose side is the height. For such a construction (easy enough to design by geometry or even simple models), $2b$ divided by h gives 3.14459..., a close approximation of *pi*.[8] (For more on *pi* and pseudo-mathematics, see page 276.)

Using his 'Pyramid inch', Smyth measured the Pyramid's internal passages, and found that they make up a complete diagram of world history, past and future! Their turnings and branchings recorded the Creation in 4004 BC, the life of Christ, and so on, up to Judgement Day, which would come in either 1881 or 1911. Among thousands of people who swallowed this were such celebrities as President Garfield (for whom history did unexpectedly end in 1881) and Charles Taze Russell, founder of the Jehovah's Witnesses.

Smyth's later followers decided that his theory was right (history really was marching up and down those stone passages) but that he had the dimensions wrong. Christ had (someone said, in 1913) secretly arrived on earth in 1874. Later a British engineer named David Davidson used revised measurements to plot a new course of history, which he published in 1924.[9] Smyth's and Davidson's ideas are still in circulation, as we'll see.

Continual readjustments of the end of the world were necessary when it kept failing to keep the date. 1874, 1914, 1920 and 1925 found the world rolling infuriatingly on. 1926 passed without a single blast of angelic trumpets, as did May 1928, 16 September 1936 and 20 August 1953. The faithful have not altogether given up hope, though, and global nuclear war may yet allow them to say they told us so.

Pyramidology now seems to be riding high on a new tsunami of occultism. Erich von Däniken and Peter Kolosimo are so eager to prop up their space-visitor theories with Cheops' Pyramid that they sometimes get Smyth's ideas garbled. Kolosimo seems to confuse the Great Pyramid of Cheops with its smaller neighbour, the Pyramid of Chephren. Von Däniken asks:

> Is it coincidence that *the area of the base* of the pyramid *divided by twice its height* gives the celebrated figure $\pi = 3.14159\ldots$?[10] (My italics)

It would be worth the price of a new Sphinx to watch him actually try this calculation.

Von Däniken notes that a 'meridian running through the pyramid divides continents and oceans into two exactly equal halves'[11] and that the Pyramid 'lies at the centre of gravity of the continents'.[12] Kolosimo puts it more dramatically:

> For centuries our scientists have been looking for an ideal meridian.... But now we know that the Great Pyramid meridian is ideal. Why? First because it passes through more land than any other meridian and secondly if we calculate the area of habitable land from the Behring Straits [sic] we find it divides exactly in two.[13]

Both men indulge themselves in no end of such gibberish, but what they seem to be trying to repeat are Smyth's ideas about the Pyramid meridian. Luckily for the Egyptians this magic meridian lay within a few miles of their capital at Memphis.

Of course they could have tried 70° west of Greenwich, a meridian which seems to pass through more land (by the look of it). The division of areas, of which Kolosimo writes in reverent syllables, is completely wrong. The land west of Cairo (30° E to 170° W) is greater than that east of Cairo by some seven million square miles. An extra South America would be needed to make up the difference.

The 'centre of gravity' statement makes no sense whatever. What may be meant is the centre of *area* of the continental shapes – as depicted on one kind of map or another. By choosing a suitable projection, and by adding or subtracting areas like Greenland, Antarctica and inland seas, one can virtually place this point anywhere one likes.

Kolosimo also claims that

> the distance of the Cheops Pyramid from the centre of the world is the same as its distance from the North Pole.[14]

This would happen to be true if the earth were a perfect sphere, but then it would be true of any structure lying on the same latitude (30° N), including New Orleans whorehouses.

Another line of argument endowing the Pyramid with mystery is that its size and quality of construction were far beyond the simple technology of the Egyptians. After all, it does contain about 2,300,000 blocks of stone, weighing on average $2\frac{1}{2}$ tons each. These had to be quarried, some at a distance, brought to the site, and lifted into place. Von Däniken:

> If the industrious workers had achieved the extraordinary daily piece rate of ten blocks piled on top of each other, they would have assembled the ... pyramid in about 250,000 days=664 years.[15]

He insists that the stone blocks must have been quarried by lasers and transported by helicopters; this equipment, naturally, being provided by extraterrestial gods. In this he disagrees with William Kingland, who feels that the stones were set upon pieces of papyrus bearing certain magic symbols which enabled them to fly.[16] Kolosimo believes that the entrance to one of the Pyramid's passages was plugged up by granite blocks *from the inside*.

This kind of tiresome nonsense comes about through a complete ignorance of serious archaeology. If any of these pyramidologists could be bothered to read I. E. S. Edwards's *The Pyramids of Egypt* or any other of the dozens of competent books on the subject, he would find each of his 'mysteries' explained in detail. The Pyramid of Cheops is no isolated, puzzling phenomenon, but a part of a long tradition of pyramid-building. All told, over eighty true pyramids still exist, in varying condition, along with enough examples of earlier burial structures to trace their development. From the First to Third Dynasties, kings were entombed in brick houses, now called 'mastabas'. In the Third and Fourth Dynasties, larger and more permanent 'step pyramids' of stone appeared. In the Fourth Dynasty, these were first encased in layers of fine limestone, building their profiles to true pyramidal shape.

The Great Pyramid was completed during the lifetime of Cheops, probably within twenty years, by a few thousand skilled masons and a large work-force of unskilled men (perhaps a hundred thousand), during the seasons when they weren't planting or harvesting.

They moved blocks of stone from a distant quarry on rafts, dragged them from the river on sledges, and slid them up earthen ramps into place. (The bulk of the Pyramid was made from stone quarried nearby, and only the outside casing came from any such distance.)[17]

Edwards points out that a crew of eight men would have had to handle only ten blocks in twelve weeks to accomplish the job. He also explains how the Egyptians could square the Pyramid with the four compass points (or rather, four true directions) using nothing more than the astronomical knowledge they clearly had, and no more modern apparatus than a stick and a mud wall. Kolosimo's granite plugs really were inserted into the tomb entrance from the inside, but this needs no occult explanation. The workmen who placed them provided themselves (with or without official approval) with an escape tunnel.

Still, pyramidology forges on. Von Däniken thinks the Pyramid couldn't have been Cheops' tomb (despite clear evidence that it was), but must have been built by spacemen as a place in which to deep-freeze, store and revive themselves. Kolosimo thinks the Pyramid might have contained the Philosopher's stone.[18] Churchward thinks, as do the Rosicrucians, that it was a temple for secret ceremonies, despite the nearby presence of a perfectly usable mortuary temple built at the same time. Churchward's opinion is that adepts passed in and out through the solid granite plugs 'with the aid of a friendly spirit'.

Others have linked the Pyramid with the numerological mysteries of the Kabbalah. Still others believe it to be a time machine or a door into that most profoundly lost land, the fourth dimension. And still others 'prove' from its dimensions the present whereabouts of

The Lost Tribes of Israel

First, how they were lost:

At the death of Solomon, the ten tribes of Israel rebelled against the new king, Rehoboam (I Kings 12). They moved off to live apart from the two tribes of Judah. Later (II Kings 6) the ten were carried off as slaves by the Assyrians. The Apocrypha (II Esdras 13) says that they later wandered out of Assyria and, after a year and a half, settled in a desert land called Arsareth. That's all we've heard so far.

The discovery of America opened up the old question: Could it be Hebrew that the American Indians were speaking? Bishop Landa was sold on the idea, and so was Oliver Cromwell. The Book of Mormon tells us that the Indians are Hebrews, though not necessarily the lost tribes.

Other candidates have been the Japanese, the Zulu and the Malaysians. In 1896 W. S. Crowdy founded his Church of God and Saints of Christ on the dogma that the lost tribes are Negro. But a rival sect (the Commandment Keepers, Holy Church of the Living God) says that blacks are actually the tribes of Judah, while whites are the ten lost tribes.

By far the most persistent theory is that two of the lost tribes, Ephraim and Manasseh, are really the Anglo-Saxons and the Celts. The Anglo-Israel movement was popular in the late eighteenth century, and shows no sign of quitting yet (see page 318). Pyramidology seemed to give it new strength. According to David Davidson's measurements of the Great Pyramid (to which he added the lengths of the reigns of Egyptian kings) the 'Final Tribulation' of the lost tribes of Britain would begin in 1928 and continue to 1936. Then we'd have Armageddon until 1953, during which the Anglo-Saxons would be tested against their many enemies. In 1953 Christ would come in person to rule the British kingdom of the world.

Davidson seems to have misread the schedule, but other Anglo-Israelites march on towards their own appointments with the Millennium. *The Plain Truth*, a slick magazine distributed by Herbert W. Armstrong's computerized fundamentalists, claims that the lost tribes are the northern Europeans, the British, and the Anglo-Saxon Americans. They're due to inherit the earth any day now (see page 321).

Pre-Columbian Astronauts, and Other Old Friends

Pseudo-archaeology ranges far from the Great Pyramid and lost tribes in search of amaze. Von Däniken begins with artifacts from Peru, Mexico or Easter Island, and deduces from them that the barely possible is absolutely certain. Of the Mayan wall carving in Figure 6–1(a), he asks:

> Could primitive imagination have produced anything so remarkably similar to a modern astronaut in his rocket? Those strange markings at the foot of the drawing *can only be* an indication of the flames and gases coming from the propulsion unit.[19]

My italics, his sleight-of-hand. I find it hard not to see this picture as a robot carrying off a beautiful girl, as in Figure 6–1(b). But then I know no more about Mayan art and civilization than von Däniken does.

On such evidence is his space-visitor theory, and Kolosimo's ancient alchemist theory, built. Do cave drawings show men with clubbed limbs, enlarged heads, circular haloes, antlers? These 'can only be' space suits, helmets, antennae! Do they show half-human, half-animal deities? Aha! Do they show winged men flying? Eureka, etc.

These two authors, and Andrew Tomas[20] leap from one startling discovery to another, secure in the knowledge that their readers couldn't possibly check out all their sources, even when these are given. A shod foot-print is found within a seam of coal 15 million years old (Tomas). Near Baghdad are found electric batteries 2,000 years old (von Däniken, Tomas). The Egyptians had penicillin 4,000 years ago (Tomas). French-

Fig. 6-1(a)   Mayan wall carving

men of 15,000 years ago wore hats and shoes, and their wives
wore petticoats (Kolosimo). The ancient Chinese had X-rays
and the ancient Incas did brain surgery (Tomas). The Egyptians made cloth so fine that 'it would only be woven today
in a special factory with great technical know-how and experience' (von Däniken).[21] It would take a considerable amount
of research to verify or disprove all of these revelations, and

Fig. 6-1(b)   Traditional Robot

it's hard to see how most of them, even if true, would prove these authors' main theses.

Damon Knight introduces a similar item which can be checked, namely, a photograph of a stone implement with this caption:

> ... *The New York Times* identified this stone carving as a 'horse-like figure found among ancient Arawak remains near Orinoco River, Venezuela'. Since horses had not yet arrived in the Americas when the figure was carved, the conclusion was that it represents a sea horse.[22]

I can't tell what Knight is driving at, unless he believes that horses or stone carvings of horses fell to earth from some Fortean island in the sky. But it seems possible that there were horses around when the object was made. As a zoologist explained in 1955:

> it is fairly certain that the early human inhabitants of the Americas [Indians] found horses abundant in many parts of the continents. It is quite certain, however, that by the time white men came to the Americas, the native horses had died out, and horses were re-introduced from Europe.[23]

In the way occult beliefs have of overlapping, Hörbiger's falling moon theory has been 'confirmed' by H. S. Bellamy and P. Allan, using the ruins of Tiahuanaco, Peru.[24] Having decided that a ceremonial arch of stone, engraved with ornate figures, is a calendar (like a stone calendar of Mexico) they proceed to show why it doesn't correspond to the movements of the sun and moon.

The 'calendar' is arranged like this:

```
XXXXXXXX     XXXXXXXX
XXXXXXXX  A  XXXXXXXX
XXXXXXXX     XXXXXXXX
 B B B B B B B B B B B
```

Here A is a large full-face figure, the Bs are smaller full-face figures, and the Xs are much smaller winged figures facing A. Every figure is decorated with tiny symbols: circles, ovals, rectangles, heads of men, birds, cats and fish. Bellamy and Allan work out Hörbiger's idea that the earth had a previous moon, which orbited 447 times per year, by counting different types of symbols in different parts of the array, and calculating their way to the desired answer. Since any number whatever can be obtained by this method,* they are completely successful.

To help themselves along, they arbitrarily disregard eighteen of the X-figures at one point. At another, they obtain an approximation of *pi* from the number of right angles in a decorative border – but only by miscounting them.

* I've obtained three values from this 'calendar' by similar calculations: The number of days in our year; the number of days in our lunar month; and 1961, the publication date of Bellamy and Allan's book, *The Calendar of Tiahuanaco*.

Von Däniken claims the figures on the arch represent space gods. Kolosimo sees them as 'automatic spacecraft using solar energy'. Inevitably, several archaeoccultists have joined these mysterious ruins with others.

Easter Island

According to von Däniken,

> Connexions between Easter Island and Tiahuanaco automatically force themselves upon us. There, as here, we find stone giants belonging to the same style.[25]

By which he seems to mean kneeling, or wearing hats. By these tokens, we may connect Easter Island with Cairo and the Vatican.

There are genuine mysteries in the remote island, especially in its huge stone 'heads' (really complete statues with squat bodies). Who built them? How were these monoliths, some weighing up to twelve tons, carved, carried across the island and erected?

Most anthropologists think the builders were Polynesians, though Thor Heyerdahl, for one, thinks that Scandinavians, after settling Peru, sailed over on a balsa *Kon-Tiki*. There is little evidence for his idea. So far as is known, the Peruvians never put to sea deliberately, while the Polynesians roamed the Pacific.

In his first book, von Däniken insisted that simple savages could not have moved and lifted these statues, without the aid of helicopters.[26] Later, Heyerdahl asked six of the present islanders to erect a fallen statue, and they did it in eighteen days. In his second book, von Däniken changes course, speaking of the incredibly hard volcanic rock of which the Easter Island statues are made. It just couldn't be cut with stone tools (such as those found lying all over the volcano quarry). Yet the de Camps say that this type of rock was chosen precisely because it was so soft.[27]

As for why the statues were made, no one but Madame Blavatsky knows for sure. They are, she claims, life-size portraits of a theosophical Root Race.

That Digital Stonehenge

Every age has its favourite Stonehenge theory. Inigo Jones

saw the rock circle as a Roman temple in the Tuscan style; occultists of the last century, re-inventing the Druids, sensed its Celtic emanations; promoters of Atlantis, Zoroaster and UFOs have had their way with it. Our own age has thrown up its characteristic gloss, in Dr Gerald Hawkins's theory: Stonehenge is, for now, an astronomical observatory and a computer.

Of course Hawkins is no pseudo-scientist, but his ideas have already been taken on by astrologers, Lemurians, etc., as ballast. His *Stonehenge Decoded*[28] takes pains to disclaim connections with the occult for either of his theories.

His first theory is that Stonehenge was an astronomical observatory where Britons of three thousand years ago sighted along pairs of stones towards interesting events in the sky. Could be. I'll have to leave genuine criticism of this theory to genuine astronomers who, unlike me, know their azimuth from their declination. But it's worth noting a few points which *Stonehenge Decoded* reveals only indirectly.

Hawkins finds a total of 32 alignments of pairs of stones, or pairs of stone arches, with various aspects of the sun and moon, such as rising and setting at midsummer, at midwinter, and at the equinoxes.[29] Of these alignments:

3 are redundant (i.e. they are fixed by the geometry of other alignments).

22 others are based on missing stones, or holes where stones or posts are presumed to have stood (at some time).

2 others involve lines of sight that may well have been blocked by a large stone (the 'slaughter stone') which has fallen over.

4 others are based on stones that have fallen over.

This would seem to leave Hawkins with only a single indisputable alignment, unless he has guessed right about the exact arrangement of stones and posts in 1500 BC. Around 1500 BC is the date Hawkins assumed Stonehenge was completed, and all his astronomical calculations are based on this date. But recent, improved dating methods now place the completion at 2500 BC. The news that Stonehenge is a thousand years older than he'd thought may deal yet another small blow to Hawkins's alignment theory.

Hawkins's 'computer' theory concerns the Aubrey holes, a ring of fifty-six shallow holes around the Stonehenge complex.

Knowing the cycles of certain lunar and solar events, he worked out a way of marking these by placing stones in some of these holes, at appropriate intervals. Then, by moving the stones around the circle, one hole per year, he could predict that, whenever any stone reached some given point, the event (say, a solar eclipse at midwinter) would take place.

This is 'computing', just as telling rosary beads or crossing off a calendar are 'computing', and it makes a fascinating game, but there's no indication that the Aubrey holes were actually used for this purpose. A more likely use has already been determined from examining the holes: Many of them contain cremations.

Hawkins would be the first to admit that his computer theory is just a guess. At the opposite pole is an article by John Michell, earnestly explaining the relationship of Stonehenge to the ruins of Glastonbury Abbey. Along the way, he brings in the Pyramid inch, dowsing, ley lines (supposed straight lines connecting various wonderful ruins in Britain),* Chinese magic, the number of the Beast (666), Australian aborigine fertility rites, and more:

> Glastonbury Abbey was erected on the line of a dragon road radiating from Stonehenge, and in the centre of the line, before the altar of the Abbey, was placed the tomb of King Arthur, the heir to the dragon throne of Britain.[30]

Michell includes useful diagrams, proving that you can draw a six-pointed star on a map of Stonehenge and that 'the Abbey is therefore contained within a rectangle of 666 feet long,' except that, in the diagram, it extends well outside the rectangle. When taken down to the Michell level, ruins cease to amaze, and begin to disappoint.

Now, about those dragons ...

* In a similar system, UFO sightings are connected with straight lines (See page 282).

Mermaids were a speciality of Phineas T. Barnum's. He exhibited several stuffed specimens over the years, beside such marvels as the petrified Cardiff Giant and Joice Heth, the 161-year-old nurse of George Washington.* Barnum's mermaids, like those displayed in Europe, were made by Japanese fishermen. But by 1858, at least one English taxidermist had caught on to the technique of sewing half a monkey to half a hake.

Gradually the naturalists have forced us to trade our fabulous beasts for disappointing substitutes. For the elegant unicorn we received a stubby rhino; for the dragon, a Chinese alligator; for the hundred-headed hydra, an octopus. The Roc that Sindi-bad saw carrying off full-grown elephants turns out to be merely a large, flightless extinct cousin of the ostrich; the Phoenix, a purple heron. And worst of all, the mermaid has become blubberized into a dugong. No wonder so many of us need Disneyland.

There are of course a few salients of animal amaze not yet captured by the naturalists ...

Much of a Loch Ness

The Loch Ness monster broke the surface in 1933. A circus and a zoological society both offered rewards for its capture, thus drawing up the true battle lines. Aldous Huxley, among others, publicly opined that it was real, and all the arguments which for centuries had surrounded sea serpents were transferred to this fresh example. Was the creature a great sea reptile left over from the Mesozoic Age? Was it a giant eel of some hitherto unknown variety? Could it be a surviving member of the extinct whale species *Zeuglodon*, alias *Basilosaurus*? Only the tabloid press knew for sure.

* Not the Cardiff Giant of the original hoax, but at least carved by the same sculptor from similar gypsum. Both 'petrified men' lay posed concealing their genitals, as if they knew they were destined to become family entertainment. Joice Heth finally died, aged 80.

One newspaper expedition was quick to spot footprints on the shore, made by someone's hippo foot ashtray. Visitors began seeing the monster regularly, in shapes as variable as those of Masartians. Most often, 'it' showed up as one or more dark humps floating on the loch's surface.

Their number ranged from one to eight, and the witnesses agreed that they must belong to some large animal moving just out of sight below the water.[1]

(This seems akin to the ufological process by which a string of lights (pieces of the Zond IV Russian spacecraft burning up in the atmosphere) are seen as connected by the observer:

He may even see a dark elongated form connecting them so that they become *lights on a cigar-shaped object*, or even *windows on a cigar-shaped object*.[2]

Probably a similar Gestalt process enabled the ancient ufologists to see gods in the constellations.)

An exhaustive analysis of reports occupied the next year in the life of Rupert T. Gould, a retired naval officer. His book *The Loch Ness Monster* appeared in 1934.[3] Commander Gould has been described elsewhere as 'an authority on matters as diverse as the development of the typewriter, perpetual motion, the transmutation of metals, the canals of Mars and the Indian Rope Trick'. He brought this formidable battery of expertise to bear on the monster and made long work of it.

His book gives fifty-one reports, several sketches and photographs, a map of the loch pinpointing all sightings and a thorough tabulation of all reports to determine their common factors.

Their common factors were, alas, only dark humps floating on the surface of the loch, elusive as the canals of Mars. Commander Gould's evidence for the monster finally rest on three points:

1 A great many people claimed to have seen dark humps on the surface.

2 A few claimed to have seen more details of the monster, or to have seen it on land.

3 One person claimed to have photographed it.

Of 51 reports, 47 took place between 4 April 1933 and 1 May 1934. The remaining four, scattered throughout the previous decade, were suddenly 'remembered' after the craze began. This seems to indicate that something was in the loch during that year. Though there have been hundreds, perhaps thousands of reports in the forty years since, Loch Ness has never seen such a short, intensive spell of consistent reports.

A monster was seen twice on dry land. Once it crossed the road in daylight in front of the car of Mr and Mrs Spicer:

> It had a thick body without any sign of legs, and a long neck which undulated up and down.... The colour of its body was grey, like a dirty elephant or a rhinoceros, and it moved in a series of jerks.[4]

Six months later, A. Grant had a similar experience, while riding his motorbike (on the same road, which leads around the loch). Though this time it was night, Grant clearly made out more of the beast's features. Its head was

> like that of an eel with large eyes set up near the crown. He also observed that the animal had strong front flippers and a rounded tail. It was black, about 18 feet in length, and moved by arching its back on front and hind flippers alternately.[5]

Both of these descriptions, even without allowing for tricks of perception and memory, apply to a single non-mythical creature, namely, a large seal. This suggestion is made by Richard Carrington, who believes the seal entered the loch one spring, by way of the River Ness, stayed until the next spring, and left by the Firth of Beauly.

The frontispiece of Commander Gould's book is the clearest and most famous photo of the monster extant. It shows a silhouette rising from the water, which could be a saurian head, the head of a goose, or almost anything. It was 'taken on Invermoriston by Mr R. K. Wilson, FRCS, on April 1, 1934, at a range of 150-200 yards.' Twenty-three years later, another photo taken by Mr Wilson on the same day turned up. The two appear as the frontispiece of Constance Whyte's *More Than a Legend*, 1957. The new picture is said to have been taken 'immediately after' the first, and to show 'the monster sinking'. It also seems to show the entire surface of the loch shrinking, since all its waves have shrunk. Either Mr Wilson retreated some distance or changed lenses. Whyte tells the whole story of the photograph, assuring us that both the doctor who took it and the chemist who developed it were very reliable chaps.[6]

By 1961 Tim Dinsdale, ARAeS, had found fresh monster proof in the first photograph:

> Looking at the picture held at arm's length, there are two kinds of ripples on the surface. The parallel lines of wind blown ripples ... and a large concentric ring of ripples caused by the central disturbance, the neck. At first glance this is all that can be seen, but looking again, it is possible to make out a second smaller ring of ripples caused by some disturbance well to the rear of the neck.[7]

Providing always that it is a neck. Dinsdale finds this second ripple, which I am unable to see at all, evidence that the 'neck' has a body below the surface. Of course, the same arguments apply whether it is a monster, a swimmer's arm, a water-logged tree with a branch sticking up, or the horn of a unicorn. Finally all Gould, Whyte and Dinsdale leave us with is a bad photo which could be anything, taken on April Fools' Day during the height of monster fever.

The monster has, since 1934, been shot at, chased in boats, sought in a submarine and detected on sonar. Yet the most positive observers are those with least experience in observing natural phenomena – weekend visitors who, seeking, find a curiosity. They generally have a far better idea of what a sea monster ought to look like, than what a water bird does look like.

Carrington's seal seems a likely explanation. Other explanations run into a series of unanswerable questions. If the creature were some large undiscovered species of mammal or reptile, and assuming that it is still there, it must have surfaced for air somewhere between 50,000 and 500,000 times. Hundreds of zoologists and thousands of photographers have spent days and weeks each looking for it. Yet no clear photograph and no positive identification has been made.

The case for sea monsters is certainly stronger. Certainly the world's oceans are large enough and rich enough in life to support such creatures, which might be either reptiles or some serpentine species of whale, long thought to be extinct. Dozens of sea serpents or sea monsters have been washed up on shore, but these inevitably turn out to be partly decomposed (or partly eaten) whales, whose decapitated spine, sticking out from a mass of flesh, resembles a long snaky neck. Gould showed a photograph of one of these in his book in 1934, and the latest was found on a New England shore a few months ago.

Rodent Removal

One small and silly myth concerning animals, still popular, is the 'suicide impulse' of lemmings. Periodically the little rodents are supposed to make a grim march from the highlands of Norway and Sweden where they live, down to the sea, where they throw themselves in. The best source for this notion is the *Encyclopaedia Britannica*, eleventh edition, which emphasizes the inexorability of it all. The lemmings

> advance steadily and slowly.... None returns and the onward march of the survivors never ceases until they reach the sea, into which they plunge and are drowned.[8]

Damon Knight, still looking for Fortean data, wonders where the next wave of lemmings comes from.

> In order to account for the continued survival of the lemmings, we must suppose either that some lemmings turn back at the last moment, an event which has never been observed, or that some lemmings in the highlands do not take part in the mass migration at all. If the latter is the case, we would suppose that the migratory instinct would have been bred out of the race long ago.[9]

He infers some kind of special creation, or else Fortean rains of rodents (which have not been 'observed' since 1578). But all this mystification depends on the words 'migratory instinct'.

There is no evidence that these migrations are instinctive at all. Bergen Evans explains them as:

> merely a crowding into the coastal plains of excess numbers that are periodically bred in the hills. It is an irregular movement of individuals and often takes years. The creatures are able to swim small streams, and it is possible that some reach the ocean, swim out beyond their power to return, and drown.[10]

Experiments with rats have shown that overcrowding can induce psychotic behaviour, so there is some possibility that the lemmings periodically run amok. But it seems at least as likely that they migrate in search of food, new places to burrow, or just to get away from the mob. No serious scientist has suggested, during the last few editions of the *Encyclopaedia Britannica*, that lemmings have a strong Will to Die.

Evolution

In 1970 the state of Tennessee finally allowed that evolution might be mentioned in the classroom without necessarily corrupting children. Of course evolution, as the fundamentalist magazine *The Plain Truth* constantly reminds its readers, is only a theory.

True, but the evidence supporting this particular theory is formidable. It's the simplest explanation so far which both fits the facts and can be tested. Moreover it explains much which the leading alternative – God scraping Adam out of mud – doesn't explain.

The Plain Truth pours out an endless stream of articles and pamphlets, however, explaining how evolution just won't work. One argument concentrates on 'Living Fossils', creatures like the coelacanth, a fish which hasn't changed substantially in seventy million years. Biologists may explain that evolution proceeds at different rates in different species, depending upon the evolutionary pressures and opportunities available in the environment, but in vain. Fundamentalists *know* the plain truth, that nothing ever evolves at all.

A second task is to ask evolutionists to explain exactly how every creature evolved to its present state, complete with such complicated mechanisms as eyes, claws, flippers, etc., which perfectly suit its present life. If an elephant needed a trunk to survive, the argument goes, how did it survive long enough to develop a trunk? Unfortunately this argument oversimplifies the evolution case until it really is meaningless. Evolutionists could, if pressed, produce a scenario of reasonable mutations, some 'documented' by fossils, living intermediate species or embryonic development, to explain a feature like the elephant's trunk. They generally avoid such speculations, however, unless there is plenty of 'documentation', just as historians generally avoid speculations about whether Alexander the Great had dandruff. The fact remains that animals which do not adapt to a changing environment, perish. And if they do adapt, they must become different animals.

In 'Evolution Gets the Horse Laugh!' plain truther Paul Kroll thinks to prove that horses have always looked exactly like Trigger and Black Beauty, and never were anything like little Eohippus. Here's his method:

> Scientist Theodosius Dobzhansky states without hesitation: 'Many textbooks and popular accounts of biology represent the evolution of the horse family as starting with eohippus and progressing in a direct line towards the modern horse *Equus* ... according to Simpson, *this over-simplification really amounts to a FALSIFICATION*' (Theodosius Dobzhansky, *Evolution, Genetics and Man*, p. 302). Did you grasp that? Here an *eminent scientist quotes another eminent scientist*.[11]

Their eminence is not enchanced by mutilated quotation, however. Following the word 'Equus', the original reads:

> This evolutionary progress involved, allegedly, the animals getting steadily larger and larger, while their feet were losing toe after toe, until just a single hoof was left. According to Simpson, this oversimplification really amounts to a falsification. In reality things happened in a far more complex, yet more meaningful way.[12]

Dobzhansky then goes on to describe the evolution of the horse from Eohippus, emphasizing the important change from a browsing to a grazing animal. In pretending that scientists completely reject Eohippus→Equus, Kroll stoops to a little *FALSIFICATION* himself. Or else, in his eagerness to accuse evolutionists out of their own mouths, he misreads what is as plain as the duck bill on a platypus. The duck-billed platypus, by the way, is seen by *The Plain Truth* as a Divine joke. No doubt we can expect future issues to explain the elephant's trunk as a Divine Freudian slip.

Noah and Co.
One of the catastrophes formerly favoured as an explanation for extinct species was the Deluge. Afterwards, either God would have started afresh with new species, or else we start climbing Mount Ararat to look for Noah's Ark.

> Since 1947 there have been half-a-dozen expeditions to Ararat to find traces of the Ark. Investigation has been handicapped by the fact that the Eastern side of Ararat stretches across the Soviet frontier, and that ascent of the mountain is dangerous, as the upper slopes are coated with a thick ice sheet which covers any possible relics ...
> The Editor nearly went on one such trip in 1950 but was held up for various reasons, mainly political.[13]

The Editor is Egerton Sykes, an Atlantologist and Hörbiger enthusiast. Every year or so since the unsuccessful attempt of Dr Aaron Smith in 1949, yet another group of hopefuls clamber the sides of Ararat, looking for the Ark. Why do they do it? Because it isn't there.

Some time back, know-it-alls began questioning the whole idea of the Ark. Walter Raleigh, having calculated that it was too small to hold all those animals, figured that Noah must have taken only the Old World animals, the New World species having evolved from them.

That was in 1616. By May 1970, *The Plain Truth* had worked up a rebuttal. John E. Portune's article takes some trouble to show that the Ark was big enough, after all. He calculates its volume as $300 \times 50 \times 30$ cubits, or (depending on the size of the cubit) between 1.5 and 3 million cubic feet. Naturally he chooses the larger figure.

Next Portune analyses the animal kingdom, finding that 60 per cent of the species live in the sea, and another 18 per cent are insects. The rest are 'of the average size of a rhesus monkey', and there are about 20,000 of these. He thus arrives at a figure of 40,000 cages capable of holding rhesus monkeys, each cage being a cube 2.5 feet on a side.

> Only 20 per cent of the Ark's three million cubic feet would provide room for 40,000 cages.... And so, viewed from the perspective of scientific fact, only *one* of the three decks was plenty to accommodate 'all those animals'.[14]

Portune has made a number of elementary mistakes. To begin with, he assumes an Ark shaped like a rectangular block, with walls of zero thickness. Making it seaworthy in shape and construction reduces its capacity by about 27 per cent (to 327,000 cubic cubits). Secondly, animal cages cannot be crammed into every available corner; the creatures must breathe, and there must be access for feeding, watering and cleaning. With the best packing, Portune can't get all his zoo on board. The best he can do is 35,000 rhesus monkeys. But, thanks to overcrowding, heat, noise, filth, lack of fresh food and exercise, Portune's Ark would soon have many fewer inhabitants. There would be no room at all for the eight humans on board, except in the aisles between cages – but then, that's where they'd spend all their time anyhow.

Caring for the animals would involve much more than live mice for the snakes, fresh eucalyptus leaves for the koala and fresh bamboo for the panda. Over this period (a hundred and fifty days or more) it would mean fetching over three tons of water per day, and more Augean chores.* It would mean blowing the husks off the budgies' seed dish, cutting fresh roses for a perverse breed of ant that refuses to eat anything else, spending time with the gorillas so they won't literally die of boredom, and bathing the hippo. No wonder Noah got drunk when he came out.

Folk Tales
The point of having an Ark is of course to deny evolution,

---

* Broom in hand, Noah faces pairs of elephants, horses, moose, okapi, giraffes, zebras, asses, American and European buffalo, benteng, yaks, musk oxen, deer, elk, reindeer, caribou, impala, ... and seven cows.

and the point of that is to deny human evolution. The attempt to split man off from the primates can be crude. *The Plain Truth* shows a picture of Neanderthal man 'cleaned up' – shaved, crewcut, wearing a nice white shirt, jacket and tie – as visible proof that the human race has always lived in the suburbs.

More sophisticated attempts include *Fossil Man*, by Frank W. Cousins. He argues that fossil evidence for man's evolution is scarce, consisting mainly of a few skulls found in far-flung locations. Some may be human, some not, but:

> the juxtapositioning of two or more skulls of different animals can have little bearing on the case for evolution unless a genealogical link is established.[15]

But the case for human evolution does not of course rest upon a few skulls and skull fragments, but upon evolution for all species, for which far more evidence exists. Man is identifiable as a primate by his embryonic development and his physical characteristics, just as the kangaroo is identifiable as a marsupial.

Most cases against human évolution either dismiss all evolution theory, as Cousins seems to do, or else allow it to operate on all species up to man, where it suddenly stops. Von Däniken favours the idea that extraterrestials mated with apes to produce man. Robert Charroux[16] prefers to think of man as himself an extraterrestial who came here and presumably forgot how to leave again. Peter Kolosimo hints that spacemen either sired our species or fabricated it out of local materials.

Such theories usually stress man's unique characteristics, e.g. speech and culture, which they say could not have arisen naturally from monkeys. Therefore speech and culture must have been brought here from some distant planet. Evidently it hasn't occurred to them to ask how these happened to be on the distant planet in the first place. All that Charroux, von Däniken and Kolosimo are doing is moving one piece of the evolutionary chain to outer space, and not explaining that piece.

In 1911, Charles Dawson, antiquarian and lawyer, found a skull in the gravel pits of Piltdown Common in Sussex. It raised an enormous scientific question about man's origins, since it showed a large brain cavity and an ape's jaw. If genuine, it would mean that man had developed a large brain over half a million years ago, *before* he had become a true man. A few sceptics held the opposite view, that man's brain had evolved after he became man, but here was Piltdown Man to disprove them.

The controversy went on for forty years, mainly because Dawson refused to let opponents examine the skull. Finally, in 1953, a fluorine test performed by J. S. Bruner, K. P. Oakley and W. E. LeGros Clark showed Piltdown Man to be a fake, a human skull fastened to an ape's jaw.

Just who buried the Piltdown skull in that gravel pit is still a mystery. But there is some evidence that Dawson did occasionally stain bones and otherwise fabricate such fossils.

In 1937 Dr G. G. Simpson had the misfortune to be the author of a 287-page bulletin for the US National Museum entitled 'The Fort Union of the Crazy Mountain Field, Montana, and Its Mammalian Faunas'. Somewhere in this document he described the oldest known primates, which he had found in this palaeontological survey. The book was long and technical, so it seems that few newsmen bothered reading it. Instead, they immediately began misquoting a press handout by the musem. Dr Simpson had stressed that the primates concerned were not to be considered direct ancestors of man. But the Associated Press wire service opened their story:

> Man instead of having descended from the monkey probably ascended from a four-inch-long tree-dwelling animal which was the great grand-daddy of all mammals on the earth today.[17]

Simpson had remarked that the animals were as small as rats and mice. It was all the press needed:

MONKEY FATHER OF MAN? NOPE, A MOUSE – Sacramento, California, *Union*.
FOUR-INCH TREE ANIMAL SEEN AS MAN'S ANCESTOR – Shreveport, Louisiana, *Times*.
STUDY OF MAMMALS BRINGS ABOUT NEW EVOLUTION THEORY – Newport News, Virginia, *Press*.[18]

Several newspapers claimed that Simpson had found the 'missing link' which has so fascinated the press for a century. The missing link has been everything, found everywhere: In the 'Pliocene skull' found in a California mine (where it had been placed by a California druggist) and immortalized by Bret Harte's ode; in the pygmy fossils of Bombay, which never existed at all, outside the local rumour circuit and the world press; in the hairy giants menacing British Columbia in the 1930s, who vanished without a trace; and in the Ameranthropoid reportedly killed by Francis de Loys in 1929. De Loys somehow lost the skin of his specimen, retaining only an ambiguous photograph which looked to sceptics like a spider monkey.[19]

Many, however, insist that the missing link lives high in the Himalayas, avoiding publicity. Or so *he* thinks.

Abominables Anonymous

The dust jacket of Odette Tchernine's *The Yeti* promises much: 'Russian Expeditions manned by Scientists are close to discovering the Identity of the ABOMINABLE SNOWMAN.'[20] The book inside delivers slightly less. Most of the 'expeditions' discussed are conspicuously manned by non-scientists: explorer, engineer, amateur photographer, etc. The scientists only appear now and then, usually interviewing mountain tribes or else repeating travellers' tales.

All the Tchernine tales seem to come under four headings. The first, tribal myths and legends, includes all stories beginning 'an old man of the ———— tribe says'. These may be set aside as arguably fiction.

The second includes hearsay. Tchernine repeats a story told her by someone who knew someone else in East Africa who once may have seen a strange silhouette or strange tracks. These are about as evidentially useful as shaggy dog jokes.

The third includes stories backed with physical evidence, which, in every case, turns out to be spurious. A yeti scalp is made of goatskin. A supposed dried yeti hand in a casket is found to be the dried paws of a fox. (This in the account of a Dr Porshnev, who remarks with childlike optimism, 'But the relic hand must be somewhere.') A yeti killed in the Pamir Mountains, where so many manifestations are reported, turns out to be a large male rhesus monkey (this time Dr Porshnev takes the same line as John Keel took towards UFO hoaxes: Someone must be trying to conceal *the truth* by false evidence).

The final group consists of thirteen first-hand stories. These yarns bear a family resemblance to one another, and to good ghost stories. The narrator is told about a local 'wild man' legend. He then awakens to find Something in his or her bed-chamber, or else is summoned from sleep by terrified peasant guides who point out the monster to him. Often he sees the creature while alone, at night, and for a few seconds' time. He may wish to track or chase the creature, but his super-stitious guides refuse to cooperate. Few of the narrators seemed to know anything about local fauna, and only two were in any way connected with zoology. Four stories also involved hearsay. Table 7–1 sets out similarities to ghost stories.

Table 7–1   Points of similarity between yeti experiences and ghost stories

Yeti experience:

	A	B	C	D	E	F	G	H	I	J	K	L	M
Awakened by the scared guides, who show him the creature	x					x			x				
In bedroom				x									x
Alone		x		x									x
A stranger, and not a zoologist or biological scientist	x	x	x	x	x	x	x	x	x	x	x		x
Guides 'refuse to go on'	x		x	x					x		x		
Glimpses 'it' for only a few seconds	x		x	x	x							x	x
Possible man or local animal				x	x	x						x	x
Hearsay or legend involved							x	x		x		x	
No. Points	4	2	3	6	3	3	2	2	3	2	2	3	4

(Average No. Points=3)

This does not of course discount yeti stories, but it does seem to imply that there is no more (and no less) reason to believe in Tchernine's yeti than in ghosts.

Some stories are clearly *not* about yeti. One person describes a 'wild man' of the southern Manchurian forest who has been captured and domesticated by a Chinese hunter. His face

> resembled the face of a beast of prey, and this impression was enhanced by the huge open mouth, in the depths of which sparkled rows of powerful fangs.... His wild, insane-looking eyes shone in the dark like those of a wolf.[21]

He also growls, his hair is a mess, and he eats raw squirrels. When his master takes him to town, he generally ends up killing some dog: 'it strangles the dog in a trice and bites through its windpipe.'[22] One night the guide awakens the narrator and they steal forth from their tent to witness 'it' howling at the moon and running with a wolf pack.

Now, this belongs to a class of well-known tales popular over the past century. When they can be checked, their wild men, wolf men and baboon boys inevitably turn out to be pathetic, feeble-minded human beings. Bergen Evans mentions one damning fact about such tales:

> the wolves they behaved like were not ordinary four-footed wolves, or even a particular species of ordinary wolves ... but were genuine funny-paper wolves, *Lupus vulgus fantasticus*, running in packs, howling by the clock, and emitting a 'weird light' from their eyes.[23]

If such is to be evidence for yeti, we may as well include the legends of the Three Little Pigs, Tarzan, and that colossal ape-man last seen clambering up the Empire State Building.

The Yeti does include some photographic evidence, mainly of 'yeti tracks' which closely resemble the monster tracks I used to, as a child, stamp out carefully in the snow, in hopes of scaring the postman. In California, two men took twenty seconds of film of a fleeing 'Snowwoman', so-called because 'she' seems to have something flapping which are taken to be breasts. The frame reproduced closely resembles a man in a bearskin rug running away from the camera. Various scientists examined the film and were unimpressed. Eventually the men who took it said that they just didn't want to talk about it any more.

The Tchernine stories vary in locale and description. Like UFO occupants, yeti are said to be short, stunted, hunched, huge, five feet tall, and seven feet tall. Their fur comes in red-brown, very red, grey-brown, yellow, white and dark shades. They live in the Himalayas, the Pamir, the Tien' Shan, Kenya, California and in the Caucasus. As Tchernine describes the yeti,

> He can live anywhere, in any landscape, at any altitude.... He escapes the effects of cold and lack of winter food by hibernating in caves or in pits.... Such creatures can run like horses, and swim rivers and fast mountain torrents. In the process of transition to the biped manner of movement, the females, unlike the apes, developed long mammary glands, so, throwing their breasts over their shoulders, they can, while walking along, feed the young hanging on their backs.[24]

If one of these females ever comes loping into any well-populated town, it should cause, in UFO parlance, quite a flap.

Of the Flesh

> You got to go by yourself to the middle of the woods,
> where you know there's a spunk-water stump, and just as
> it's midnight you back up against the stump and jam
> your hand in and say:
>> Barley-corn, barley-corn, injun-meal shorts
>> Spunk-water, spunk-water, swaller these warts
> And then walk away quick, eleven steps, with your eyes
> shut, and then turn around three times and walk home
> without speaking to nobody.

Tom Sawyer's cure for warts sounds ideal for those dissatis-
fied with conventional medicine. First, it is completely *natural*,
involving no compounded drugs, no surgery and no doctor.
Second, it works by the 'law of similia', whereby 'like cures
like': a rotten stump full of stagnant water could resemble
a wart. Third, it sounds like an old injun remedy, and everyone knows how clever primitive people are at curing everything.
Fourth, it might even work – though in that case it runs the
risk of being adopted by 'straight' practitioners and thereby
losing its appeal.

Pseudo-medicine often seems designed on just such principles. Its popular success surpasses that of almost any other
crank system. Millions of people who chuckle over flat earth
notions or pyramidology still wear copper bracelets to ward
off arthritis, rub on worthless hair restorers, allow quacks to
pummel their spines, swallow unnecessary tonics and vitamins,
avoid meats or foods of a certain colour, and visit faith healers.

Martin Gardner explains two secrets of quack success:

1 That many illnesses pass away anyway, and the quack
can take credit for the 'cure'.

2 That many illnesses have a psychological basis, so their
cure is largely a matter of faith.[1]

While conventional doctors may also effect the occasional
cure by accident, and while they may prescribe worthless
'placebos' to patients they believe to have no organic disorders,

there is no general attempt on the part of the medical profession to conceal these facts. At the same time, the bulk of orthodox medical practice rests on no such fringe cases, but on facts and scientific theories which have withstood severe testing; theories which, except on scientific grounds, are hardly debatable.

Why then, do people move from orthodox, or 'allopathic'* therapy, to devious quack systems? Aside from Gardner's reasons, Table 8–1 may explain some differences in the way people see the two choices.

Table 8–1   Orthodox vs 'fringe' medicine:
Differences from the patient's point of view

Orthodox medicine	*Fringe medicine*
Hard to understand, technical, specialized. (Patient has no idea what a virus, an EEG, or hydrocortisone might be.)	Easy to understand. One simple principle. (Patient can see how 'like cures like', how magnets draw pain from the body, or how God might effect direct miracle cures.)
Brusque, unsympathetic or busy doctor (especially with hypochondriacs).	Sympathetic healer who takes a personal interest in his patient, has time for a chat (especially since he has little else on his mind).
May admit defeat on cases which are 'hopeless', chronic, or beyond his science.	Never gives up.
Never guarantees cure.	Certain of diagnosis and cure.

* A name still given to orthodox medicine by its opponents. Brian Inglis feels that 'allopathy began to make itself redundant by its own achievement in bringing most of the infectious diseases under control' (p. 52, *Fringe Medicine*) and that it consequently has made all its best discoveries and now ought to leave the field to fringe doctors. This curiously echoes the nineteenth-century feeling that science had made all the discoveries it was ever going to make, so that it ought to turn over the search for knowledge to occultists.

Orthodox medicine	Fringe medicine
Doctors' methods become stereotyped. They're 'all the same', taking blood pressures, writing prescriptions ...	Exotic new methods (at least at first, and for any one system).
Cure may be unpleasant (injections), frightening (surgery) or difficult (dieting for obesity).	Cure is pleasant (a herbal drink), simple (spinal adjustments) or easy ('miracle' diets).
Success is never advertised by the profession.	Success is widely advertised by practitioner, as well as the aunt everyone has who 'swears by him'.
Failure is widely reported (e.g. thalidomide, malpractice suits, and the hypochondriacal boast that 'six doctors gave up on me').	Failures are seldom reported, since, as in roulette, they are usually expected.

Like Conquers All

Homeopathy was invented in the early nineteenth century by a German doctor, Samuel Hahnemann, whose great 'Law of Similia' ('like cures like') rules the system still. By the Law of Similia, a sick man is cured by giving him a drug that would make him sick if he were well. It is necessary, as one homeopath put it, 'to assist the disease in order to quell it'.

This reversal appears in many pseudo-sciences: Gravity is not a pull, but a push. We're not outside the earth, but inside. Light doesn't enter the eye, it comes out of it. Homeopaths explain that symptoms are not produced by disease at all, they are merely 'Nature's reaction' to disease. If Nature isn't reacting strongly enough, we must help it along.

> If Nature's efforts are accompanied by symptoms, say A and B, then logic tells me that by ordering the patient a remedy or remedies capable of rousing in normal persons the symptoms I have called A and B, I shall undoubtedly strengthen the curative effort that is at work behind the symptoms A and B within the sick body.[2]

It might seem dangerous to give someone with a fever a drug

that induces fever, and rather callous to prescribe laxative for
a diarrhoea sufferer, but homeopathy has an answer. All drugs
are to be diluted to infinitesimal dosages.

Here is another reversal: Hahnemann and his followers
believe that, the smaller a dose is, the more powerful its effects.
Homeopathic drugs have been diluted to one decillionth* of
a grain. That is, the homeopathic apothecary takes a pint of
the pure drug, mixes it in ten pints of water, throws away
nine pints, and mixes the remainder in ten pints of water;
then he repeats the process sixty times. Obviously there is very
little left of the original drug in the mixture, but just how
little is difficult to picture. Martin Gardner compares it to
'letting a drop of medicine fall into the Pacific, mixing thoroughly, then taking a spoonful.[3]

But a decillionth is a far, far smaller dose than this. Try to
imagine a globe of water the size of our entire solar system.
Then imagine that every star in our galaxy, and in every other
visible galaxy, is surrounded by a similar globe of water. All
this water is combined, and into it we drop *one 1,000 millionth*
of a drop of medicine, mix thoroughly, and take as directed.

Actually, if the purest imaginable water is used in a real
homeopathic dilution, it must still contain far more natural
amounts of even the rarest elements on earth, than it can
possibly contain of the medicine.

Nevertheless, with a one-decillionth dose of ordinary salt,
one homeopath claimed to produce over a thousand different
symptoms in healthy persons. Since it is highly unlikely that
any of these persons actually received even a single molecule
of his salt, such cures are put down to the 'spiritual' effects
or 'radiations' of the substance, which somehow persist even
after the last of it has been poured down the drain during
the dilution process.

What are the active ingredients of homeopathic remedies?
Anything will do, from arsenic (given for diarrhoea, gout,
palsy and the itch) to graphite (given for tumours, psoriasis

*A decillion is 10^{60}, or 1 followed by sixty os. For some idea
of its size, multiply the weight of the sun (in ounces) by the age
of the earth (in seconds), and multiply the result by the number
of people who have probably lived on earth so far (about 10^{11}).
The answer is about 10^{60}.

and piles). Table 8–2 shows a few diseases and their cures, as given in a homeopathic handbook. The handbook also recommends treating insomnia with caffeine and stomach ulcer with aspirin, probably on the theory that caffeine keeps people awake and that aspirin damages the stomach lining. It even recommends – though this sounds like a bad joke – treating gout with minute doses of chalk.

Table 8–2 Homeopathic cures

	Charcoal	Chalk	Belladonna	Sod. Bicarb.	Sulphur	Iron rust	Poison sumac	Sepia*
Low blood pressure				X				
Diabetes				X		X		
Lumbago	X			X				
Arterio-sclerosis	X					X		
Constipation	X				X			
Worms		X			X			
Tuberculosis	X	X	X					
Writer's cramp		X	X					
Kidney stone			X				X	
Colitis	X						X	
Appendicitis	X	X						
Jaundice	X	X						X
Prostate infection	X							X
Tumour	X				X			

(* Sepia is cuttlebone.)

Note that the cure for jaundice involves sepia, the bone, not the pigment, though the latter might seem more magically correct. But then homeopaths seem to have no more poetry than their orthodox foes. In fact, homeopaths *are* orthodox in everything but their notions of scientific truth. Many homeopaths in Britain and America are fully qualified MDs, practising conventional medicine except in prescribing. Their establishment image in Britain seems to have come about through royal patronage. Since they rely on conventional treatments in emergencies, their homeopathy must be harmless if useless.

With the revived interest in occult matters, however, numbers of unorthodox homeopaths have set themselves up in business in both Britain and America. These, too, shoot for a kind of respectability, usually by adopting a string of letters after their names. This stubborn clinging to 'science', this refusal to see that homeopathy is rooted in simple magic, is as perverse as the behaviour of Christians who deny that Christ was a Jew. Hahnemann homeopathy's drab microdoses of cuttlebone may be instructively compared with an ancient Hindu remedy for jaundice:

> [The priest] daubed him from head to foot with a yellow porridge made of turmeric ..., set him on a bed, tied three yellow birds, to wit a parrot, a thrush and a yellow wagtail, by means of a yellow string to the foot of the bed; then pouring water over the patient, he washed off the yellow porridge, and with it no doubt the jaundice, from him to the birds. After that, by way of giving a final bloom to his complexion, he took some hairs of a red bull, wrapt them in gold leaf and glued them to the patient's skin.[4]

What patient could be so ungrateful as to die after this magnificent treatment?

The point is not that magic should replace orthodox medicine, but that homeopathy is self-deceiving in declaring itself a science. It ought either to abandon its occult basis or else embrace it honestly, admitting itself to be the cuckoo-child of magic.

Nature's Was I Ere I Saw Serutan

Who could argue against a balanced diet, fresh air, exercise and sunshine? Who could insist that antibiotics always work as hoped? Who thinks all surgery is necessary? Disciples of naturopathy, stand up and be counted!

So I paraphrase the basic arguments of this large, ill-defined cult. Probably most naturopaths don't feel that they belong to a movement at all. They may be vegetarians, naturists (who sunbathe for health), hydrotherapists (who wash themselves for health), or anti-vaccination people, but they share a common distrust of orthodox medicine and a common faith in 'nature' cures. Passwords like *natural, unadulterated, organic* and *biochemic* are sprinkled through their literature and, since each sub-cult defines such terms differently, it isn't easy to find out what they're supposed to mean. *Natural* things usually include raw foods, unpasteurized milk, herbal medicines, massage and exercise. Definitely unnatural are non-herbal medicines, processed food, vaccination and surgery. Diet cults will be discussed further in chapter 10; other naturopathic passions here.

These passions have included cold baths, hot baths, steam baths, sun baths and air baths; massage, towel-rubbing ('friction baths'), ultra-violet lamps, infra-red lamps, coloured lamps, and most certainly enemas. Dr Robert A. Wood of Chicago, a particular advocate of, as he calls it, 'colonic irrigation', used this form of nature's lavage to cure appendicitis, syphilis and TB of the bone – or so he says.[5] Barbara Cartland recommends inducing a bowel movement every twelve hours, saying that 'we all know that the setting sin of the British nation is constipation', resulting in 'people who I'm quite certain end up with every sort of disease that it's possible to have'.[6]

Aside from its Freudian possibilities, the enema obsession seems tied to an exaggerated fear of constipation. The obsessed usually demand two or three movements a day. Otherwise, they fear, 'the body absorbs from the clogged intestines poisons that would normally have been excreted' and they become 'auto-intoxicated'.[7]

It is true that (genuine) constipation may cause 'malaise, headache, coated tongue, foul breath and mental sluggishness' but medical science long ago abandoned the theory of poisoning.

> As evacuation of the bowel usually gives prompt relief ... such a cause is unlikely. A more probable explanation is that the pressure ... on the nerve endings in the colon and rectum initiates afferent impulses which lead to the symptoms.[8]

Earlier, the same source explains that

> since good health may be maintained by people who defecate only once every 2 or 3 days, it is unwise to insist that a daily bowel movement is always essential.[9]

Ignoring such reliable advice, however, because it comes from

their old enemy, medicine, naturopaths continue to imagine
they are being perfectly natural in using 'colonic irrigation'.
It might be worthwhile calling their attention to the hero of
Joris-Karl Huysman's novel *Against Nature*, who found his
broth enema a perverse delight:

> his taste for the artificial had now ... attained its supreme
> fulfilment. No one, he thought, would ever go any further;
> taking nourishment in this way was undoubtedly the ulti-
> mate deviation from the norm.[10]

Fasting is another continuing pastime for naturopaths, no
doubt explaining a good deal of their constipation. Short fasts
can do no harm to healthy people of course, but extended
fasts can obviously cause malnutrition and lower resistance to
infection. But then naturopaths have rather chaotic ideas about
nutrition anyway – their notions range from nerve tonics to
fruit-nut diets to an almost pathological fear of white foods –
and doubtless most of them don't believe in infection.

According to one naturopathic school, germs don't cause
disease, disease causes germs. George Bernard Shaw among
others subscribed to this inverse theory, claiming that germs
were just an inimical form of body cell, spontaneously
generated during disease:

> These specialized cells, called germs, microbes, bacilli,
> spirochetes, leucocytes, phagocytes, and what not, can
> escape into the air by the breath, the spittle, the handker-
> chief, the excretions, the clothes ...[11]

Shaw felt that the two modern causes of epidemics were
handkerchiefs and drains. The former carried the germs to
the laundry and ultimately to victims, and the latter, being
dismal, dark, damp places, multiplied these evil cells. Evidently
disease could not be conquered until people spat and blew
their noses on the ground, and until sewers discharged their
waste directly into open streams and rivers, where sunlight,
he said, would kill the germs in seconds. He was all against
pasteurizing milk, because 'heat destroys the creative cell and
the pathogenic one indiscriminately', and he was dead against
vaccination. As far as I can imagine the results of his reforms,

they ought to produce a natural world of TB, cholera, typhus, smallpox and putrid lifeless rivers.

A recent indictment of vaccination is *The Blood Poisoners*, by Lionel Dole. According to Dole, the BBC, the press, and all the deluded doctors who follow Pasteur are engaged in one grand conspiracy to sell vaccine to an unsuspecting public.

> While the people are being lied to in every known language, and drugged and inoculated for the benefit of the huge chemical combines who own the Press and the Radio, it is obviously necessary to hit back with the truth.[12]

And the truth, as Dole sees it, is that vaccination just won't work. To show how worthless it really is, Dole carefully culls news stories from the past fifty years, for cases where something seems to have gone wrong. Several facts make his work easier:

1 The press, often as ignorant about vaccines as the rest of us, can make silly errors. Thus one case of an epidemic said to be averted by mass inoculation really is nonsense – the press report is given days before the inoculation could have taken effect.

2 There have been cases of bad (ineffective or dangerous) vaccines, especially in early applications. By picking out instances such as a misapplication of diphtheria toxin in 1925 (which did not give immunity) and a dangerous batch of Salk polio vaccine, Dole builds up a picture of all vaccine as all poison.

3 No one can ever prove that vaccine has warded off a disease in a particular patient. Vaccines are proven by statistical analysis of experiments using large groups. Dole seems to confuse these statistics with raw statistics on diseases in the whole population. The latter, however, are complicated by other factors: Not everyone gets vaccinated, vaccinations don't always 'take', and some vaccinations (such as smallpox) do not guarantee lifelong immunity.

Dole's alternative to vaccination is cleanliness, fresh air, sunshine and fruit and vegetable juices.

> In Athens ... monkeys fed upon natural foods and living in the open air were able to bear poliovirus injected right into their brains, and not one of them developed polio,

whereas, the same kind of animals, kept in small, dark cages in Paris, and fed upon laboratory (pasteurized?) food succumbed to the injections at the rate of 9 out of 10! As this is by far the most important laboratory information ever published in the whole vast literature of the subject ...[13]

Is it? This item was taken by Dole from a 1950 book on polio, by a man who worked on polio vaccine, and who at that time thought a vaccine impossible to make. It very likely reflects his opinion that fresh air and vitamins were the only available defence against polio.

As presented by Dole, the two experiments are meaningless. How many monkeys were used in each experiment, their general health, etc., are not mentioned. It could easily be that the Paris monkeys were reduced to a state where they might have succumbed to such injections of anything, even water. We have Dole's word for it that they actually died from the injections, but not that they died of polio.

He infers from these two unrelated experiments that fresh air, sunshine and health foods can ward off polio. If a vaccine inventor drew such an inference to 'prove' the value of his product, he'd be laughed out of the medical profession.

Obviously fresh fruits and vegetables, sunshine and fresh air are valuable to health in general, but they proved singularly ineffectual against polio before vaccines. It's worth noting that, across America, healthy, sturdy, suntanned farm children were struck down by polio every summer (when they were getting plenty of naturopathic medicines of all types).

Sometimes it's hard to see how naturopaths think. They find the fluoridation of water, for example, 'unnatural' and dangerous, despite the presence of even larger concentrations of fluorides in some natural water supplies. Evidently their theory is, if nature wants you to have rotten teeth, you should have them.

Again, opposition to pasteurized milk is difficult to understand. Unpasteurized milk has been known to carry TB, diphtheria, scarlet fever and undulant fever – unpleasant diseases to catch in the service of nature. It can be protected only by pasteurizing (heating) or by curdling to make it into yoghurt or cheese. If naturopaths approve the second process, why not the first?

Finally, those who reject pasteurizing milk as unnatural, find it perfectly natural to drink juice which has been (a) extracted by an electric machine from fruit which (b) only exists in its present, tasty form because of centuries of cultivation, that is, meddling with nature. Grapefruit and Delicious apples are human inventions no less than penicillin and vaccine. Even closer to penicillin are those strains of yeast so necessary to the health of health food shops, strains perfected by, I'm afraid, that old unnatural potterer, Man.

A Strong Glance

Gayelord Hauser's diet views are discussed in chapter 10. He espouses many naturopathic principles, such as the air bath (based on the erroneous notion that the skin's pores can breathe), vegetable juice cocktails, 'elimination diets' and of course colonic irrigation. Besides, Hauser promotes the strange 'eye exercises' of Dr William Horatio Bates.

Dr Bates was an ophthalmologist who practised intermittently in New York from 1885 until his death in 1931. The intermissions were occasioned by spells of amnesia, when Bates wandered off to places like London or North Dakota. Having thus lost eight years and two wives, he privately published his magnum opus, *Cure of Imperfect Eyesight by Treatment without Glasses*, in 1920. It became an immediate hit with lovers of the natural, and spawned a small literature of pseudo-ophthalmics.

His system is based on a completely wrong idea of how the human eye accommodates, or changes its focal length to look at objects at varying distances. The actual process works like this:

> In man and a few other mammals [accommodation] occurs by changing curvature of the lens; at rest, lens is focused for distant objects; it is focused for near objects by becoming more convex with the contraction of ciliary muscles in ciliary body ... Few mammals can accommodate ... In fish and amphibians, the lens is moved backwards and forwards in relation to the retina (as in focusing a camera).[14]

The ciliary muscles are tiny muscles inside the eyeball. This process of accommodation has been established beyond dispute, by photographic and other evidence.

Bates, of course, disputes it. According to him, the eye of man focuses exactly like the eye of a fish: the whole eye is shortened or lengthened by large *external* muscles, and the lens is 'not a factor in accommodation'. This he proves by experiments with the eye of a fish.

Later Batesians were forced to abandon this central theory, since it is demonstrably absurd. They have not, however, abandoned the notions that spring from it.

In the Bates system, all sight defects are caused by eye-strain, which is in turn caused by wrong thoughts. The cure is not to wear glasses, but to learn to see without strain, through eye exercises. Hauser urges:

> give your eye muscles every chance to relax, which they cannot do as long as they have glasses in front of them. Even if you cannot do without them, take off your glases from time to time during the day ... close your eyes, cup the palms of your hands gently before them, shutting out all light, but being careful never to press on the eyeballs, and take a few deep breaths. Let go mentally. Think *black*. Talk to yourself about black. Shut out everything in the world except the idea of black.[15]

This is *palming*, one of Bates's essential techniques. Others include *swinging*, which means simply standing up and sway-ing from side to side: and *blinking*. As Batesian Harry Ben-jamin explains, this is an important remedy for defective vision:

> Learn to blink once or twice every ten seconds (but with-out effort), no matter what you may be doing at the time, and especially when reading.[16]

I suppose this is better than Bates's suggestion that the eyes be strengthened by looking directly at the sun (which can, of course, burn the retina and cause permanent blindness). It takes Gayelord Hauser to top that one, attributing cataracts to constipation! Harry Benjamin agrees:

> The root cause of cataract is a toxic condition of the system due to continued wrong feeding and general wrong

living; and constipation of long standing is almost always a predisposing factor in the case, just as it is with other highly toxic conditions, such as rheumatism. The blood-stream becomes full of toxic matter, which is carried through the body to find lodgement in any spot available to it.... It is a silting-up of the lens of the eye, over a period of years, as the gradual outcome, generally, of a highly toxic condition.[17]

There is of course no evidence at all for any connection between constipation and cataract, and neither toxins in the blood nor silt in the lens have ever been detected in either condition.

Ophthalmologists may be surprised to hear that detached retina can be caused by 'the constant wearing of very strong glasses',[18] as Benjamin claims. This makes about as much sense as saying that a strong cup of coffee will tear a hole in the tablecloth. Dieticians will be further flabbergasted by Benjamin's cure for certain eye disorders which may be due to vitamin A deficiency: fasting.

None of Bates's followers seems to have the faintest idea how real, physical eyes operate, what are the real causes of eye defects and diseases, and why people wear glasses. For people who are merely near-sighted, who throw away their glasses and blunder through life on Batesian principles, the method probably results in little more than discomfort.

The real tragedies occur, however, when a Bates enthusiast suffers from glaucoma, atrophy of the optic nerve, or some other ailment which may demand immediate medical attention before it leads to blindness. Such tragedies cluster about the work of every medical pseudo-scientist.[19]

Yet the near-blind continue to lead the near-blind. I have little doubt that Bates-inspired cults will continue to flourish for some time. Perhaps eventually a monument will be erected, of Dr Bates triumphantly crushing bifocals under foot. On the base there could be panels depicting the master curing the blind by palming, swinging, and blinking, and by enemas.

All the Old Familiar Places

Another great tradition in home cures is based on sympathetic magic, i.e., magical correspondences. Whatever happens inside the body is reflected by symptoms in, and cured by treating, some more accessible part. The principle applies to voodoo dolls and, as we'll see, palmistry and phrenology. Here it is shown in zone therapy, iridiagnosis, acupuncture, osteopathy and chiropractic.

Zone therapy divides the body into ten zones, so arranged that body parts are connected to fingers and toes (one finger and one toe per zone). Pain can thus be relieved in any part by simply applying pressure to the correct finger or toe. Earache or deafness, for example, requires squeezing the ring finger, labour pains can be cured by rubber bands around the first two toes of both feet, while the site for sore eyes is the first or second finger. Parts of the mouth come into the zone system, too, so that menstrual pains can be relieved by pressure on parts of the tongue.

Naturally zone therapists do not claim merely to relieve pain. Naturopathist Benedict Lust has claimed zone cures of cancer, polio, goiter and falling hair.[20]

Iridiagnosis, invented by a nineteenth-century doctor in Budapest, has recently resurfaced as an Oriental cure. It means diagnosing disease from the appearance of the patient's iris. As in zone therapy, the iris is divided into a number of segments, each corresponding to some part of the body. The iris is supposed to be connected to the rest of the body by fine nerves (so fine as to thus far escape detection by all anatomists). A spot on the iris (a 'lesion') is taken to mean bodily disorder. Since such spots are amenable to suggestion, like the canals of Mars, the iridiagnostician's job seems to be one of creative imagination and bold guesswork.

A recent craze related to iridiagnosis is telling whether or not someone is 'sanpaku'. Sanpaku people reason poorly, are chronically tired, sleep badly, have bad memories and are impotent. All this can be detected from the condition of the iris. According to Sakurasawa Nyoti's *You Are All Sanpaku*, the fatal symptoms can be detected in John F. Kennedy, Ngo Dinh Diem and Marilyn Monroe, all of whom died violently. They might have averted their fate by simply eating macrobiotic foods (see chapter 10), if they had only looked at their irises in time.

'ARE YOU SANPAKU?' asks the cover blurb.

Look in a mirror. Sanpaku is a condition in which the white of the eye can be seen between the pupil and the lower lid – a condition which connotes a grave state of physical and spiritual illness ... and an extraordinary susceptibility to disease, accidents and tragic death.[21]

By simply leaning forward slightly to peer anxiously in a mirror, of course, anyone can become dangerously sanpaku.

Sharp Remedy
Acupuncture uses much the same system of correspondences as zone therapy. Various organs of the body are said to be connected, through a system of tubes which *Acupuncture News* calls 'a fourth circulatory system' to certain 'nodes' on the skin. By inserting needles under the skin at the appropriate node, the afflicted organ can be charged with 'healing energy'.

Since the nodes may be located some distance from the seat of the disorder, much of the art of acupuncture lies in finding them. The Chinese have for centuries trained their acupuncturists with models. Western practitioners try feeling for the invisible nodes, or else locate them with an electronic gadget similar to the 'neurocalometer' used by chiropractors. Others, according to Brian Inglis, use a 'sixth sense', by which he may mean guesswork. Inglis discusses acupuncture among other unorthodox therapies in *Fringe Medicine*, most of which he sees as viable alternatives to 'allopathy'. While admitting that acupuncture theory sounds improbable, he says:

it sounds rather less eccentric in the light of discoveries about atomic energy. It is not impossible that the life force does operate through predetermined medians; and if a prick with a needle is known to be enough, in certain circumstances, to induce a variant of artificial insemination in frogs, it is not stretching credulity too far to concede that it might have stimulating effects on the human body.[22]

Nor is it stretching credulity too far to suppose that a fish's eye works exactly like a human eye – until they are shown to have different mechanisms entirely. What acupuncturists claim to be able to do is neither to produce reactions between atomic particles nor to fertilize frogs, but to cure human ailments.

Acupuncturists claim to cure arthritis, rheumatism, menstrual disorders, migraine, asthma, hay fever and facial paralysis. As with iridiagnosis, their theory is completely groundless, since no anatomist has ever managed to find their magic tube network. This would not of itself rule out possible therapeutic effects, any more than the magical theories of the original quinine users would rule out quinine's real effects.

On the other hand, it's going too far to explain acupuncture by invoking radioactivity and the prick of a needle that causes artificial parthenogenesis, or virgin birth, in frogs, until it can be established that acupuncture does really heal. Significantly, the above diseases are characterized by pain or discomfort, the relief of which would probably be counted by most patients as a 'cure'. The one exception is facial paralysis, which often clears up without any treatment.

Acupuncture does seem to alleviate pain. In China it has been used to anaesthetize patients for surgery. During the operation, the patient can remain awake, talking, completely aware of everything going on around him – but insensitive to the surgical pain. Professor Pat Wall of the University of London believes that this effect may be achieved by hypnosis.

> This in no way dismisses or diminishes the value of acupuncture, but is does place it in a class of phenomena with which we are partly familiar. To put this in its historical perspective, we should remember that major surgery under mesmerism was widely practised in the London teaching hospitals 100 years ago until it was displaced by ether, and then chloroform general anaesthesia.[23]

He shows four ways in which acupuncture operates like hypnosis:

1 The mesmerized patients, like acupuncture patients, were awake and talking during their operations. Like them, they felt no pain (and showed no reflexes) in parts under surgery, though other regions were normal.

2 Hypnosis doesn't work on everyone. Acupuncture in

China is only used on patients who request it, but even then it doesn't work on all of them.

3 Children cannot be hypnotized successfully, and acupuncture is seldom used on children.

Some degree of suggestibility below the level of hypnosis may also be involved. Wall mentions the 'placebo reaction', by which people, seemingly, can be persuaded out of pain. In one hospital test, half the patients were given injections of morphine; the other half, injections of salt water. While 80 per cent of the morphine group felt better, so did 60 per cent of the salt water group. This may be due to their expectation of relief from pain via the magic needle. The needles of acupuncture may well be held in similar esteem in China.

Acupuncture has already been investigated as an anaesthetic technique by a few doctors, and more investigations are almost sure to come. Surgery under hypnosis, when it works, has obvious advantages over both general and local anaesthetics. Wall suggests that, if hypnosis is to be used extensively in surgery, more people will first have to be made amenable to it. The real value of acupuncture may finally lie not in its technique at all, but in the investigations it could open up into new ideas in drugless pain relief.

Lumbar Jacks
Osteopathy was developed in 1874 by an American, Andrew Still, as an adaptation of the then-popular Swedish massage. Still's idea was that virtually every ailment could be traced to a blockage of the artery (causing the blood, being static, to 'sour') or else a similarly blocked nerve; and both blockages could be traced directly to the spine. When spinal vertebrae became dislocated, as they so often were in Still's theory, they caused 'lesions' or 'subluxations', leading to blockages as above. The remedy was to massage the spine in some special way known only to Still, and 'adjust' the lesions out of existence. Still thus claimed to cure TB, epilepsy, gallstones, tumour, yellow fever, malaria, diphtheria, rickets, piles, diabetes, practically anything, by finding and adjusting subluxations. In the 1890s, he founded a school which has since carried osteopathy all over the United States.

Still rejected of course the germ theory of disease, and he rejected likewise homeopathy, other massage systems, and everything else but his method. Nor did his fanaticism confine itself to physiology, for Still became a convert from Methodism to the Millerite end-of-the-world cult (see chapter 25).

Osteopathy has moved towards respectability since Still's day, and many American osteopaths are now licensed to dispense drugs or perform surgery. Spinal adjustments are still their specialty, but now they make less sensational claims (Still swore that he'd once grown three inches of hair on a bald man in one week). They have not, of course, given up the mystique of subluxations.

Since no one but an osteopathic disciple has ever been able to positively detect a subluxation, osteopaths clearly have little trouble in adjusting them to oblivion. And when miraculous cures don't ensue, they can either find more adjustments necessary, or else blame the patient:

> if a patient has an illness which has reached the organic stage, it may be too late for manipulation to work satisfactorily; but if the patient had visited an osteopath in time . . .[24]

Chiropractic is a far more popular variety of spine-kneading than osteopathy (from which it was copied), largely due to the ease of becoming a chiropractor. In most parts of America, a chiropractor needs only eighteen months of training and no licence to practise. Founded in 1895 by D. D. Palmer, an Iowa grocer, chiropractic is today represented by hundreds of schools, which seem unable to agree as to which adjustments effect which marvellous cures. Two different chiropractic texts recommend treating the same disease by manipulating completely different vertebrae.

Brian Inglis seems to feel that, as with acupuncture, 'osteopractic' may be theoretically unsound, but that – whether by directing the 'life force' or simply placebo reaction – it works. And since it is an art rather than a science, he feels that osteopractors should *avoid* learning too much about physiology, lest it cramp their native style. As an analogy, he wonders what would have happened if James Thurber had taken drawing lessons early in his cartoon career.

I think this is a false analogy, since most of medical knowledge is not 'how to heal', but 'how the body works' knowledge.

And there is no evidence that any artist was, or might have been, hindered by understanding, say, the effects of light on foliage, or by a knowledge of human anatomy. Even lessons in healing need not hinder 'natural talent', if – to extend the analogy still further – we remember that Picasso submitted to drawing lessons.

But no doubt chiropractors would feel confined by an understanding that germs can cause disease, that the body is filled with glands and organs related to one another in complex ways, and that they must deal with patients who are much more than stacks of vertebrae control handles linked to life force pumps.

H. L. Mencken once suggested that chiropractic might function as a form of eugenics. Chiropractors, by trying to adjust the subluxations of deluded patients who really had cancer, TB and the like, might hasten their deaths, tending thus to raise the IQ of the American public. He failed to reckon with the depth and breadth of the delusion, however. I figure that by the end of the century, nearly every American ought to have an aunt whose hay fever vanished after one miraculous adjustment.

Between 1901 and his death in 1945, the American mystic Edgar Cayce diagnosed thousands of illnesses psychically. He would lie down, put himself into a hypnotic trance, and reel out his diagnosis while a stenographer took it all down. Since Cayce (pronounced 'Casey') associated in waking life with osteopaths, his diagnoses frequently mentioned spinal subluxations. The diets he dreamed up resembled naturopathic cures for similar reasons. Cayce also thought highly of therapeutic doses of electricity, as did many turn-of-the-century quacks.* Indeed, he covered all bets: '... there is good in all methods, and they all have their place', he said, and recommended 'healing that is sincere, of whatever nature – whether spiritual, magnetic, mechanical, allopathic, electrical or thermal'.[1]

The reason man's lifespan has been reduced from the Biblical thousand years to a mere eighty, he explained, is sin. Especially the sin of self-gratification: 'Just as great a sin to overeat as to overdrink; to over think as to over act!'[2] Evidently he saw no paradox in the long average lifespan in the over-indulgent United States vs the shorter spans in poorer nations.

Cayce gave 14,246 readings in all, advising clients on matters of health, religion, philosophy, man's non-descendance from the monkey, Atlantis, the Great Pyramid, automatic writing, astrology, warnings in dreams, reincarnation and all other sub-

---

*A contemporary advertisement for 'Harness' Electropathic Belts' claims that they 'Renew Exhausted Nerve Force', promoting health, vigour, and 'the highest condition of intellectual strength.... It cures Rheumatism, Gout, Sciatica, Lumbago, Nervous Exhaustion, Neuralgia, Indigestion, Constipation, Torpid Liver, Sleeplessness, Ladies' Ailments, Hysteria, and all Kidney Diseases.' For other electrical cures, see chapter 21.

jects of occult interest, not forgetting a delicate reference now and then to naturopathy's old standby:

> Do not at any time allow the system to pass days, or even a day, without the body throwing off the dross through natural channels.[3]

Faith Healing

Dr Louis Rose, a psychiatrist, has been studying faith healing for several years. Surely Dr Rose is the very open-minded man healers have been asking for. He maintains a carefully neutral 'agnosticism' on the subject despite the scarcity of evidence in healing's favour, and his book, *Faith Healing*, is a model of determined impartiality.[4]

Rose discusses faith healing in the broadest sense, listing Roman Catholic miracles, Mesmer's animal magnetism, Christian Science and Reich's orgone therapy, as well as more familiar forms. In trying to work out general principles, he admits there are more questions asked than answered:

Is the faith of the patient important? Are some schools more effective than others? If so, do their techniques differ? Are the cures permanent? Are some illnesses more often cured than others?

The historical answer to the last question seems to be, yes. Even in the apocryphal miracles of early saints, Dr Rose finds that organic cures are far fewer than functional cures. For example, plague (infectious disease) cures are rare, and few saints claim the restoration of sight to eyeless persons. The majority seem to be cures of lameness, blindness, deafness and other disorders which might have hysterical origins.

The fundamental question is, of course, does it work? Rose meets it head-on:

> What is needed ... is not more affirmations of creeds, more sensationalized 'human stories' ... more blasts of unyielding scepticism, more claims such as 'thirty per cent of my patients get better', more attempts at mechanical measurements of healing forces ... [but] rather for a painstaking examination of actual cases to see if any cures remain which cannot be reasonably explained.[5]

Testing any therapy is difficult. One way might be to send

genuine cases to healers and let them try their skill. In 1955 this type of test was organized by a medical institute in Germany. 650 patients cooperated, receiving treatment by a spirit healer for six months. Most had organic complaints such as heart diseases, bone diseases, intestinal ailments; none had improved under orthodox treatment. The results:

61 per cent believed that they had improved.

22 per cent showed improvements which were only temporary.

10 per cent grew worse.

9 per cent showed genuine improvement. But these were mostly 'cases of gastro-intestinal illness – and there, it seemed, conventional treatment was equally effective'.[6]

One group were told that they were receiving 'absent healing' when they were not. These patients said that they felt better, but showed no improvement.

A second test of effectiveness would be to track down cases which sound like spectacular cures. Dr Rose engaged on this long, tedious process, trying to verify claims by a set of criteria similar to those used to verify Lourdes miracles:

1 The illness should be organic.

2 It should be verified beforehand by a physician.

3 There should be a marked improvement in the physical condition.

4 The improvement should begin within a reasonably short time after the healing session(s).

5 A physician should verify the improvement.

6 The improvement should be permanent, without a relapse.

7 The improvement should not be explicable in medical terms (e.g., as spontaneous remission or due to orthodox treatment).

After several years, Rose had collected ninety-five cases, which I have listed in Table 9–1. It must be remembered that these are not average faith-healing cases, but cases represented by healers or the press as 'miraculous cures'. Most came to Dr Rose's attention either through healers themselves or through sensational newspaper and magazine stories. Only the last three cases are worth recounting:

Table 9–1 Ninety-five healing cases investigated
by Dr Louis Rose

Number of Cases	Result
58	Medical records unavailable.
22	Records contradict claim.
3	Improved, but relapsed.
1	No improvement; deteriorated.
4	Improved, but possibly from concurrent medical treatment.
4	Improved in function, but no change in organic state.
2	Possible help from faith healing (*see text*: A, B).
1	Relief or cure after faith healing (*see text*: C).

A. A man who had been blind for fifty years in his right eye suddenly recovered his sight. He reported both an optician and an oculist as saying it was 'miraculous'. On checking with the ophthalmologist, it was learned that this was no miracle, but a spontaneous dislocation of the lens, which had a cataract. This is an old operation known as 'couching' (pushing the cataract aside), which can also occur through violent exercise or a sudden jerk.

B. A man underwent a biopsy (surgical removal of tissue for inspection) for a suspected throat cancer. Cancer was found, and he was scheduled for surgery to remove it. Meanwhile he saw a healer, and his voice improved. When re-examined, no cancer was found. Surgeons claimed that this was a case of 'cure by biopsy', where, by chance, all the cancerous tissue had been removed for inspection. Dr Rose also happened upon an identical case which involved no faith healing. Apparently such cures by biopsy are more common than formerly thought.

C. A doctor claimed cure of a slipped disc by one faith healer and of hernia by another. Said Rose:

In the first illness described it is obvious that acute pain was the major factor, and neurologists and orthopaedic surgeons are familiar with the vagaries of the so-called 'slipped disc' syndrome.[7]

Hernias are likewise known to heal without any treatment.

Case C appeared in the headlines as 'Doctor cured in three treatments'. Other cases investigated had been called 'Permanently cured', 'Psychic healing succeeded when doctors failed', and 'Deformity melted away'. None of this was substantiated. One rickets case, successfully treated by orthodox methods, became exaggerated to 'He was born paralysed in legs and arms ...'

The popular healer Harry Edwards claimed to have cured about a hundred thousand people in Britain. Dr Rose set out to find a single one of these, or a single cure by any healer. What he found instead is perhaps best illustrated by an account of his visit to a Harry Edwards session in 1951:

> Later, as I was leaving the hall, I saw a woman walking with the help of two sticks on which she leaned heavily.... I suddenly realized that this was the same woman who, an hour or so earlier, had walked down the steps from the platform to the auditorium without the aid of her sticks, glowing with joy at her 'cure' and taking her first unaided paces for several years.[8]

Bennett Cerf had a similar experience at a Hollywood banquet addressed by Aldous Huxley, who had been trying for years to correct his serious vision defect with Bates eye exercises. Huxley placed his paper on the lectern and 'rattled glibly on', without the aid of glasses. But when he suddenly faltered, it became obvious that he had simply memorized the speech.

> To refresh his memory he brought the paper closer and closer to his eyes. When it was only an inch away he still couldn't read it, and had to fish for a magnifying glass in his pocket to make the typing visible to him.[9]

It would take a fair-sized encyclopaedia to trace the history of food cults from Adam's taboo apple to Zen macrobiotics. Entries might include the 'clean food' rules in Leviticus, the Pythagoreans' abstention from beans,* and the story of a fourteenth-century wonder food, antimony.† Famous vegetarians of the past two centuries, including Shelley, Shaw, Montessori and half of the revolutionaries named in Herzen's memoirs (the other half being devoted to phrenology), would occupy nearly a volume. Even then there might be no room for side excursions, say, into the food ideas of the futurist poet Marinetti. (When he wasn't boosting Mussolini's fascism, Marinetti devised such recipes for the new order as salami served in hot black coffee sprinkled with eau-de-cologne.)

Such an encyclopaedia could never be kept up to date, however, for new cults appear almost daily. Some have to be brought down from inaccessible tribes in the Alps, Urals or Himalayas, and some are found in obscure Japanese monasteries, but a great many cults seem to spring full-bloom from the foreheads of California chiropractors. Lesser men stand ready to try each new system in turn, forgetting past disappointments.

Pseudo-nutritionists not only claim to have all the answers, they claim the answers are so simple that any half-educated layman can understand them. Almost every food cult comprises some simple-minded system wherein one or two wonder foods are to be eaten in quantity, while one or two poisonous foods are to be avoided. As in chiropractic, all considerations

---

* Robert Graves, in *The Greek Myths*, says the Pythagoreans thought that ghosts entered into beans. They avoided them, therefore, taking no chances on eating an ancestor.

† The alchemist Basil Valentine is said to have tried fattening groups of pigs and groups of monks on antimony. The pigs prospered, but the monks died; hence the name *antimoine*.

of the human body's complexity are waved aside as so much orthodox clap-trap.

Food Taboos

Fasting, like drugs, sleep deprivation, extreme pain or partial asphyxiation, can produce hallucinations. This has always made it a valuable technique in mystical religion, though the Buddha and other reformers rejected starvation as meaningless. Still, the basic idea that fasting is good for you has remained with the food cultists, being handed down reverently like an inheritance of Confederate dollars.

Around 1910 a fasting cult, espoused by Hereward Carrington (whose spiritualist work appears in chapter 16) and Upton Sinclair, proposed to cure TB, cancer, syphilis, etc., by simply starving the patient. This particular cult is temporarily dead, but many naturopaths still recommend fasts to 'purge' the system, before undertaking some vogue diet.

Brief fasts probably do no harm to healthy people, nor any good. Obesity has been tackled by fasts of up to thirty weeks, but only in hospitals under medical supervision. The amateur attempting a long fast runs a serious risk of vitamin deficiency diseases, at best.

The pattern of food taboos is clear in the diet promoted in 1933 by Dr William Howard Hay. Here Martin Gardner summarizes the Hay diet, according to which

> almost all body ills are the result of 'acidosis'. This in turn is caused by (1) too much protein, (2) too much adulterated food, like white bread, (3) combinations in the diet of protein and carbohydrates, (4) retention in the bowels of food beyond twenty-four hours after eating. He also recommended fasting, apparently unaware that fasting *really* causes acidosis.[1]

All the Hay diet notions are still in currency among other food cults, especially his taboo on 'adulterated foods'. The definition of adulteration varies, but there seems to be general agreement that 'pale foods make pale people' the title of an article in a naturopathic magazine called *Here's Health*. Elsewhere a television actress writes: 'No white bread – that's just waste; no salt – that retains liquids; no white sugar – that's mainly chemicals.'[2]

In every particular, this taboo on white foods is wrong, and as meaningless as the ancient Greek taboo on red foods. The fad for brown eggs, brown sugar and brown bread helps keep the prices of these items artificially high, for if there is one genuine difference between them and their pale equivalents, it is scarcity.

White sugar isn't 'mainly' chemicals, it is one hundred per cent chemicals – as are all foods, and all TV actresses. 'Chemicals' is of course meant to be a pejorative; the idea is that white sugar is concocted in some laboratory retort, while brown sugar grows 'naturally'. The truth is that both are refined from the same sugar cane by the same factory process. The trace of chemicals that gives brown sugar its colour and pleasing taste has been removed from white. Both varieties are, simply, sugar, and have no other nutritive value.

That salt retains liquids, far from being a reason to avoid it, is one of the reasons we need it. Fortunately for cultists who abstain from salt, they probably take in a small amount in other foods.

The superiority of wholemeal bread over white is obvious; it has been demonstrated in both animal feeding tests and by analysis. Wholemeal flour contains greater amounts of niacin, thiamine, riboflavine, and several other nutrients than non-enriched white flour. Moreover it contains amounts of pyridoxine, pantothenic acid, biotin and folic acid which do not exist even in enriched white flour. White bread is not, however, 'waste', since it contains roughly the same amount of protein (8 per cent) as wholemeal bread (8.2 per cent). As part of a balanced diet, there is little reason to suppose that white bread is wasteful or harmful. Indeed, one test seems to have shown that any kind of bread is an excellent protein-carbohydrate food for growing children.[3] Where waste actually comes in is the milling and extraction processes, where, for purely technical considerations (white flour stores better than wholemeal), some of the best parts of the wheat are removed.

The all-time favourite among food taboos is vegetarianism. Here the main argument is presented by another television actress:

I don't believe in the slaughter of animals – but even more I just don't think meat is good for you. It takes a long time to digest, and while it's digesting it releases toxic poisons – the kind you get from any dead flesh – into the blood.[4]

The 'toxic poisons' in question are probably uric acid and what naturopaths call 'necrones'. Uric acid is always present in the body. About half of it is manufactured by the body itself, irrespective of diet. The remainder comes from foods rich in purines. According to a standard reference:

> As liver, kidney, sweetbreads, roe, sardines and sprats are the only foods rich in purines, these are the foods from which an excess urinary output of uric acid might be derived.[5]

For sufferers from gout or kidney stones, it might be of purpose to cut out these six foods, but healthy persons have nothing to fear from uric acid. It is not known to cause any disease. 'Necrones' seem to exist only in the imaginations of vegetarians.

Cholesterol provides a stronger case, but the evidence that eating animal products causes heart disease is not conclusive. Animal fats from meat, butter, milk, etc. raise the level of plasma cholesterol, and this level can be lowered by replacing them in the diet by polyunsaturated fats, such as peanut oil or corn oil. To the vegetarian the message is clear: Eating meat causes ischaemic heart disease. The actual situation is more complicated. Other factors affect the level of plasma cholesterol – one's age and sex, types of carbohydrates in the diet, exercise and glandular factors – and factors like smoking and obesity obviously affect heart disease. One nomadic tribe in Africa consume large amounts of animal fats without raising the level of cholesterol in their blood plasma.[6]

> 'Blood cholesterol' is a subject which is 'news'. This is because of its undoubted association with atherosclerosis and its sequel, ischaemic heart disease ... Like all other 'news' its clinical importance has at times been exaggerated and distorted in newspapers, on television and on the radio.... Although much has been learned about cholesterol and lipoproteins in the last 20 years, much more information must

be acquired before their role in health and disease can be clearly stated.[7]

The cholesterol scare started people doing quite a few silly things such as taking corn-oil capsules (which cannot of themselves *replace* animal fats unless one stops eating animal fats) and using expensive corn-oil margarines, some of which had been hydrogenated (that is, made identical with animal fats).

Some vegetarians allow animal products such as eggs and milk, others forbid them. Some avoid citrus fruits ('acidosis' again) while others are exclusively fruitarians. Many sects promote some sort of vitamin or mineral supplement, taken as tonic syrup or pills. By thus making the vegetarian a kind of invalid, whose delicate constitution needs pampering with vegetable juices, bone-meal pills, multiple vitamins and herbal tonics, health-food establishments cater for the hypochondriacs who probably make up a good part of their clientele. One issue of *Here's Health* lists over eighty products or groups of products, including 'hair food' and herbal foods for pets (!)

The level of nutritional ignorance runs high among vegetarians, if we judge by the revelations of Edgar Cayce:

> Plenty of lettuce should always be eaten by most everybody; for this supplies an effluvium in the blood stream that is a destructive force to most of those influences that attack the blood stream. It's a purifier.

> Keep plenty of those foods that supply calcium to the body. These we would find especially in raw carrots, cooked turnip greens, all characters of salads, especially salads of watercress, mustard greens and the like.[8]

Lettuce's special effluvium has so far gone undetected by conventional nutritionists, who lack Cayce's aethereal sources of information. These sources have, in turn, overlooked cheddar cheese, which contains sixteen times as much calcium as carrots, four times as much as watercress, and a third more than any vegetable. Which is fine unless you consider milk products dangerously unvegetarian.

Dr Melvin Page, a Florida dentist, believes that milk is responsible for many adult ills. He points out the high incidence of cancer in Wisconsin, a dairy state. Says Martin Gardner:

> This illustrates one of the most elementary of statistical fallacies. People of Wisconsin tend to be long-lived and since cancer is a disease of middle and elderly years, it is a more frequent cause of death in Wisconsin than in many other states. An area low in cancer deaths is likely to be an area of poor health where inhabitants tend to die young.[9]

A similar argument is advanced by vegetarian Dr Joseph D. Hollo in *Snap Back from Your Heart Attack*, 1967, explaining the value of exercise:

> Let us follow the example of the English miners among whom only very few are stricken by arteriosclerosis. On the other hand, statistics show that nine times more coronary cases can be found among the physicians of England.[10]

Many doctors obviously do lead sedentary and stressful lives which contribute to heart disease. But the English miners have not been saved from heart attacks by exercise, but by early deaths from silicosis, lung cancer and other mining hazards, including accidents. Hollo's readers, not realizing that he is neither a statistician nor a medical doctor, are liable to perform his dangerous experiment of (following a heart attack) trying to climb twenty-five flights of stairs.

Recently the milk taboo has led to the production of 'plant-milk', by boiling and pressing grass and other fodder into a milky substance which is then canned and sold in natural food shops. Evidently in this case, 'Nature' is taken to be a factory process, opposed to the artifices of Daisy and Buttercup.

One of the great enemies of sugar, milk and wheat, and the originator of 'organic' food, was Jerome Irving Rodale, who died in 1971 aged seventy-two. Rodale built up a health empire worth $9 million, most of it from publishing two magazines. *Prevention* (circulation: 1 million) and *Organic Gardening* (700,000).

Cooking was absolutely taboo with Rodale, who explains that 'No animal eats cooked food'. When readers have absorbed

that surprising truth, Rodale hits them with another: Hitler
was a sugar addict.

> Hitler was a typical example of sugar addiction relating
> to a tendency towards crime.... The evidence is there.
> There can be no question about it. Hitler must have suffered
> from low blood sugar due to an overconsumption of sugar.[11]

So he says in *Natural Health, Sugar and the Criminal Mind*, in
which he finds many other strange connections between crime
and the hated sucrose. Can it be a coincidence that a fancy
cake was named after Napoleon? That in the book depository
whence Oswald shot President Kennedy, the FBI found *an
empty Coke bottle*? That the Boston Strangler liked chocolate?
To Rodale, the answer is as obvious as fudge: addiction to
sugar, not heroin, is responsible for the rising crime rate in
America, the high suicide rate in Denmark,* and a host of
diseases from cancer to hay fever. Well, maybe.

Another Rodale worry is that we're being emasculated by
certain foods. He explains that experimental animals have lost
their sex distinctions through impoverished diet, the males
becoming smaller, the females losing their 'pelvic capacity for
easy child bearing'. Obviously humans are on the same path:

> Observations among our young people shows [*sic*] that
> humans become subject to the same deficiencies as a con-
> sequence of depleted foods, used since the roller flour mill
> was invented.... Canning, pasteurizing, and refinements of
> many kinds have contributed to the hereditary breakdown.
> The increase of the use of white sugar no doubt is also a

* 'Denmark,' he misinforms us, 'has the highest suicide rate in
the world.' (His world evidently doesn't include Czechoslovakia,
Finland, West Germany, Hungary or Switzerland.) He then lists
eight nations in order of increasing sugar consumption: Japan,
Spain, Italy, West Germany, France, US, UK and *Denmark*. Had
he shown each nation's suicide rate, it would be obvious that his
theory misfires, for:

	Sugar consumption (lb/person)	Suicide rate (per 100,000 persons)
Japan	43	14
UK	122.2	9.7

contributory cause. You will notice the uniformity of build
between boys and girls if you attend any 'hippie' or 'beatnik'
gathering.[12]

The peculiar logic of this passage is so murky that comment
on it is almost impossible. But the percentage of live births
to total births has gone up considerably since the invention
of the rolling mill. There is no evidence of any physical
deterioration of our species through heredity (not that it would
show up this soon), and no evidence that pelvic narrowness
affects child-bearing seriously. Finally it's curious that a proportion of Rodale's followers are the boys and girls whom he
finds so ominously sexless.

Loaves and Fishes
Many food cults counterbalance taboos with special wonder
foods. With Rodale, the emphasis is on 'organically grown'
fruits and vegetables, meaning those grown without the aid of
artificial ('chemical') fertilizers, and without pesticides.

Of course a genuine case can be made against pesticides,
at least those types which are wiping out wildlife at an alarm-
ing rate. Hopefully the worst of these are going out of style.

Nitrate fertilizers have also been shown dangerous to the
environment in two ways: They cause the soil to lose its ability
to fix nitrogen, making it in effect poorer soil, and they wash
down into rivers and streams to poison fish. The effects of
artificial fertilizers on the actual crops grown, however, appear
to be positive. The only evident difference between an apple
grown with the aid of horse manure and an apple grown with
the aid of some artificial manure is that the latter fruit is
larger, tastier and generally better. Chemically, an apple is an
apple.

A favourite wonder food seems to be kelp, commonly known
as seaweed. A booklet called *Kelp*, by Eric F. W. Powell, puts
its case:

> It seems logical to assume that as life began in the waters
> the seas must contain vital agents ... and that whatever
> comes from the seas should be rich in life-sustaining pro-
> perties.[13]

For instance, the sludge from oil tankers. Powell hints at
kelp cures for a variety of diseases, but the examples he cites

are all of a type: Lady of fifty who cannot sleep, woman in excellent health except for severe headaches, and so on.

I recall one case of neurasthenia where the sufferer, a young man of 24, was utterly exhausted. He had a nervous dyspepsia with much flatulence, complained of pain in his back, was constipated and could not sleep except in fitful snatches.[14]

This description fits many reactors to placebo medicine well, lacking only a chronic sinus condition, vagarious pains and allergic rashes. Powell treats cases with homeopathic microdoses of kelp.

Eaten in greater than Tom Thumb portions, kelp is a good source of iodine and other minerals. An easier way of staving off goiter is to eat sea fish once or twice a week, or to simply use iodized salt. Unless one is suffering from a mineral deficiency, however (as is almost no one with access to meat, milk, cheese, eggs and green vegetables) kelp is simply a useless luxury.

Powell makes much of kelp's vitamin content, but the only three it contains (carotene, riboflavin and niacin) are available in common, cheap foods which also contain other vitamins.

Honey is widely believed to be far more nutritious than plain sugar. Rodale cites honey and molasses as healthful replacements for the sucrose scourge. Cecil Tonsley, in *Honey for Health*, 1969, gives honey remarkable curative powers. In one piece of hearsay evidence he describes the cure of a gangrenous foot, at the point of amputation, by tying it in a bag of honey.[15] A remarkable cure indeed, considering that honey is mainly sugar and water.*

Five different wonder foods are the health secret of Helmut Eugene Benjamin Gellert Hauser, better known as Gayelord Hauser. These are skim milk, wheat germ, black molasses

---

* Honey is 76.4 per cent sugar and 23 per cent water. It contains traces of several vitamins and minerals, but less of these than almost any other foods. Its lack of water (the bees fan it with their wings to dry it) and slight acidity kill enough bacteria to keep it from spoiling, usually, but as a cure for gangrene it's probably about as effective as tying your foot in a bag of jelly beans.

(treacle), brewers' yeast and yoghurt. An advertisement tells of his discovery:

> Gayelord was the eleventh son of a Tübingen school-master and had a normal, happy childhood until he was sixteen, when he developed a tubercular infection of the hip, which was pronounced to be incurable. As a final measure, he was sent to the sanatorium in Switzerland run by Dr Benedict Lust. Dr Lust watched him eating lunch one day and startled him by saying, 'If you keep on eating dead foods, you will certainly die. Only living foods can make a living body.'[16]

Lust, you may recall, is the founder of American naturopathy and author of a book on zone therapy. Hauser's other influences included Dr Auguste Rollier, curer of TB with sunbaths; and the science of chiropractic.

In the 1920s he went to Hollywood, still a great magnet for self-appointed health authorities. If anything, food cranks were thicker on the ground than now. Among Hauser's famous clients were Greta Garbo and the Duchess of Windsor, while his competitor, Lelord Kordel, has had to be content with Eva Gabor.

Hauser's *Look Younger, Live Longer*, first published in 1951, presents his medical theories, a grab-bag of sun baths, sitz baths, massage, herbal laxatives, enemas, vitamin supplements (sold by his organization) and Bates eye exercises. He thinks we should sleep on slanting ironing boards, head downwards, that cataract can be cured by massive doses of riboflavine, and that B vitamins may be just the cancer cure science has been looking for.[17] As for his five wonder foods, which 'used daily, can add five youthful years to your life', they seem remarkably ordinary on closer inspection:

1 Yoghurt is a delicious form of soured milk containing no nutrients except those in milk. Hauser's ideas on yoghurt seem to be taken from the nineteenth-century Russian scientist, Metchnikoff, who thought the bacteria in live yoghurt would replace our normal intestinal bacteria, which, he believed, were poisoning us. They aren't, as everyone but Hauser knew, half a century ago. He tells us it comes from Bulgaria, where formerly 'for each million inhabitants, 16 lived 100 years or

more; whereas here in the United States only 9 in a million reach the century mark.' I've been unable to find current comparable statistics, but more affluent, degenerate Americans (6.1 per thousand) now live to over 85 than do rural Bulgarians (4.4 per thousand) who still eat plenty of yoghurt.

2 Skim milk is of obvious value to fat people, and a cheap replacement for milk in cooking. Otherwise it is less nourishing than whole milk, since it lacks vitamins A and D. Of course Hauser will be glad to sell you expensive vitamin supplements to make up this deficiency.

3 Wheat germ and

4 Brewer's yeast are good sources of protein, as good as meat or cheese. They're also more expensive. But then Hauser, who sells them, can hardly be expected to see a disadvantage in that.

5 Black molasses, or treacle, is, Hauser says,

not only an excellent source of many B vitamins, but also of iron, calcium and other minerals. Black treacle is a by-product of sugar refining and contains all of the minerals and heat-stable vitamins of the original cane juice.[18]

It does contain fair amounts of minerals, but not from sugar cane. The chief sources of its iron and copper are factory machinery and boiling kettles; of its calcium, the lime-water used in the refinery. Even at that, it contains less of these and other minerals than ordinary beans (several varieties). As for B vitamins, it's one of the poorest sources: Martin Gardner explains that the average adult would require a gallon of black treacle per day to keep fit.[19] Since treacle is 67 per cent sugar, this would entail a 9,350 calorie daily diet, with a consequent weight gain of around 12 lb per week (not allowing for diabetes and iron poisoning). Hauser mainly boosts treacle as a source of vitamin B6, but most normal diets already contain three to ten times the B6 that most adults need.

Over the years the Hauser empire has grown. Today his 'Life & Beauty' stores sell vitamins, wonder foods expensive electric machines for extracting vegetable juice, and a range of the master's books.

Other wonder foods have become fads from time to time,

then disappeared. Who remembers chlorophyll, royal jelly, 'safflower' oil? Who, in a few years' time, will remember bone meal, silver pills, sunflower seeds, garlic oil, or any of the tonics and elixirs that must finally go the way of Hadacol (which owed its curative powers to a tasty percentage of alcohol)?

For the over forties, the search for natural health takes some strange and unnatural turnings. In Barbara Cartland's *The Youth Secret* are listed over thirty 'natural' beauty preparations, from Almond Skin Food, Algemain Seaweed Elixir and Avocado Satin Cream to a preparation actually called Winston's Placenta Cream with Wheat Germ Oil. Miss Cartland sounds very silly. No, I shouldn't have said that. For that, I should be pelted with Egg Wrinkle Cream, or have my mouth washed out with nutritious Culpepper's Green Lettuce Soap.

Zen Macrobiotics

Anyone who knows what's good for him has been infected by the macrobe, they say. Despite rumours of malnutrition, despite the closure of a few restaurants by hygiene-conscious health authorities, this craze continues to find new converts wherever Ohsawa books are sold.

The basis of Zen macrobiotics is unbelievably simple. Some foods are 'yin' and others are 'yang'. George Ohsawa explains it all in *Zen Macrobiotics*:

> According to our philosophy, there is nothing but Yin and Yang in this world. Yin and Yang, physically speaking, are CENTRIFUGAL and CENTRIPETAL force, respectively. Centrifugal force is expansive; it produces silence, calmness, cold and darkness. Centripetal force, on the other hand, is constrictive and produces sound, action, heat and light in turn. The following fundamental phenomena are consequences of these two fundamental forces: [20]

He then goes on to sort physical opposites, such as hot/cold and light/heavy, into Yin and Yang lists. Purple is Yin, for some reason, while red is Yang. All the elements of the periodic table are Yin, except hydrogen, arsenic, carbon, lithium, sodium and magnesium. Diet comes into the system because the vegetable kingdom is Yin; the animal, Yang. Yet salads are Yin and cereals Yang, and this exception is compounded by sweet or sour tastes being Yin; salty or bitter, Yang. Evidently the country of origin of the food complicates things further, being tropical (Yin) or frigid (Yang).

Ohsawa explains the importance of a balanced diet of Yin and Yang. Oddly enough, this balance seems most often achieved by a diet of one food, whole grain cereal. The occasional salad or meat dish is allowed, but liquids are severely restricted. Ohsawa seems to have the notion that drinking liquids puts a strain on the kidneys (akin to saying that allowing yourself to have blood puts a strain on the heart).

Miraculous cures are claimed, of course. Ohsawa strongly hints that macrobiotics cured radiation victims of Hiroshima, and lists eighty other diseases curable by Yin and Yang. On the list is every major disease known, except of course malnutrition. Here's the cure for the common cold, heart disease, leprosy, leukaemia and cataract. Banish frigidity, impotence, syphilis and gonorrhea all at once! Say goodbye to paranoia and polio! Haemophilia, long supposed by the ignorant medical profession to be hereditary, is shown here to be just another case of not enough brown rice (or too much salad).

> No illness is more simple to cure than cancer (this also applies to mental diseases and heart trouble) through a return to the most elementary and natural eating and drinking: Diet No. 7.[21]

Diet No. 7 turns out to be a hundred per cent whole grain cereals and sips of liquid ('as little as possible'). Ohsawa thus invites the cancer patient to compound his condition with scurvy and possible dehydration. Jesus Christ.

Time was when everyone knew what a drug fiend was: a criminal monster, a prowling night creature in whose fevered brain flickered unholy desires. In 1955 Bergen Evans wrote of the popular misconception of the addict as 'a wild-eyed, gibbering, desperate creature';[1] the popular misconception hasn't improved much since. Not only journalists (who, after all, are trying to entertain their public) but policemen, churchmen and even a few doctors are willing to indulge in a little wild-eyed gibbering of their own, when pronouncing upon drugs they have neither used nor seen used. And it would be hard to match the desperation of the Texas judge who handed out a twenty-year sentence to a kid caught with three joints.

There is a popular attempt to associate drugs with violence in one way or another. Pot used to lead to teenage gang wars, and, as we're continually reminded, Charles Manson dropped acid. No such significance is found in the addiction of Perry Smith, the killer of *In Cold Blood*, to aspirin.* Instead, we get headlines like 'LSD BOY KICKED TEACHER' followed by a story of how a boy, allegedly on acid, swore at and kicked a PT instructor, who retaliated by breaking his jaw in two places. So it seems there is some relation between drugs and violence after all: In ancient Mexico they executed drunkards, while in Russia they used to execute tobacco smokers, after torturing them to get the names of their pushers.

Pot (marijuana or cannabis) for those who can distinguish it from heroin, is the drug that leads to heroin addiction. The canon of anti-pot absurdities goes like this:

1   I heard of one case, a nineteen-year-old dancing girl who was taken to a 'reefer club' by a party of friends. Soon a man was at her side, offering her a cigarette. It was a decoy. Soon she became one of his best customers ...[2]

* But Rodale, the great enemy of sugar, finds it ominous that Perry Smith washed down his aspirin with Coca-Colas.

2 Marijuana is only and always a scourge which under-
mines its victims and degrades them mentally, morally and
physically. A small dose taken by one subject may bring
about intense intoxication, raving fits, criminal assaults. It
is this unpredictable effect which makes marijuana one of
the most dangerous drugs known. The moral barricades
[sic] are broken down and often debauchery and sexuality
result.[3]

3 In recent months, scientific research has brought to light
the frightening fact that LSD drastically alters the genetic
organization of human germ cells – and consequently could
cause horrendous mutations in the offspring of users. Some
evidence indicates that a similar ... genetic alteration may
also be induced by marijuana. Dr Luis Souza ... found
that after the first experiences with marijuana there was a
seemingly complete destruction of DNA ...[4]

4 A 2nd Marine Division communications N.C.O. recently
told *Plain Truth* that in a year of Vietnam duty he saw
several corpses who had been killed by marijuana-crazed
individuals. But in that year he saw none killed by Communist attack.[5]

5 The argument was succinctly put by the Home Secretary, Mr Reginald Maudling ... two months ago, when he
said that he could not forsee marijuana ever being legalized
because 'the evidence that soft drugs can lead users on to
hard drugs is too compelling to be ignored.'[6]

6 Does marijuana lead to heroin addiction? The Los
Angeles County Sheriff Department affirmed a direct connection: 'Our experience has proved that well in excess of
90 per cent of all narcotics addicts in this country have
graduated to the use of heroin through the use of marijuana.'[7]

No. 1 comes from a lurid 1939 news story entitled 'Just a
cigarette you'd think, but it was made from a sinister weed,
and an innocent girl falls victim to the TERROR!' Like much
later material, it assures us that marijuana is addictive, that
users become violent criminals of abnormal strength, and that
(paradoxically) they also become enervated, depressed and
suicidal.

Other quotations come from people who ought to know

better. No. 2 is by a former US Commissioner of Narcotics. We might expect from him a few pieces of evidence or at least sober statistics. Instead we get the ranting of a half-literate Temperance preacher. Oddly enough, the preacher would be more justified, since moral degradation, 'criminal assaults' and 'debauchery' are all proven effects of alcohol, while none is yet proven for pot.

No. 3 is a wild misinterpretation of an inconclusive experiment, to be discussed later. No. 4 deserves little comment, except that not even Sherlock Holmes could look at a corpse and deduce that its killer was (a) using a certain drug, and (b) not a Communist.

Nos 5 and 6 show law enforcement people in Britain and the US at their dumbest. The L.A. cop is easily the stupider; in a single sentence he manages to handcuff meaning and bludgeon logic to death. He begins by saying that ninety per cent of narcotics addicts use heroin, which makes nonsense of all that follows. (The majority of real addicts are 'legitimate' users of prescribed

> sleeping pills, tranquillizers, slimming pills, anti-depressants, and stimulants. Others take regular doses of aspirins or other medicines for which a prescription is not needed. ... The man who spends pounds a week which he can ill afford on cigarettes which are harmful to his health is seriously addicted.[8])

Next, the L.A. cop concludes that, because ninety per cent of (heroin) addicts previously used pot, pot leads to heroin. The phoney logic of this can be shown by letting A be 'heroin addicts later' and B be 'earlier users of pot'. Then (he reasons) *if most A are B, then most B are A.* In other words, 'If most ducks are birds, then most birds are ducks.' He may argue that that isn't what he meant at all, that he really meant that *some* proportion of heroin addicts wouldn't be in their present condition if they hadn't first smoked pot. This may be true, or it may not, but we'll never find out from his ninety per cent statistic.

Maudling's supposedly 'compelling' evidence is probably a graph prepared by W. D. M. Paton, comparing the number of arrests for cannabis in Britain with the number of registered heroin addicts, for the years 1954 to 1966. The two seem connected in some way, but Michael Schofield, in *The Strange Case of Pot*, 1971, points out three reasons for not jumping to conclusions:

1 Two dissimilar groups are being compared: One is virtually all the heroin addicts, while the other is a small minority of cannabis users, those who get caught.

2 There is no reason to assume that cannabis users who get caught are typical of all users, or that their number is a fixed percentage of the total number of users.

3 A cause-effect relationship needs more than simple statistics of this type. We could also infer that when an addict registers, this somehow 'causes' the police to arrest a pot smoker.

Of course there is *some* connection between the two drugs. For one thing, both are illegal, making it convenient for them to be sold by the same persons. Some people might possibly 'graduate' from pot to H. But then many heroin users seem to be drug experimenters anyway. In one study,[9] 98 per cent had used amphetamines, 95 per cent sedatives, 81 per cent tranquillizers and 94 per cent cocaine. In another,[10] 73 per cent had used barbiturates, 100 per cent alcohol, and 95 per cent tobacco. A study of prison addicts[11] showed similar histories.

There seems to be no hard evidence for the 'graduation' theory. Hong Kong's alarmingly high number of heroin addicts managed to begin without cannabis, and a survey of Vancouver addicts showed that less than ten per cent had previously used it. On the other hand, heroin addiction is still rare in Morocco, where cannabis has been widely used for years. Finally Dr Roger Lewin points out that 'there is no biological evidence that the use of one drug leads to a craving for another'. He goes on to say:

It begins to look as if the anti-marijuana lobby will have increasingly to turn to non-scientific arguments to back its case.[12]

In fact they do seem to be graduating from hard evidence to soft. Premature announcement that science had proved pot causing brain damage, genetic damage and so on, have looked less conclusive in the light of later research. In large doses, pot may do who knows what physiological damage, but then so may large doses of water. The final condemnation – that pot is an unwholesome escape from the problems of real life – sounds peculiar coming from *The Plain Truth*, itself a purveyor of millennarian religion.

LSD and DNA

A persistent and frightening belief about LSD is that it causes severe damage to human DNA, leading to 'horrendous mutations'. This belief should be around for some time to come, since LSD is not widely available for clinical trials.

The research which started this rumour took place in the United States in the late 1960s. There were four types of experiment:

1   Human cells were exposed to LSD in test tubes.

2   Laboratory animals were given massive doses of LSD.

3   Genetic material from the germ cells of heavy or habitual users of LSD was examined.

4 LSD was administered to test people, and genetic material from their germ cells was examined.

Four California scientists have disputed the conclusion that LSD causes genetic damage.[13] They argue that pure LSD taken in moderate amounts does no damage to chromosomes in living tissue, causes no genetic damage, and causes no tumours or cancer in humans. They base this argument on their own work, and on a complete review of all work on LSD done up to 1971, which showed that:

1   When human cells were exposed to LSD in test tubes, the reported damage may have been done by the examination process itself. Even if it wasn't, the dose each cell received varied from 10 to 10,000 times the dose it would receive in a living body. Moreover, the dead cells were unable to excrete or detoxify poisons as do living cells.

2   Laboratory animals were given doses far larger than humans usually take.

3   The damage detected in human users only occurred in those who took LSD in uncontrolled forms and dosages, or who also used other drugs. Illicit LSD is often adulterated (only fifty-four per cent of samples analysed contained relatively pure LSD). Finally, experimenters had only the users'

word for how many doses they had taken, and how large the doses had been. Were they heavy users, light users, or users at all?

4   When relatively pure LSD was given to human subjects, there was no evidence that any chromosome damage took place.

As for malformed babies, spontaneous abortions and so on, pregnant women would be wise to avoid *any* unnecessary drug – though no specific case has been proven against LSD.

Before the genetic scare, there were plenty of other LSD horror stories. It has been blamed for mental breakdowns, for which, like any psychotropic drug (e.g., alcohol) it may well be responsible.

At the same time, the public often seems eager to scare itself with stories like these:

> One man slept on a floor because he thought his bed was only two inches long. Another man felt he had to offer a human sacrifice and tried to throw his girl friend off a building. A third man was standing on a cliff; he wanted to dive into the waves below because they resembled a silk scarf! [14]

The last is of course the familiar I-can-fly story formerly told about other drugs. In some versions the victim wants to commit suicide; in others, he fails to apprehend the danger. In this 1939 version, we get it both ways:

> A young and lovely woman, her clothes in shreds, stood perilously perched on a window ledge. Behind her was a man. He, too, was wild-looking and dishevelled. Several times the girl made an effort to jump and the man feebly held her back. Soon, a third man appeared, coloured and strong, and hauled them both back. They were both marijuana addicts. As she disappeared, she could be heard screaming, 'I can fly. Well, I don't care if I die!' [15]

Any real psychological dangers in LSD are completely masked by such rumours, in which names, dates and places are never given. The mechanism of rumour will appear again in chapter 24. Here it can be seen in the story of the six University of

Pennsylvania students who were supposed to have taken LSD
and then stared steadily at the sun until their retina were
damaged, and they went blind. The story was enthusiastically
told by even less sensational newspapers. Eventually it was
traced to a University health official, who, after admitting it
was untrue, committed himself to a mental hospital. One or
two newspapers even bothered to retract the story.

The real or imagined horrors of LSD have to be seen in
perspective.

> The fact that among alcoholics the suicide rate is 80
> times greater than the normal population seems to escape
> notice. The possible relationship between drug-taking and
> crime, and particularly crimes of violence, received attention,
> but the relationship between alcohol and crime seldom
> seems to obtrude upon the public consciousness. There is
> fairly good research evidence to suggest that alcohol intoxi-
> cation is particularly associated with aggressive and sexual
> crimes,[16]

writes Dr Griffith Edwards. The point being not that we
should ignore LSD psychoses and concentrate on alcohol psychoses, or that we should forget about Killer Heroin and fight
Killer Tobacco, but that real concern about drugs and drug
problems should lead to careful and thorough research. So far
we've had little of that in regard to LSD. The same authorities
who condemn it because 'we know so little about it' are busy
passing legislation to make LSD clinical research all but impossible.

Of course there should be caution in dispensing or permit-
ting any drug which acts on the central nervous system. And
that caution might start in the British and American prisons
where inmates are being given massive doses of Thorazine, and
in the Nebraska schools where children who misbehaved were
dosed with Ritalin.

(When I planned this chapter, I meant to present a balance
of drug myths, overground vs underground. But the establishment's beliefs have far-reaching implications, while those
of the underground are, in general, merely a pathetic list of
new ways to get high. The use of morning-glory seeds, nutmeg
and burnt banana skins seems to have passed, and I hope to

hear of no more cases of misinformed children dying with peanut butter in their veins. There remains only one discovered high to talk about.)

Soreheads

In 1965 a Dutch medical student who had failed his exams drilled a hole in his head, in order to change his psychological state. Some may find this a rough road to insight, but the student, Bart Huges, explains the 'third eye' in his book *Trepanation*.[17]

Huges's theory is that opening the head reduces pressure in the cerebro-spinal fluid, allowing the blood vessels of the brain to expand. The effect of this increase of 'bloodbrain-volume' is a kind of high, he says, comparable to a permanent acid trip, standing on one's head, Yoga breathing, etc.

According to Huges, a hole in the head is the most natural thing in the world. Children, after all, have open sutures in their skulls, but when they grow up, these close, turning them into hard-faced, materialistic, war-mongering adults. 'Awareness, spontaneity and intimacy have vanished.'[18]

The reason animals act so childlike and natural (though many of them have closed, adult heads) is that they walk on all fours, keeping their spines horizontal. Man loses all by standing upright, which increases the pressure in his cerebro-spinal fluid.

I'm not sure how much sense this makes medically, or even hydrostatically. Huges never does get around to explaining a number of things:

1 Whether spinal taps, which certainly reduce pressure in the cerebro-spinal fluid, have 'third eye effects', and if not, why not?

2 Why no one seems to have noticed expanded consciousness in people whose heads have been opened accidentally or surgically for other reasons?

3 Why kangaroo adults seem to act as aware, spontaneous and intimate as any creature with a horizontal spine?

4 Why humans don't automatically become less materialistic when they lie down?

Huges has been able to interest a few other I'll-try-anything-once people in having their heads drilled. That he has not managed to interest the medical profession in awareness surgery would not of itself cast doubt on the trepanation movement, but for one curious contradiction:

It is repeatedly emphasized, as with LSD, that if you haven't tried trepanation, you can't possibly understand it, except in an academic sense. On page 23 of *Trepanation*, Huges's pal R. H. Hübner claims that sophisticated demonstrations of the theory would not be necessary 'if one medical doctor ventured to stand on his head and draw his own conclusions'. But on page 10, Huges explains that his father (a doctor) and a student psychiatrist he knows have gone further than that – both have skull holes, from former injuries. Do they, at least, understand his theory?

> No. For both of them my authority carries too little weight for them to pay attention to my writings. I have several times tried to explain the mechanism to the student, but *he was too little aware of the facts of psycho-analysis* and the findings of Pavlov to grasp the meaning of the words.[19] (my italics)

Huges's new awareness evidently has its limits. But Trepanation drills on, to the triocular tunes of Joe Mellen:

> It was lost and now it's found again,
> Don't drive it underground again,
> Bloodbrainvolume ...
> Headstands have been done for
> The whole thing was begun for
> It's what the world was made for
> The price must be paid for
> Bloodbrainvolume.[20]

Of the Head

There are six main systems for finding out a man's character without necessarily making his acquaintance. This chapter covers four: phrenology, physiognomy, palmistry and graphology. Astrology and numerology will be covered in later chapters.

Each system has claimed allegiance from generations of the occult-minded; some have temporarily reigned as serious sciences. Each, of course, claims to be the one true way to overpower and mystify your friends by reading their most secret thoughts.

All in the Head
Ever since they abandoned Aristotle's notion that the head was a kind of cooling tower filled with water, people have been explaining the brain. Most of us are familiar with the analogies of clockwork ('you can hear the wheels turning'), telephone exchange ('getting his wires crossed'), radio ('not on the same wavelength') and the computer. Each analogy is a monument to the state of contemporary knowledge and ignorance about our cooling towers.

The exciting analogy in the eighteenth century seems to have been the pigeon-hole desk. Talk of the 'faculty' of this and that led naturally to phrenology, and in 1800 the Austrian Franz Josef Gall introduced the theory that the pigeon-holes, or faculties, were located in twenty-seven different parts of the brain's surface. These he mapped and numbered, to the delight of today's antique dealers.

It stood to reason that a large faculty of cautiousness (No. 10) should show up as a swelling of that part of the brain, which should in turn require a protuberance of the skull to accommodate it. Therefore, feel the bumps and know the man.

Gall's pupil, Johann Gaspar Spurzheim, revised his system, adding favourite bumps of his own and re-classifying the head. There were *Feelings* (from 1, *Amativeness* to 21, *Imitation*), and *Intellective Faculties* (from 22, *Individuality* to 35,

Causality), with many interesting traits in between, such as No. 4, *Adhesiveness*, or urge for a soul-mate.[1]

Phrenology caught on like pox, and received nearly as much medical approbation. In 1807 a commission from the Paris Institute found the Gall-Spurzheim theory unworkable. All through the nineteenth century, phrenological systems kept appearing, and kept being disproved, until it became clear to all but determined believers that the brain was not a pigeon-hole desk. This slow dawning took over a century. Meanwhile, phrenology commanded the belief of people like Walt Whitman, who referred to it in his poems; Sir Isaac Pitman,* whose large hat size was taken to correlate with his shorthand and phonetic inventiveness; and Sir Arthur Conan Doyle. But gradually the system made its way from the laboratory to the believer's parlour, and thence to the fortune-teller's tent, helped by the discovery in 1901 that brain lesions cause disorders completely unrelated to any phrenological map.

Facting Faces

Physiognomy has a long and honourable history. It was popular with the Greeks, and Renaissance men wrote volumes on the subject, contradicting one another. Most of us probably practise a kind of makeshift physiognomy in daily life, though we seldom check or systematize our guesses.

When there is truth to be found in such observations, it is probably the truth of caricature (swart Dick Nixon, equine de Gaulle) or the truth of descriptions in cheap fiction ('thin, cruel lips', 'pale, rheumy eyes', 'a great bull neck'). Each feature is classified according to its resemblance (a) to some animal supposed to have the quality we're looking for; or (b) to the distortion of features by powerful emotions. Using method *a*, we find the sly man with his long fox's nose, possibly because we endow the fox itself with exaggerated slyness. Ditto the long doltish donkey face, the timid rabbit face, and the wise owl face (before spectacles, the owl was more reason-

---

* Pitman seems to have been taken with physiognomy, alphabet reform (as was Bernard Shaw) and vegetarianism. He described his vegetarian views in a letter to *The Times* in 1879, which began: 'Ser,—A frend sujests tu me that I ought tu reit a leter tu *The Times*, plasing mei leif-eksperiens in kontrast with ...' Signed: 'Eizak Pitman'.

ably endowed with cruelty and nocturnal ghostliness). Using *b*,

> A red ... eye denotes the person to be selfish, deceitful and proud, furious in anger, fertile in the invention of plots, and indefatigable in his resolution to bring them to bear.[2]

The classification systems are numerous and contradictory. 'Sibyl', quoted above, gives thin lips to mean 'a quick and lively imagination' and 'not too much attached to money', while another physiognomist says the same features mean 'prim and penurious'.

The nineteenth-century occultist Cesare Lombroso attempted a statistical study of criminality and faces, but his results were unreliable. In the 1930s the anthropologist E. A. Hooton tried to establish some link between criminality and body features. His research foundered on two counts:

1 While it's easy enough to show that a proportion of convicted criminals have some particular feature, it's not so easy to show that the population in general doesn't have the same feature in the same proportion.

2 'Criminality' usually depends upon the setting of the act, existing mores, getting caught and getting convicted. Thus the fictional Jean Valjean was a 'thief', and Sacco and Vanzetti were 'murderers' only in certain contexts. Any theory which proposes a genetic explanation of criminality must define and eliminate the influences of these contexts.

The best summary of physiology currently available is John Brophy's *The Human Face Reconsidered*, 1962, which says:

> We do read character in faces, and sometimes accurately and with penetration, but this is when we either know the owner of the face intimately or possess other evidence about him from words spoken or written, from his actions, and reactions, with the mutable expressions of the face which accompany them, from the voice, from the total physical presence.[3]

A few other factors might also come into play. A person's outlook might shape his habitual expression. It may be that a person who has a particular face would provoke reactions in others that might determine in part his character. For instance, a man with a 'determined' jaw may find that people approach him as if they expect a conflict; their aggressiveness could make him stubborn. Finally, a person who finds certain facial expressions useful in daily life may adopt them more or less permanently. We all know the waiter with downcast eyes, the salesman who smiles too much, the politician on TV who uses ageing and seediness as tokens of wisdom and homely warmth. I leave it to the reader to decide how happy the salesman, how humble the waiter, or how wise and fatherly the politician really is, 'offstage'.

Brophy gives a brief summary of the tenets of popular physiognomy:

1   Large, well-spaced eyes: Candour and honesty.
2   Small eyes, set close together: Cunning and treachery.
3   Eyes which avoid your glance: Unreliability or guilt.
4   Eyes with deep upper lids: Secrecy, suspiciousness.
5   Long nose: Inquisitiveness.
6   Nose with down-curving tip: Avarice.
7   Wide mouth: Generosity, affability.
8   Thick lips: Sensuality.
9   Thin lips: Envy.
10 Narrow mouth: Primness, self-righteousness.
11 Square or jutting chin: Determination, heroism.
12 Receding chin: Weakness, indecision.

He finds no evidence for accepting any of these, and points out how misleading real faces can be. If a picture of Winston Churchill were shown to someone who'd never heard of him, they would see every evidence of sensuality and none of leadership potential. If we remove Hitler's moustache and comb back his hair, he looks remarkably like a plump Kirk Douglas.

Honeymoon in the Hand

It's interesting to see modern writers on palmistry trying to relate this ancient superstition to scientific principles. Noel Jaquin, in *The Hand of Man*, 1933, has no hesitation in furnishing the universe with the necessary forces.

All activity is electromagnetic, whether it be a lover's kiss, an explosion of dynamite, or the falling of a comet. We know that light, heat, sound, wireless waves, ultra-violet waves, etc., are all electromagnetic. How far then are we affected, our actions influenced by the radiations emanating from the far distant planets?[4]

He points out that all life needs energy from the sun, and invokes moon madness, yet another hard-dying superstition. That all living creatures derive energy ultimately from our sun does not explain planetary influences, nor would these serve to explain lines in the hand. Jaquin therefore introduces yet another dubious link, phrenology:

> Each part of the hand has its counterpart, or department, in the brain; thus, the emotions connected with our amorous impulses are shewn in the formation of the Cardiac or Heart lines, while the logical abilities and the degree of will-power are indicated by the formation of the Cerebral or Head line.[5]

Jaquin feels it's unfair to dismiss his 'science' just because we associate it with gipsies and old ladies' tea parties; for 'we do not deride orthodox medicine even though its early practitioners were blood-letting barbers'.[6]

On the other hand, 'Cheiro' (Count Louis Hamon) feels that it was only the blood-letting barbers who knew their business, while modern doctors are ignoramuses. He bewails the replacement of early all-round craftsmen by modern specialist doctors:

> This specialization ... may give greater knowledge on particular things, but it confines men to a narrower line of thought. It therefore happens that a physician may know little about anatomy, whereas the surgeon may know next to nothing of medicine.[7]

Of course the reverse is true. The surgeon is always a fully-trained doctor, and every physician studies anatomy extensively. Indeed, the most inept, ill-trained and fumbling doctor of today knows more about the human body than all the blood-letters, bone-setters and poultice-mixers even suspected. Cheiro's point is that we should ignore the advice of our misinformed family doctors and trust to the diagnoses of palmists.

Palmistry makes three claims: that it can diagnose disease; that it can judge character (*chirognomy*); and that it can foretell the future (*chiromancy*). Since palmist diagnosticians show little awareness of developments in medicine since the last century (Cheiro quotes a scientific opinion of the 1820s that the nerves are channels for 'nervous fluid' which might be related to electricity), let's see how they do in other areas.

Chiromancy is plain fortune-telling, having no particular advantages over cartomancy, rhabdomancy, geomancy, hydromancy (divination by cards, sticks, dirt and pools of water) or reading entrails, crystal balls or tea leaves. The palmist need not argue his case with the scientist, if he will submit to a simple test. All he has to do is make fifty specific predictions, to come true within a certain time, under test conditions. If even five come true, he'll find the scientist's supposed scepticism will vanish.

Many who reject fortune-telling still feel that chirognomy may have 'something in it'. It makes sense to think of the mechanic as having short, square hands; the artist, long, tapering fingers and so on. And could not a long life-line indicate an hereditary disposition to longevity? It would be nice if it worked out that way, but reading character from the hand has several deficiencies:

1 Character is a vague ghost, hard to grasp. We're all generous to a degree, methodical about certain things, artistic at times. Everyone loves, invents, calculates, dreams.

Moreover, character varies in context. Pride and ambition are virtues to a Cheyenne, vices to a Hopi. What is seen as thrift in a poor man's hand must also look like miserliness in a rich man's hand.

2 Flattery guarantees the palmist a certain 'success' in almost any reading. Looking into a palm he sees well-developed mounts of Jupiter and Mercury, and tells the owner that he has ambition, pride, enthusiasm and an urge to power (Jupiter); that he is quick-witted, and likes change, travel and excitement. Naturally the client concentrates on those traits he has or would like to have, ignoring the others.

3 The palmist may know his client, or be able to guess something of his character, and direct his reading accordingly.

The hand of George Bernard Shaw (frontispiece of Jaquin) has a spatulate ring finger which, we're told, 'indicates dramatic ability'. But the hand of Sarah Bernhardt (in Cheiro) shows no such indication. Undaunted, Cheiro finds that her dramatic ability has moved elsewhere; it is now located in the open space between her Line of Life and Line of Head. That space, incidentally, is missing in Shaw's hand.

4 If the geometry of the hand is significant, it ought to be geometrical. How long is a 'long' life-line? When does a head-line 'slope', and in relation to what? How big is a 'well-developed' mount of Mars? Palmists don't say. Perhaps, as they indicate, it depends upon experience, but then experience doesn't seem to lend precision to their judgements.

Chirognomy has been tested many times by psychologists, with negative results. In a televised test, palmists examined the hands of persons thrust through a curtain, and their assessments were compared to those of psychiatrists. The two did not tally.

Palmists are of course in no doubt as to who was right. As with all cranks, they feel they haven't been given a fair hearing, and that orthodoxy is ganging up on them.

> The reward of the pioneer is so often the ridicule of his fellow-men. We are not very much more just today. Of recent years men of genius have been deprived of their living and literally hounded to death [!] by the ridicule of their more ignorant brethren.[8]

How true, how true. They laughed at Galileo, they laughed at Darwin, they laughed at Edison ... and they laughed at Punch and Judy.

The Written Character
Graphology, or handwriting analysis, could be found to have a sound psychological basis. The strongest arguments in its favour seem to be:

1 There may be some connection between the overall pattern of a person's handwriting and his personality. An artist might be expected to make a pattern of visual interest; an orderly, methodical person could write slowly and neatly, and so on.

2 There may be unconscious reasons for some writing

mannerisms. Take the two examples in Figure 12–1. Example
A can be seen to rise on certain letters to the highest layer.
According to graphological theory, this indicates spiritual
aspirations, creativity, dreams and illusions. Example B sinks
below the deepest layer, indicating expression of the sexual
impulses and other repressed material of the unconscious.

Imagination
Mind and spirit
Actuality
Biological demands
The unconscious

A   B

Figure 12–1   Graphology examples

Graphologists have similarly analysed tendencies to lean the
handwriting right or left, the writing's size and proportions,
its angularity or roundness, the shape and length of connecting
strokes, the weight of strokes and many other factors, in terms
of unconscious behaviour.

Most graphologists seem to carry the idea pretty far. Klara
G. Roman, in *Handwriting Analysis: A Key to Personality*,
1961, uses a worksheet listing forty-one characteristics to look
for, making up an elaborate and impressive 'personality
profile'.[9] Whether each profile corresponds to some actual
personality is another question. Unfortunately, a graphology
system isn't usually subjected to systematic experiments on a
large scale, as are conventional psychological tests. We have
therefore no guarantee that it tests what it's supposed to test;
that it works consistently on large numbers of people; or that
its findings correlate with those of other tests.

Graphology seems to have grown out of earlier studies of
unconscious behaviour. So have the thousands on thousands
of 'projective' tests in popular magazines. Weekly or monthly,
we're invited to become any animal we like; to rank a set of
colours; to draw a tree; to notice whether we strike matches
away from us or towards us; to spend a million; to draw
ourselves; to notice the asymmetry of our faces; to rank some
Chinese symbols; to choose a new pet, name, house, spouse or
career; and so on. Each 'test' promises genuine insight into
one's own character, and, monkeys to mirrors, we find all of
them fascinating.

It's difficult to discuss astrology simply as character analysis, without taking account of its claim to predict the future. If the movements of planets guide human actions, they must guide most of the human interactions on which 'fate' depends. There are astrologers who go further, maintaining that *every* event is completely determined by planetary influences, but this, as we'll see, leads to ridiculous conclusions. For now, it will be enough to examine the root notion of some guiding influence from Out There.

In 1971 BBC presented a radio discussion of astrology.[1] Some of the arguments for astrology were trivial, but some were ingenious, and deserve a longer answer than the programme allowed time for.

A owned an employment agency and used astrology in her work. She claimed that it predicted a business merger, and that it was right in long-term trends, though not always on specific points.

B, an astrologer, saw himself as picking likely scenarios (like an astrological Herman Kahn) rather than making exact, detailed forecasts.

C saw science as an accretion of facts, data, while astrology took the larger view, trying to relate man to time, to understand the nature of time and the universe.

D claimed that empirical proofs of astrology were numerous. He quoted a 1965 study of the relation of the moon to rainfall which is now accepted as valid, but which, he said, was originally inspired by astrology. He also mentioned research by Michel Gauquelin into planetary influences.

A's argument is unanswerable. If astrology works for her, it works for her. However, we might ask how she distinguishes long-term trends from specific predictions. If her horoscope predicts, say, that business will slump, then pick up, it cannot be said to be a prediction at all, unless it names dates. Every business everywhere is almost certain to have a slump, then pick up, at some future time.

The same applies to B's scenarios. When Herman Kahn and Anthony J. Wiener set out to make their framework for speculation,[2] they had no special access to information about the future. All they could do was extrapolate present trends, to extend the curves of GNP, population, etc., and see what would happen if ... Their scenarios of 'surprise-free' futures are really equivalent to predicting that a coin will either come down *heads or tails* (making no allowances for it to land on edge, disappear down a crack, or be snatched by a thief in mid-air). If this is really what B is doing, then he is also admitting that astrology provides no special knowledge whatever about the future. Moreover, he could draw his scenarios without the aid of astrology, for this kind of speculation amounts to an exercise in logic.

C is wrong about science. Contrary to the popular picture of science, it is not an accretion of facts. According to Peter Medawar,

> the ballast of factual information, so far from being just about to sink us, is growing daily less. The factual burden of a science varies inversely with its degree of maturity. As a science advances, particular facts are comprehended within, and therefore in a sense annihilated by, general statements of steadily increasing explanatory power and compass – whereupon the facts need no longer be known explicitly, i.e. spelled out and kept in mind. In all sciences we are being progressively relieved of the burden of singular instances, the tyranny of the particular. We need no longer record the fall of every apple.[3]

Furthermore, if astrology is not a science but a philosophy, we have no right to expect it to make any kind of prediction, or to deal with facts at all. Where it does condescend to dirty its hands with facts and predictions, it is a science, and may therefore be judged like any other science, on performance.

Which brings us to D's assertion that astrology is an empirically testable science. Before looking at some ways of testing astrology, it's necessary to examine some of its claims to being a science.

1   *Millions of people believe in it.* Well, millions of people

have believed the earth was flat. Like other occult sciences, astrology offers certainty about the future, insights into one's own and others' personalities, and medical advice. If one can't understand another's behaviour, it's always easier to attribute it to astral influences, than to try to find out what makes him so contrary here and now.

2 *Astrology is based on millions of observations of the movements of the planets, from Chaldean times up to the present.* It is, rather, a metaphysical construction, made by men, and imposed upon their observations. Even the same constellations have different meanings for different peoples. Leo, for example, is not seen by South American Indians as a lion,

> because they disregard what we would call the animal's tail and hind legs and make of the rest a lobster seen from above.[4]

Observations of planetary movements, when subjected to projection of this kind, fare no better than Leo the Lobster. Using identical data, two newspapers managed to come up with unrelated predictions for the same day:

CONSTANCE SHARPE
Gemini A new interest – a hobby perhaps – will begin to occupy your leisure. A piece of good news comes to you by a roundabout means.

Cancer This promises to be a bright, cheerful week in which you succeed in winning the approval of important people.

DOROTHY ADAMS
Gemini A settlement is made which will bring long-lasting security as well as hard work. Life will move faster, with plenty of variety to keep you happy.

Cancer News you will hear will put your mind at rest. There are pronounced indications of a windfall which could go a long way towards settling a domestic problem. An elderly friend will be extremely helpful.

3 *Astrological predictions aren't always absolutely right,*

but then neither are weather predictions. But at least, weather
forecasters know how to improve their predictions. Lack of
sufficient data seems to be their main problem. By contrast,
the movements of planets are now known far more accurately
than astrologers need to know them. Apparently they could
only improve their accuracy by changing their basic theory,
which has remained static for millennia.

Another difference is that we always know when weather
forecasters are wrong, while astrologers are so vague as to
make some of their predictions meaningless. The weather
bureau doesn't say that it could be a propitious day for enterprises possibly involving the family, with perhaps some travel
indicated. It says the day will be warm and sunny enough
for a picnic.

Finally, the weather forecaster exerts no psychological pressure on the weather, while telling a man to expect bad news
can act to make him see any news in the worst light. At least
some astrological predictions are self-fulfilling.

4 *Some astrological predictions are absolutely right.* The
cases most often cited are predictions of the assassination of
Kennedy and of an assassination attempt on Hitler.

One American astrologer who claims to have predicted the
assassination of John F. Kennedy was interviewed on BBC
radio in 1972. She also claimed to have predicted the death of
Robert Kennedy, and other events in the lives of the Kennedy
family. Her story sounded convincing, though she offered no
proof that her predictions had actually pre-dated the events in
question.

Oddly, she said nothing about the future of the Kennedy
family. It was a perfect opportunity to make her point to
millions of listeners, by simply saying that ——— was going
to happen to ———, within a certain time.

Less than a week after her broadcast, Robert Kennedy's
son was aboard an airliner hijacked to the Middle East, an
event which made world headlines for days.

One question remains unanswered. Thousands, perhaps tens
of thousands of horoscopes must have been cast for JFK,
during the years when he was the No. 1 man in American
politics. If astrology is to get the credit for this single correct
prediction, how are we to explain the thousands of failures?

The prediction of an attempt on Hitler's life seems to be

true. The astrologer and Nostradamus scholar Karl Ernst Krafft predicted on 2 November 1939

> that Hitler's life would be in danger between 7-10 November and actually used the expression 'possibility of an attempt of assassination by the use of explosive material'.[5]

On 8 November 1939, just such an attempt was made. Krafft promptly wrote to the government, calling attention to the accuracy of his prediction. The Gestapo promptly arrested him. Evidently he managed to convince them that he wasn't in on the plot, for they later released him.

This prediction seems startlingly accurate. But Ellic Howe, who traces Krafft's entire career, explains that he cast hundreds of horoscopes for Hitler, for Germany, for the Third Reich and for other Nazi leaders. At no time did any of these horoscopes produce a single useful prediction. As we've seen, Krafft was a great self-publicist, so we may be sure that other true prophecies would have been trumpeted. A man must have considerable faith in his system to use it for nineteen years before it works once.

No single correct prediction is enough to show that astrology has a scientific basis. A large number of indisputable predictions could provide the basis for a revision of astrological theories. This in turn could provide for more successes, leading to further refinements and consolidations of theory, and so on. But that is a path few astrologers wish to take, the path of science.

It gives a rather strange twist to D's statement that astrology *is* science, to realize that the only serious investigations being carried out are by non-believers. Michel Gauquelin[6] prefaces his own research by stories of earlier, abortive attempts to prove astrology.

Commandant Paul Choisnard 'proved' several of its theories by an ignorance of statistics and by failing to understand that Europe is not on the equator. Karl Ernst Krafft published his *Treatise on Astrobiology* in 1939. His findings were marred by his utter innocence about basic astronomy.

The three most important factors in a horoscope are the sun sign, the moon sign and the ascendant. The sun sign is determined by which twelfth of the year one is born in, the moon sign changes every two or three days, and the ascendant is determined by the hour of birth. Michel Gauquelin examined these signs for 25,000 celebrities' births, and found a random distribution. No extra soldiers were born in Aries, no extra musicians in Libra, and so on.

In one test, the birth charts of three celebrities (a TV announcer plagued by bad luck, a bicycle race champion and an entertainer) were given to fourteen astrologers, to be matched with the celebrities' names. All failed. Another test showed astrologers unable to select the birth charts of murderers from those of other people.

Gauquelin examined the birth times of 576 French doctors, and found that the number born when either Saturn or Mars was either rising or at zenith, was higher than expected by chance. He then tried another group of 508 doctors, and found the same peculiar bias.

Gauquelin next extended his research to cover other occupations and other countries. He collected the birth times of 25,000 celebrities from Germany, Italy, Belgium and Holland. These times were matched with the rising or zenith of the moon, Saturn, Jupiter and Mars. The positive and negative correlations found are shown in Table 13-1.

Gauquelin realized that these careers seemed to show some mysterious planetary influence, but an influence having nothing to do with astrology. He also realized that no hypothetical 'ray' could account for sudden changes in the inherited character of a fully developed feotus which is ready to be born. But discarding this theory still left his strange statistics unexplained.

Finally he settled on a theory of 'planetary heredity'. He assumed that heredity played a large part in determining whether a child would grow up to be a doctor or a general, and he proposed that a planetary ray or influence might trigger off the births of children with the appropriate genes.

If heredity does select the children to be born at a particular hour and day, then we might expect to find parents' skies at birth similar to the skies at birth of their children. Gauquelin checked 15,000 parent-child pairs and found a correlation between their skies at birth. This planetary heredity seemed to follow 'certain familiar genetic laws'.[7]

It would be rash to jump to the conclusion that Gauquelin's theory is proved – he would be the first to deny it – but it

Table 13-1 Celebrity births and planet positions

+ indicates a higher than expected number of births at the rising or zenith of this planet.
− indicates a lower than expected number of births at the rising or zenith of this planet.

	Mars (♂)	Jupiter (♃)	Saturn (♄)	Moon (☾)
Scientists	+	−	+	
Doctors	+	−	+	
Team athletes	+	+		−
Solo athletes	+			−
Soldiers	+	+		−
Ministers		+		+
Actors		+	−	
Journalists		+	−	
Writers	−		−	+
Painters	−		−	
Musicians	−			

does seem as though more research along planetary heredity lines is needed. Several objections to his theory can be raised:

1   The 'moment of birth' is a fiction. Shall we count the moment when the baby's head is visible? When it emerges? When the rest of him emerges? The delivery of the placenta?

2   Recorded times of birth are notoriously inaccurate. The obstetrician, midwife, or hospital office worker who fills in this information is no astronomer. He or she may be tired, rushed, too busy to fill it in for hours or even days.

3   Whatever triggers it off, labour may be of any duration, from a few minutes to more than a day. The planetary ray would have to determine the probable length of labour and then align it with the birth sky in advance. It can only do this if length of labour is an hereditary factor, or if large numbers of women are close to some average labour duration.

4   So many factors are involved in becoming a celebrated member of any profession that it is surprising that planetary heredity should show up at all. Admission to medical school in many countries, for example, may depend greatly on social standing as well as on aptitude. So far as I know, Britain has only one black policeman, and the US has one or two black generals, recently appointed.

5   Womb environment may be powerful enough to over-ride many hereditary factors. Gauquelin's theory will have to take account of:

   a. Seasonal variations during gestation.
   b. The mother's use of drugs while pregnant – even aspirin.
   c. The rate of spontaneous abortion, and its changes.
   d. Seasonal variation in birth times.
   e. Effects, if any, of sun's and moon's gravity. These might be felt indirectly, through weather variations.
   f. Effects of diet and prenatal care.

In view of these objections, it is optimistic to hope that Gauquelin has discovered any link between planet movements and human traits.

In *The Case for Astrology*,[8] J. A. West and J. G. Toonder sum up what they feel is the scientific evidence favouring this system. They begin with Gauquelin, then cite an astrologer's 'statistical' study without giving his statistics. This is followed by a mixed batch of scientific and pseudo-scientific items:

Biologist Frank A. Brown found that oysters seem to open

and close their shells in a rhythm adjusted to the passing of the moon overhead. He also found changes in the activity rates of other organisms which seemed to correspond to lunar and solar cycles.[9]

Dr L. J. Ravitz tested what West and Toonder call 'the electrical potential emitted by the body in normal and insane people'[10] and found lunar phase cycles. By this I think we may understand that he used a skin galvanometer to test skin moisture, hence agitation (on the lines of a lie detector). This kind of test is notoriously delicate and unreliable.

The Czech psychiatrist Eugen Jonas, plainly a believer in ancient mysteries, is claimed to have guessed the sexes of 217 out of 250 individuals, from their birth charts. This extremely good result cannot have arisen by chance. Either Jonas has found a genuine sex-guessing method (in which case we're bound to hear much, much more of him) or his experiment was faulty. No details are given as to how he obtained all those birth charts without knowing the sexes of their owners.[11]

Electrical engineer John H. Nelson found possible connections between magnetic storms on the earth and the positions of other planets with respect to the earth and sun. This sounds reasonable, since the sun seems to cause magnetic storms, and since planets, which produce magnetic fields, may affect them. Hardly evidence for astrology, since, as Nelson says, it makes no difference which planet is in the critical position.[12]

Another authority quoted is Rudolphe Tomaschek, a physicist and an astrologer, here represented as 'chairman of the International Geophysical Society'.[13] Tomaschek was also a fanatical Nazi, and inclined to substitute Nazi 'truths' for facts (for his views on physics, see page 234).

Professor Giorgio Piccardi has shown by a long series of experiments that the speeds of some chemical reactions seem to vary in regular cycles, perhaps tied to sunspot cycles. West and Toonder follow this up with other, less reliable studies of cycles, which we'll see in chapter 22.

The attempt to put astrology on a scientific footing probably goes something like this: Planetary influence→chemical reactions→nucleotides→genes→heredity→human character. It's a brave effort, but unsupported by evidential links. Even if it were found to be the case that planets shape human character in some way, the astrology story is implausible. For we are told that they alone have worked out the details of planetary influence, and that they did so in ancient days (at about the time the Egyptians considered the earth flat and the sky a box-shaped tent).

But even the possibility of planetary influence on our genes is so remote as to be a fantasy. Mars is expected to create a soldier by being selective enough to alter the arrangement of 150,000 nucleotides in certain of the 30,000 genes in certain of his 46 chromosomes – from a distance of over 40 million miles – while leaving the rest of his genes or chromosomes alone – and all by 'vibrations'. Maybe so, but then maybe the moon has a wooden leg.

Fate against Freedom
The astrologer Joseph Goodavage devotes an entire chapter of his book[14] to an attack on free will and a defence of plane-tary determinism. Suppose he, and other characterologists, are right, and all our most trivial actions are mapped out in advance in our genes, stars or numbers. In that case, there's no reason to read your daily horoscope or have your head bumps felt, since knowing your future can't affect it. Why bother over-coming those domestic difficulties or waiting for that important letter, as advised? Your ultimate destiny, and all steps leading up to it, are completely fixed, locked into the universe com-puter. The only excuse for taking astrological advice is that you can't help but take it – nor can the astrologer help but give it.

Other astrologers and characterologists allow us *limited* free will, not much of an improvement. If a man has a 'murderer's hand', a large bump of destructiveness, or sinister stars, can he really be blamed for his actions?

Psychologically, this fatalism accounts for much of the appeal of such systems. There's a kind of security in knowing you just can't help it, you're moved by the stars. Responsibility vanishes into the firmament. So did Cromwell imagine that not he, but the hand of God, was slaughtering the Irish thousands. So did Eichmann blame 'higher orders' for his slaughtering the Jewish millions. So do we all, whenever we succumb to the Fates, and give over a part of our humanity to some Great Inevitable.

Experiments with extra-sensory perception, or ESP, began nearly a century ago, as part of the work of the new Society for Psychical Research. The first experiments were simply demonstrations. A panel of eminent scientists and civil servants from the SPR were invited to watch the show and write a report. In their enthusiasm, these good men made only the clumsiest attempts to prevent or detect cheating. Not surprisingly, some of their most positive cases turned out to be frauds. Such were the Smith-Blackburn experiments of 1882-92:

Smith was seated at a table. His eyes were padded with cotton and covered with a thick cloth, and his ears were stuffed with cotton and putty. Thick rugs beneath his chair were intended to deaden vibration. Finally, his whole body and the chair were wrapped in two thick blankets.

Blackburn, at the opposite side of the large room, was shown a complex abstract drawing devised by the committee. He was allowed to copy it several times, to fix it in his mind. Then, without speaking or touching Smith, he stood behind Smith's chair, while the latter drew a copy of the figure. His copy was almost always perfect.

The SPR committee men were astounded. They began citing this case as irrefutable proof of telepathy. They continued saying so right through 1908, when Blackburn admitted it was all a hoax; right up to 1911, when he publicly explained his method.

While copying the drawing to fix it in his mind, Blackburn had secretly made a tiny copy of it on a cigarette paper. He palmed this and inserted it into the end of his pencil. When ready, he would stumble against the edge of the rug near Smith. At this signal, Smith would call out 'Where's my pencil?' Blackburn would lay his pencil on the table, and Smith would reach out from under his blankets and pick it up.

Under the blankets, Smith had concealed in his clothes a spiritualist's luminous slate. He would push up the blindfold from one eye, lay the cigarette paper on the slate, and copy the figure from it.

Earnest ESP research really began with the arrival at Duke University (Durham, North Carolina) of Dr Joseph Banks Rhine, a botanist. Dr Rhine's first paper on telepathy,* published in 1929, concerns Lady Wonder, a telepathic horse owned by Mrs Claudia Fonda. Lady could spell out the answers to various questions by touching her nose to lettered or numbered blocks. Oddly enough, she was only successful at this when Mrs Fonda was nearby. At one point in his research, Rhine caught the owner giving Lady signals. Still, he believed that Lady had once had truly psychic powers, but that these had mysteriously faded.†

In 1930 Rhine began using the now-famous 'ESP cards', bearing the symbols: cross, circle, square, star and wavy lines. In his general ESP experiments, the pack of twenty-five cards

---

*Psychic abilities are usually broken down into four categories:
1 *Telepathy*, or thought transference.
2 *Clairvoyance*, or 'seeing without eyes', as in finding lost objects.
3 *Precognition*, or knowledge of the future.
4 *Psychokinesis*, or the ability to influence a physical object by thought alone.
'ESP' usually refers to No. 1, sometimes to Nos 2 or 3.

† Lady Wonder lived a long, probably profitable life. In 1952, the police tried asking her to locate the body of a missing child. Bergen Evans says she replied: 'Pittsfield Water Wheel'. But no body was found at the Pittsfield water wheel. Then the police chief suddenly realized that this was, as Evans says, 'an enquinopsychic blunder or horsegraphical error' for 'Field and Wilde's water pit', an abandoned quarry near the boy's home. There the boy's body was found. That the chief hadn't thought of looking there in the first place probably explains why he needed advice from a psychic horse (Evans, *The Spoor of Spooks*).

In 1956, a professional magician named Milbourne Christopher found Mrs Fonda and Lady still at it. He caught Mrs Fonda using a standard stage trick called 'pencil reading', i.e. guessing the number a person writes down by the movements of his pencil. She had provided a special long pencil. Christopher pretended to write one number while secretly writing another. Lady Wonder wrongly guessed the number indicated by the motion of his pencil (Gardner, *Fads and Fallacies*).

(five of each kind) is shuffled and cut. The agent (A) then looks at each card in turn, without showing it to the subject (S), who tries to guess it. A high number of correct guesses, or 'hits' may indicate either telepathy or clairvoyance ('second sight').

A. J. Linzmayer was one of Rhine's early successes. In guessing at 4,505 cards, Linzmayer made 1,212 hits. By pure chance, he should have made only about 901. To the novice, his score may not seem spectacular, but in fact the odds against its arising accidentally are 17,000,000,000 to 1!

Obviously Linzmayer either used ESP or else he learned by normal means what some of the cards were. At first, Rhine exerted only the crudest controls to insure against the latter possibility. Linzmayer was tested under absurd conditions, such as sitting with Rhine in the front seat of his car, or simply being asked to gaze out a window while Rhine handled the cards. As soon as the experimental conditions became more reasonable, Linzmayer's ESP ability vanished. Nevertheless, Rhine believed in Linzmayer, as he'd believed in Lady Wonder.[1]

The Pratt-Pierce Experiment

H. E. Pearce, a divinity student, and J. G. Pratt, a graduate in psychology, performed a 'classic' long-distance experiment in ESP on the Duke campus in 1933. Pratt remained in his room while Pearce crossed the campus to the library (which Pratt could see him enter, from his window). Pratt used two packs of ESP cards, this time not looking at their faces at all, but simply going through them one by one, face-down (this was a test of pure clairvoyance), beginning at an agreed time. Then he turned the fifty cards over and recorded their order. In the library, Pearce was presumably recording his guesses. Then each man made a copy of his record, sealed it and delivered it to Rhine's office, before they met to compare results.* In 37 such sittings, for three of which Rhine was in Pratt's room acting as observer, the two students produced significant scores: 558 hits out of 1,850 trials. The odds

---

* But in all reports of the experiments made between 1934 and 1940, no mention is made of the duplicate records in sealed envelopes.

against so high a score are well over 10^{12} (or 1 followed by 12 zeroes) to 1.

Again, it should be obvious that chance alone was not at work. C. E. M. Hansel investigated the Duke campus and found that it would have been perfectly easy for Pearce to have left the library during the experiment, approached Pratt's room, and watched him turn over the cards for recording. The room had a clear window giving on to the corridor, a trap door with a hole in it situated right above Pratt's table, and Hansel found that he could stand on a chair in the corridor and peer through a crack at the top of the door to see the cards.[2]

Rhine and Pratt replied to this objection by pointing out the three sittings when Rhine was in the room. 'He, like J.G.P. [Pratt] could see the subject from the window as the latter entered the library (and of course could see him exit as well).'[3] Hansel then asked how Rhine could have watched everything at once. If he continually looked out the window for Pearce, Pratt could fake his records to give a high score. If he watched Pearce, Pratt could sneak back from the library. Moreover, no report of the experiment says that Rhine *actually did see* Pratt enter and leave the library.

The Pratt–Woodruff Experiment

This complicated classic was designed to eliminate certain kinds of trickery by making it 'double-blind'. That is, the experimenter (E) is ignorant of the guesses of the subject (S), while S is ignorant of the cards. Figure 14–1 shows both sides of the table used, which was divided by a screen. On the S side, five 'key cards' are hanging on pegs. Each bears one of the ESP symbols, and E does not know which is which. Below them on the table lie five blank cards (which may as well be five painted squares) marking their positions. A slot at the bottom of the screen enables both S and E to see these blanks. A smaller, slanting screen prevents S from seeing what E is doing.

E shuffles and cuts an ESP pack, keeping it face down. S guesses the top card, indicating his choice by pointing at a blank. If his guess is a cross (+), he points at the blank below the key card bearing a cross (see Figure 14–1). E takes the top ESP card and places it opposite the blank indicated.

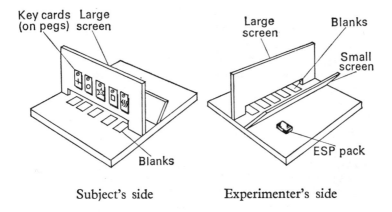

Fig. 14–1   Table used in the Pratt-Woodruff ESP experiment

When they have gone through the pack, E should have five piles of cards before him. He now turns over each pile and tallies it, recording how many cards of each symbol it contains. An observer (O) has been sitting behind S, keeping him honest. O now records the positions of the key cards on their pegs. E does not see this record. O and E now clip their records together and lock them away. Now the screen is laid on its side. The three persons present all note the positions of the key cards again, and the number of hits in each pile.

Pratt and Rhine believed this system to be foolproof. Obviously S couldn't see the ESP pack, and E probably couldn't see the faces of the cards he was handling, either, so he couldn't pass signals. And since E placed the cards in piles according to S's directions, without knowing which pile corresponded to which ESP symbol, he couldn't cheat by slipping cards into the 'right' pile.

32 subjects were tested by this method. Their total score, for 60,000 trials, was 12,489 hits. Though this is only 489 hits above average, the odds against it are over a million to one. The odds against one of the subject's scores was over 20 million to one.

Again, there is a serious weakness in the method, as used. If E can learn the position of even one of the key cards, he can increase the number of hits. Hansel investigated this possibility.

He found that, though the key cards are hung on their pegs in a different order for each run (each twenty-five trials), it is certainly possible for E to guess the new positions of one or two of them. When the screen is laid on its side after a run, E notes that the key card in Position 1 (the right- or left-hand end) is, say, a cross. The screen is then set up for the next run. S or O then removes the key cards from their pegs and replaces them in a different order. But E can see from his movements in what order he removes them (left to right or right to left). Then, unless the key cards are shuffled before replacing them, E can guess that the first or last card replaced will be the cross.

E then completes the run as usual, and begins his tally. At this point, neither S nor O can see what he's doing. It's easy enough for him to slip a card or two (bearing a cross) into the 'cross' pile without being detected.

This may sound far-fetched, but Hansel showed by another experiment, using the Duke apparatus, that this deception could easily be carried out. He found five variant methods by which E could determine the positions of one or more key cards.[4] Moreover, he found a statistical indication that this may have happened. He observed that, in a typical high-scoring run, certain symbols seemed to get more than their fair share of hits. More often than not, these symbols had occupied Positions 1 and 5 (the end positions) in the previous run. It's significant that the subject who obtained the unusually high score mentioned above scored far higher on symbols that had previously occupied these two positions than might be expected by chance. The odds against her score's being arranged as it was are 10^{11} to 1 against. This leaves us with only two possibilities:

1   Someone actually cheated, or
2   The subject demonstrated ESP, but ESP with a peculiar bias, and that bias just happened to be in the direction of the only discoverable way of cheating.

Which it was, could easily have been found out by repeating the experiment with shuffled or randomized key cards. Instead, in the forty years since, the Duke experimenters have preferred argument to experiment.

More Classics
The Turner-Owenby experiment was an early long-distance

test performed by Sarah Owenby, a Duke graduate assistant, and Frances May Turner, a student. Turner acted as agent in the Duke Parapsychology laboratory, while Owenby received her transmissions 250 miles away. A 'pure telepathy' technique was used, that is, Turner merely thought of a symbol and wrote it down, while Owenby wrote down her guesses. The plan was to send both records direct to Rhine.

The early scores were sensational: 19 out of 25 on the first run alone (odds against: 5,000 million to 1). But Owenby did not send her records to Rhine, she sent them to Turner, who of course could simply have written her own record to agree with it. Rhine was unable to see this.

> I will state that the recording was unmistakably in Miss Turner's own hand and ink, and no changes were evident. The notes that were written under the record were unmistakably those of Miss Turner. The point is, if one of these excellent young ladies were to be suspected, both would have to be.[5]

But when, for later runs, Owenby sent her records direct to Rhine, her scores dropped to average.

The final Duke classic was performed by Lucien Warner and Mildred Raible. The subject was locked in a room with a switch controlling a signal light elsewhere, with which he could signal that he was ready to guess another card. Ten runs with ESP cards were performed, on which he achieved 93 hits (43 more than expected by chance). J. L. Kennedy[6] pointed out two weaknesses in this experiment: First, the duration of the light signal could be varied, so that the subject could call for specific symbols. Second, some symbols came up far more often than others, indicating poor shuffling of the cards, or else card manipulation.

ESP Cards

Three types of cards were used at Duke. None was really satisfactory for experimental purposes. The first were cut by hand from card stock. They were probably of unequal size, and difficult to shuffle properly. The second were blank playing cards, rubber-stamped with ESP symbols. In 1936, R. H. Thouless examined two packs of these, and found that he could read the symbols from the back.

The third type, professionally printed, could also be read from the back, a fact discovered by B. F. Skinner and others. Besides, due to the way the pattern on the backs of the cards had been printed, some of them could be identified by their edges.

It's astonishing that playing cards should have been chosen for ESP research at all. They are, after all, the instrument of stage magicians and second-dealing gamblers; they can be marked and manipulated in many traditional ways. At the best of times, card-shuffling is a poor way of getting a random distribution of symbols. Still, when it came to tests of psychokinesis (the ability to influence physical events by thought), Rhine chose another old gambling instrument, dice.

PK and Dice

Rhine's penchant for acronym has shortened psychokinesis to PK. His research used dice, with subjects 'willing' them to fall a certain way. Not only can dice be drilled, shaved, falsely numbered and manipulated, but even straight dice often show a bias in the long run. Casinos for this reason retire dice often, but at Duke, subjects continued to try for the same effect on the same dice over long experimental runs. Not surprisingly, PK appeared at Duke and nowhere else.

But whenever testing continued and varied, PK vanished. Rhine saw this as a mysterious 'decline effect', but it seems rather to have been due to pure chance. He began by testing batches of people for PK. Then he selected those who happened to have above-average scores for further testing. Naturally, as the law of averages caught up with him, their scores sank.

H. Forwald of the Swiss Federal Institute of Technology tried to calculate the 'psychic force' necessary to make a die skitter a certain distance sideways as it bounces on a surface. Since Forwald seemed ignorant of the ordinary *physical* forces involved, his results were unrealistic. Elsewhere, others tried coin-flipping PK experiments, without success.

An American dice expert suggested that, rather than have a PK subject tire out his psyche trying to push dice around for thousands of trials, it might be better to try a simple all-or-nothing test: Why not have a subject try making a delicately-

balanced arrow, inside a vacuum jar, turn? The force required
would be small, and the results indisputable. But PK experimenters have preferred to ignore this advice, and concentrate
on statistical tests with dice.[7]

Gardner describes a gambling game in Chicago in which the
object, as in PK tests, is to make a certain number come up
more often than average. Yet the 'tally sheets, year after year,
show precisely the percentage of house take allowed by the
laws of chance'.[8] If PK works at all, it doesn't seem to work on
dice.

Dr S. G. Soal, a mathematician, is the British counterpart of Dr Rhine. As Rhine had his Linzmayer, Soal had his star performer, Basil Shackleton. According to Arthur Koestler,[1] Soal was originally sceptical about ESP; he tested 160 subjects, including Shackleton, without striking pay dirt. This must be seen as the same kind of 'scepticism' with which an Edison would set out to disprove the electric light. No one tries to disprove so complex a theory as ESP by five years' exhaustive research.

The conversion of Soal came in 1939, it's said, when someone persuaded him to look, not just at hits on target cards, but at hits 'one card ahead'. In this situation:

Target:

$+$ $+$ $\bigcirc$ $*$ $\square$ $\bigcirc$

Guess:

$+$ $\bigcirc$ $+$ $\square$ $+$ $\square$

there's only one hit on target, but three hits on the next card ahead, which might demonstrate a kind of precognition. Soal scanned the records of Shackleton's average performance for these '+1 hits' and, lo, their number was large. That he hadn't designed the test to look for them made no difference to his triumphant conclusions. This seems somewhat like building a space rocket and, when it fails and flops into the sea, calling it a submarine.

Thereafter Soal was a believer, and his experimental conditions began a slow deterioration over the years. He began to cast his net wider, looking for +2 hits, +3 hits, and for hits on previous cards (−1, −2 and −3 hits). Naturally this multiplied his chances of finding significant scores.

The point can be illustrated by comparing sets of random

numbers, from tables which have been deliberately drawn up to give a patternless, chance distribution. I took two sets of 400 random numbers from such a table,[2] divided them into ten 'runs' of 40 numbers each, and compared each run for -2, -1, direct, $+1$ and $+2$ hits. The best run showed 16 hits of the $+1$, and 16 of the $+2$ type. By the standards of some parapsychologists, the odds against this happening by chance are 100,000 to 1. The actual odds are about 2,000 to 1 against. *Can this be mere coincidence?* It can (see page 273).

Soal's experiments with Shackleton were performed under very strict conditions. The agent (A) and subject (S) sat in adjoining rooms, each watched by an experimenter (EA and ES). A sat at a table across from EA. Between them was a screen with a hole in it. EA would take a number from a list of random numbers prepared by Soal and display it at the hole. The numbers ran from 1 to 5. A would have previously laid five cards (bearing animal pictures) before him, hidden from EA's view. When the number appeared in the hole, A would turn up the card in that position and begin 'sending'. In the other room, to which the door was ajar, S would write down his guess, while ES watched him. After fifty trials, A's five cards were turned up and their positions recorded by EA, in front of witnesses. Then the random number tables, EA's record, and S's record would all be clipped together and mailed to Professor C. D. Broad at Cambridge.

These conditions sound fairly foolproof, but Hansel has shown three ways in which even this test could be rigged, and G. R. Price, a medical research associate, has shown six other ways.[3]

Soal thus experimented with Shackleton and other subjects, but his controls were often less strict than the above. During one series, an agent looked through the hole in the screen and saw Soal, who was acting as EA, writing on the prepared sheet of random numbers. Soal claimed later that he was merely tidying up some numbers, but the possibility remains that he was helping someone to a better score. Whatever was happening, a careless experiment cannot be used as scientific evidence for ESP. In 1939 the possibility of fraud in Soal's research was a cloud on the horizon, no bigger than a hand (of ESP cards). But by 1955 it would grow to an overcast sky.

Childsplay

From 1955 to 1957, Soal used his animal cards on two Welsh boys, aged thirteen. He and his associate Bowden thought highly of the series, and described it at length in their book.[4]

One boy demonstrated the most amazing powers of guessing cards seen by his cousin, under a variety of conditions, even when behind screens or across a field from each other. He scored 21 hits in 25 guesses, the odds against so high a score being about 2×10^{12} to 1. The boys were offered small sums of money for high scores.

At one point, they were caught (by Soal) using a code of coughs, chair creaks and sniffs. Incredibly, the experiments did not cease. After a reprimand and a delay of four months, the series continued. As Soal and Bowden put it, 'Why make an undue fuss over a mere childish peccadillo?'

When the experiments resumed, the scores were high again. Critics and sceptics witnessed many demonstrations, and confessed themselves unable to detect any code being used. The boys performed well under all conditions – except when out of earshot.

Soal had assumed that a likely place to look for ESP was among rural, more 'primitive' people, and children. A fond hope among parapsychologists is that ESP may be a 'lost' trait, commoner in children, primitive people, and animals.

Hansel pointed out that children and animals have one other special ability lost to adults: acute hearing of high frequency sounds. He performed an 'ESP demonstration' of his own, duplicating Soal's conditions, with other Welsh kids. Two girls, aged eight and nine, stood fifty feet apart in a field. The subject was screened from the agent's view; both were watched by critical observers, who detected no code. The score was 16 out of 25. A second run, with a boy, gave 23 out of 25.

Hansel then explained the trick. He had a dog whistle of the high-frequency 'silent' type in his pocket, which he could sound by squeezing a rubber bulb.

I arranged with the agent that on each trial I would sound pips on the whistle until she signalled me to stop by making a small movement of her foot when she had heard the requisite number of pips according to a prearranged code. The [subject] also heard the whistle.[5]

None of the adults present heard it, however. High-frequency sounds (which can be produced by a dog whistle, or even by a boy whistling between his teeth) cannot be heard by many persons over the age of forty. Soal and Bowden were by this time around seventy. It seems certain that, living in sheep country, the boys would have seen silent dog whistles in use at sheepdog trials.

Great Believers

A list of pro-ESP people today would include the names of many eminent scholars and men of science, including Arthur Koestler, Sir Cyril Burt and H. J. Eysenck. Koestler and Burt[6] think that ESP may be bound up in some fundamental way with the nature of matter and time. Since an electron seems capable of being in two places at the same time, they reason, why shouldn't a thought be able to do it?

But if thoughts are capable of quantum jumps from place to place (and time to time) then all our notions of cause and effect must be wrong. And if this is so, then conventional science must be scrapped, and of course ESP research, which is conventional science, must be scrapped along with it. Which would leave no basis for believing in ESP. It's an interesting paradox.

Koestler boosts ESP by listing great names (*all* the past presidents of the Society for Psychical Research, with all the honours after their names), much as cigarette companies used to advertise the healthfulness of smoking by testimonials from sports celebrities. He also quotes Eysenck, saying that either ESP exists or else there is a 'gigantic conspiracy' involving dozens of universities and respected scientists. Eysenck is himself a respected psychologist, but that hasn't prevented him from making this rather silly statement.

Such an either/or simply doesn't apply. The fact is, there have been all kinds of unsatisfactory experiments in ESP performed by men of the highest reputation. There are at least seven alternatives which Eysenck has not mentioned, experiments in which:

1 Conditions allow the unconscious passing of cues from agent to subject.

2 The subject can cheat.

3 The agent can cheat.

4 Results are non-random because the target information is also non-random (i.e., deliberately or accidentally encoded).

5 'Good' statistics have been selected from average batches (the earth is flat, too, in spots).

6 Conditions allowed recording errors to raise some scores.

7 All conditions were scrupulously fair, and where no ESP was shown.

Notice that none of these involves the slightest conspiracy, even a two-person plot (as seems to have been the case with Soal's Welsh boys).

Koestler leaves the subject of tedious card experiments and takes up an experiment from the 1880s, performed by two respected men who tried transmitting 246 drawings to 'gifted subjects'.[7] I've traced Koestler's tracing of six successful transmissions (see Figure 15-1). Ten more were also said to be successful. There were also 'partial successes', but these are hard to verify by any standards.

Of the drawings in Figure 17-1, I haven't the faintest idea

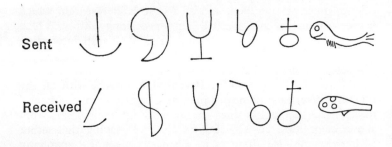

Fig. 15-1 Drawings from an ESP experiment (after Koestler)

how they came to be transmitted. One odd thing about them is that the types of mistakes the subject made, which are the same types we might expect from someone who has hastily memorized a set of drawings and later reproduced them. If ESP were a cognitive process, we might expect to see cognitive errors (e.g., the goblet becoming a teacup); if it were a kind of mental xerography, we might expect fuzzy or shaky approximations of the original shapes. But it is mainly memory which tidies figures, reverses unimportant parts, and makes ellipses into circles.

By contrast, Figure 15-2 (traced from *Mind to Mind*, by René Warcollier[8]) shows errors of a cognitive type, and provides a far more convincing argument for telepathic transmission of figures. Warcollier also shows transmissions where only parts of figures are received, where parts are jumbled, and where the shape of the figure is reproduced, but not the actual object transmitted. Had such events taken place under anything like controlled experimental conditions, they would constitute powerful evidence for ESP. Unfortunately, like the picture transmissions of Upton Sinclair,[9] most of Warcollier's drawings have occurred in parlour-game conditions, and are therefore of only anecdotal importance.

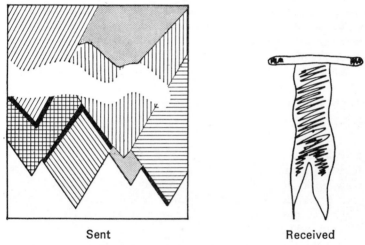

Sent   Received

Fig. 15-2 Drawings from an ESP experiment (after Warcollier)

Returning to his theme of greatness, Koestler discusses a demonstration conducted by Gilbert Murray (LL.D., Litt.D., O.M.),

> not only the most prominent classical scholar of his time, but ... he drafted the Covenant of the League of Nations, and was showered with honours by learned societies from all over the world.[10]

Professor Murray would leave the room while someone chose a subject which was written down. The subject was usually a quotation, a scene from literature, or an item in the news. Murray's guess would be written down, and the two compared. Since all his 'agents' were close friends and his daughter, we should not be shocked to learn that many of his guesses were correct. In fact, sixty per cent were 'evidential', in their opinions. One example of a successful guess is the thought subject 'the sinking of the *Lusitania*'. It should be pointed out that these experiments began in 1916, a year after this historic event. It is about as remote an item to guess as someone's thought 'the battle of Waterloo' in 1816. Hansel, as usual has the last word:

> If Murray's success was due to telepathy, he should have had no difficulty in convincing sceptics by demonstration rather than by discussion and persuasion; but ... he made no attempt to display his abilities under reasonable test conditions.[11]

Could it be that, after all, Professor Murray was only playing a parlour game?

ESP Today

Koestler mentions a test at the Maimonides Medical Centre, New York, in the 1960s, an attempt by Drs Krippner, Ullman and associates to induce telepathic dreams in subjects, using EEG readings to tell when they were dreaming. He mentions no worthwhile results.

In 1963 the US Air Force used a computer to conduct a Rhine-Soal type experiment, but with stricter conditions. The computer, VERITAC, generated random numbers (0 through 9) to be used as targets. These were displayed one at a time on a console in the agent's room. The agent could do nothing but look at each number, concentrate on it, and hope to transmit it. In another room, the subject made his guess by pressing a button. This would automatically record his guess, compare it with the target, compute his score so far, and bring the next number into view for the agent. Both VERITAC and the random numbers it generated were checked.

On the theory that believers might score higher than sceptics, experimenters divided the subjects into these groups. They were tested for clairvoyance (no one in the agent's room), precognition (guessing one digit ahead) and general ESP. After 55,000 trials, neither group had produced a score significantly above or below average, and the difference between the two groups' scores was also insignificant.

Dr Helmut Schmidt, the physicist who has succeeded Dr Rhine as director of the Institute for Parapsychology at Duke University, has designed two clever machines for testing paranormal powers, both using randomizing devices. One is intended to test precognition. It looks like a box with four lights and four buttons. The lights flicker on at random, and the game is to guess which will go on next, and to press the button under it.

Inside the box is a sophisticated random number generator using the radioactive decay of strontium 90 and fast electronic switching to distribute impulses among the four lights evenly. The pushbuttons are designed so that they only work when their respective lights are off, to prevent one obvious cheat. The number of trials and of hits is registered automatically.

Schmidt checked the randomness of his box against random numbers generated by a computer, and he also tried pressing one button continuously. Both methods produced only the expected average result of about one hit in four trials.

In one experiment (63,066 trials) the number of hits was about 652 greater than expected by chance. The odds against getting a score this high are 200 million to 1. In a second experiment, subjects could choose to 'hit' or 'miss' deliberately. This time the score was even better, the odds against it being about 10,000 million to 1.

This, I think, is the first convincing indication of precognition. Without question, Schmidt's apparatus produces random information. It is almost certain that none of his subjects knew how the apparatus worked, so it seems unlikely that they could have influenced it by normal means. There may be a small possibility that one of them could have tampered with the 'hits' register, but this, too, seems unlikely. If it were the case, or if the two tests represented a simple statistical variation, then future tests will of course put the record straight. Otherwise, I see only two possibilities:

1 That some people are capable of detecting complex patterns in apparently random data, or

2 That some people are capable of seeing into the future, at least ·00000025 second, and for at least once in 175 tries.

Schmidt's other machine performs a non-dice test for possible PK. This time the subject is shown a circle of lights, again operated by radioactive decay. This time the light jumps from one lamp to the next, one step at a time. The step may be clockwise or counterclockwise; this is randomly determined. The subject is asked to 'will' the light to move one way or the other (the direction chosen being constant for all trials).

First he tested 18 people and found most scoring below average; the light moved more often against their chosen direction. In a further test, 15 people performed 32,768 trials, 50·9 per cent of these again being negative. The odds against a score this *low* are about 900 : 1.

Schmidt then pitted a high-scorer against a low-scorer, comparing their results for 6,400 trials. The high-scorer got 52·5 per cent right (odds against, 16,000 : 1) and the low-scorer, 47·75 per cent right (odds against, 3,000 : 1). Schmidt points out that the odds against so great a *difference* in their scores are 10 million to 1, but this seems to me a peculiar statistic. It should be pointed out that, taken together, the two scores show 12,800 trials and 6,416 hits, and that the odds in favour of this high a score are 13 : 1. One has to be particularly careful in using statistics of this type, and in trying to relate them to reality. For example, the odds against an American's having a social security number whose digits are all the same, e.g., 777-77-7777, are 1,000 million to 1, yet several Americans must have them.

The Grand Idea

Thought-transmission, knowing the future, and thought-control of the physical world are certainly desirable abilities to have. At present, however, they are only metaphysical ideas. Forty years of ESP research have so far failed to turn up conclusive evidence of their existence, let alone any of their properties. Schmidt's experiments have indicated so far only that *some* relation obtains between deliberate human actions and events on a subatomic level, a short way into the future. It's an exciting idea, but its verification, and its meaning, must be left to further research.

The ESP hypothesis demands a healthy agnosticism. The sceptic is just as wrong-headed in imagining that it is impossible, as the believer who insists on having it. If, on the one it turns out to exist, in violation of fundamental laws of physics, so much the worse for those laws. If, on the other hand, it isn't demonstrated in the next forty years, that won't discourage the long march of ESP research along its – what? Path to understanding? Or treadmill?

Of the Spirit

Modern spiritualism, unlike parapsychology, has no claim to the name 'science'. It is, as Harry Price put it, 'at its best, a religion; at its worst, a "racket".'[1] Almost from the beginning, however, popular interest has centred not on spiritualist beliefs, but on the material evidence of miracles.

With Emmanuel Swedenborg (1688-1772) it was still very much a religion. Swedenborg was at first an inventor and experimental scientist.

His investigations ranged from the composition of matter to the seat of the soul in the human body; and his studies embraced mathematics, physics, mechanics, astronomy, metallurgy, chemistry, geology, magnetism and anatomy.[2]

One of his primary philosophic concerns was the union of science and theology, of knowing by reason and knowing by faith. He wrote a number of theological works and kept a record of his dreams and a *Spiritual Diary* of his religious experiences. Unexpectedly

this intelligent, learned and pious man began to have intercourse with spirits. He made no secret of this, but frequently at table, even in large companies, and in the midst of the most rational and scientific conversations, would say, 'On this point I conversed not long ago with the Apostle Paul ...'[3]

He spoke also with the inhabitants of Mars, Mercury, Saturn, Venus, Jupiter and the moon. His descriptions of them tend to be rather vague, since he was primarily interested in their spiritual wellbeing. He was said to have been a seer, and to have made a number of well-attested revelations. He brought the Queen of Sweden a message from her departed brother which, according to one version, made her faint. He is said to have known the exact time and extent of a great fire in

Stockholm, and commented upon it at the time, while he was three hundred miles away.* He also is said to have revealed to the widow of a Dutch ambassador where her husband had hidden a missing document, in a secret drawer of his desk.

Swedenborgians generally maintain that there are only two possibilities: Either the eminent theologian was a fraud, or else he was a genuine psychic seer. That we are viewing his wonders through the obscuring dust of two centuries makes comment on the genuineness of his miracles meaningless; but I see no reason for him to have been anything but a good, even holy man, about whose life legends have been accreting through no fault of his own.

Many seers who appeared in the nineteenth century were several cuts below Swedenborg. Following the publication in 1847 of a popular book by Andrew Jackson Davis, the 'Poughkeepsie Seer', strange rapping noises came from the bedroom of a farmhouse in New York state, the room of Margaret and Kate Fox (aged eight and six).

The story spread that a murder had been committed in the house, though this was never verified. The Fox sisters went on tour all over the United States, making upwards of $100 per night from immense crowds. 'During the next few years,' writes Simeon Edmunds, 'a positive epidemic of "rappings" broke out all over the United States.' A Supreme Court justice wrote a book on the subject, and other prominent people became involved, either as commentators or seers.

It was not until 1888 that Margaret Fox confessed in a newspaper article that she and her sister had produced the raps by cracking their finger and toe joints. This had indeed been alleged thirty-seven years earlier by some investigators, but the public would have none of it. In fact, Margaret toured the country a second time, demonstrating the trick, to no avail. The public, having been convinced of spirit raps, was not to be conned by the truth. A large number of scientists showed, again and again, that it was easy enough to produce the joint-cracking raps without visible motion. Yet, for most people, this was all cancelled by the single statement from

---

* This account from a letter by Immanuel Kant could itself make psychic history. Dated August 1758, it claims the fire took place in September 1759. Actually the fire was on 19 July 1759. Two slips of the quill, evidently.

the famous physicist William Crookes, that he thought some of the phenomena genuine.

In the 1850s, the American mediums Mrs Hayden and Mrs Roberts set up business in Britain. Their methods included going through the alphabet until a rap was heard (the Fox girls had had to answer only yes-or-no questions) and table-turning. Table-turning became the new epidemic.

The physicist Michael Faraday gave his attention to trying to learn where the table movements originated.

> He arranged two flat boards, separated by glass rollers, in such a way that pressure on either board caused it to roll away from the other. An indicator formed from a hay-stalk enabled the slightest movement to be detected.... Faraday showed that as the upper board invariably moved first when the table tilted, the motivating force came, not from spirits, but from the hands of the sitters.[4]

The involuntary nature of the movements could also be shown, for when the sitters were allowed to watch the haystalk, the movements ceased. From these and other experiments, Faraday concluded that table-turning could not be caused directly by spirits.

William Crookes conducted an investigation of a quite different kind, of the Scottish medium Daniel Dunglass Home (1833-86). He concluded that Home had:

1 Levitated heavy objects into the air by touching, without lifting, them.

2 Caused raps and knocks by non-physical means.

3 Changed the weight of objects.

4 Moved around heavy furniture at a distance, without touching it.

5 Lifted tables and chairs into the air without touching them.

6 Levitated human beings.

7 Persuaded an accordion to float in the air and play, without touching it.

8 Produced luminous clouds and lights.

9 Materialized human forms and faces.

10 Materialized hands (luminous or visible in light).

11 Performed automatic writing.

12 Produced information (by ouija planchette and automatic writing) to which he did not have access.

13 Performed miscellaneous actions (e.g., transporting an object from another room, through solid doors and walls – in spiritualist parlance, 'apports').

A formidable list, and if Home had actually been able to perform almost anything on it, there would be no room for scepticism. Alas, most of these phenomena were observed by Crookes alone, and no independent evidence exists of their having worked. When a man attests to incredible feats like levitation, we must be sure that he isn't lying, that he hasn't been hallucinating, drugged or hypnotized, that he hasn't been fooled by conjuring tricks, and that he hasn't been coerced or persuaded into his testimony.

D. D. Home flourished for many years. For a time, a wealthy Mrs Lyons patronized him, settling £60,000 pounds on him. She later sued to get it back, claiming that Home had persuaded her that her departed husband wanted her to give him the money.

Later, he drifted into the company of several young aristocrats in London (having already toured Europe and impressed several monarchs). It was in London, on the night of 13 December 1868, that three of them, Viscount Adare, his cousin Captain Wynne, and Lord Lindsay, witnessed a levitation.

Home was asleep in one room when the three withdrew to the next room. Both rooms had windows on the same side of the building. Suddenly Home appeared outside the window, opened it and entered. Adare says:

> It was so dark I could not see clearly how he was supported outside. He did not appear to grasp, or rest upon, the balustrade, but rather to be swung out and in. Outside each window is a small balcony or ledge, 19 inches deep, bounded by stone balustrades 18 inches high. The balustrades of the two windows are 7 feet 4 inches apart, measuring from the nearest points.[5]

The accounts of the three witnesses disagree, however, on both trivial and important details. Indeed, Adare and Lindsay gave several accounts each, contradicting each other and even themselves. The following composite will give some idea of their vagueness:

The incident took place at 5 Buckingham Gate, Kensington (Adare); at Ashley Place, Westminster (Adare); at Victoria Street, Westminster (Lindsay). There was a ledge 4 inches wide below the windows (Adare); a ledge $1\frac{1}{2}$ inches wide (Lindsay); no foothold at all (Lindsay); balconies 7 feet apart (Adare); no balconies at all (Lindsay). The windows were 85 feet from the street (Lindsay); 70 feet (Lindsay); 80 feet (Home); on the third floor (Adare); on the first floor (Adare). It was dark (Adare); there was bright moonlight (Lindsay). Home was asleep in one room and the witnesses went into the next (Adare); Home left the witnesses in one room and went himself into the next (Adare). T. H. Hall, in *New Light on Old Ghosts*, 1965, has fairly established that the event took place at Ashley House, Ashley Place, Westminster, which had balconies 4 to 7 feet apart, on the third floor, which was 35-40 feet from the street. There was a new moon on the night in question.

Hall also showed that Adare, besides sharing his bed with Home, was otherwise under his influence. Lindsay's versions contradict both those of Adare and certain facts. Wynne's only statement, prepared at the request of Home, says only that Home went out of one window and came in through another. We are finally left with no evidence that anything supernatural actually occurred.

This hasn't stopped believers from saying that D. D. Home's abilities have been proved beyond doubt. Similar claims have been made about Florence Cook.

When an eminent scientist gets involved with the super- natural in any capacity, believers rejoice. And when William Crookes, later knighted for his contributions to physics, pro- nounced Florence Cook to be a genuine medium, believers took the case as proved. T. H. Hall, however, has shown a number of reasons for suspecting that Crookes was either co- operating or being used.

First, Florence Cook (Mrs Elgie Corner) was certainly capable of fraud.

She was trained by and associated with mediums who were known to be flagrant tricksters; the accounts of her early career in periodicals of the time are clearly indicative of her palpable fraud; she was exposed more than once in circumstances which seemed to allow for no other explanation than that of gross trickery, and she was a member of a dishonest family who deliberately conspired together to make bogus spiritualism into a profitable career.[6]

Crookes was forty-one, and his wife was pregnant with their tenth child. Florence was eighteen and pretty, and willing to spend considerable time at the Crookes home, locked into a dark room alone with him, while beautiful apparitions were shown to him. The man Florence had secretly married, Captain Corner, put an unspiritual construction on the proceedings, and gave Crookes a beating. By 1875 the situation was becoming obvious to outsiders, who published hints that the next manifestation might be an infant phenomenon.

As for the apparitions, no one but Crookes is reported to have ever seen them. Florence would go into her cabinet, either alone or with her friend Mary Showers (later caught putting on a fraudulent seance) and go into a trance. Subsequently the ghost of a beautiful young girl (or two, when Mary participated) would emerge and float about the room. Crookes rhapsodized about these spirits, and tested their solidity by 'such intimacies as embracing and walking arm-in-arm ... and even feeling whether it was wearing corsets'.[7]

During this period, Florence was receiving large sums of money from another benefactor, the wealthy and credulous Charles Blackburn. Eventually Blackburn grew suspicious and cut her out of his will before he died.

By 1880 Florence had been exposed as a fraud by Sir Charles Sitwell. In 1893 she was back in business, though by then her spirits had little to say, beyond harping on Blackburn's hard-heartedness. Blackburn himself was conjured up, but did not apologize.

Madame Blavatsky took the seance to India, which enhanced greatly the reputation of her Theosophical Society back in England. That reputation has not, apparently been diminished by her being caught, repeatedly, producing fraudulent spirits. One book devoted to her memory[8] seems to spend half its sixty pages refuting one fraud-detector, by stating at great length that a certain secret panel in her seance room had been bricked up *before* she performed her wonders. At least that's what I think it says, for the statement is mingled with long asides about the bad karma of the investigator.

Another flamboyant medium, still the darling of many spirit believers, was Eusapia Palladino (1854-1918). Coarse, voluptuous, and a bold opportunist, Eusapia blew like a fresh breeze through the stuffy Victorian seance parlour. She was 'discovered' by Cesare Lombroso, the promoter of criminal physiognomy, who, evidently, was unable to detect deception in her striking good looks.

The cabinet in Eusapia's case was a curtained-off corner of the room, containing a table and various musical instruments. The medium sat with her back to it at another light table, with investigators either side of her. The light was dimmed, and, with investigators holding her hands and pressing her feet with theirs, Eusapia caused the table before her to rise, the curtains behind her to bulge out towards her, raps on the hidden table, and noises from the instruments.

The results of investigations in Milan, Paris, Cambridge and Naples were inconclusive, though the men at Cambridge suspected something. Eusapia continually pinched the hands of the men holding her and otherwise distracted their attention, which was already divided between restraining the writhing of a sexy woman and watching for phenomena. Seances always took place at night, when they were tired and she (a day sleeper) fresh.

In 1909, in the United States, Eusapia was finally caught. Unknown to her, a third investigator was smuggled into the room to lie on the floor and watch everything. He'd expected to see wires or some other sophisticated apparatus.

> What a surprise when he saw that she had simply freed her foot from her shoe and with an athletic backward movement of the leg was reaching out and fishing for the guitar and the table in the cabinet! ... Her achievement was splendid.[9]

Far from being hampered by the men holding her hands, she actually leaned on them for support during these contortions.

Realizing that believers would simply say that *some* of her phenomena were bogus, but the rest genuine, other investigators at Columbia University set a different test. They introduced to her a pair of amateur magicians as fellow professors and allowed them to pretend to be astounded by Eusapia's psychic powers, while they studied her. Two other men were hidden in the room to watch her tricks again. Then, in a second seance, the magicians deliberately kept the conditions lax at first, while wonders appeared. At a prearranged signal they used stricter controls, and all manifestations stopped.

Eusapia's vocabulary of tricks was large. She could man-oeuvre herself so that two men's feet were in contact with only one of hers, freeing her other leg for action. She kicked up the curtain to make it bulge out, drew the table from the cabinet with her foot and turned it over, and so on.

A third investigation in 1910 showed her using only tricks. But the credulous have clung stubbornly to their goddess, refusing to see why a poor peasant girl should wish to deceive the public at $125 a seance, plus the flattery of publicity, in preference to spending her life as a servant.

The rubes never learn. As late as 1972 an article in *Nova* magazine cited Eusapia's seances as amazing proof of the supernatural.[10] Eusapia was amazing, all right.

Eusapia's manager, Hereward Carrington, once said that ninety-eight per cent of all psychic phenomena were faked. Archie Jarman[11] thinks that Carrington may have under-estimated the percentage. Jarman looked into three London mediums in 1957, and caught all of them cheating. Sometimes the deceptions were hilariously simple.

One medium produced the floating luminous faces of Blue Water, an Indian brave, and then Tong Ling, a Tartar. Against orders, Jarman left his chair and inspected these faces close up. For both, he could clearly see the line across the forehead where the mask met the skin.

A second medium had a cold, and his ghosts, as they roamed the room, sniffled. This man's luminous trumpet floated around the circle of sitters, delivering messages from the other side, until it came to Jarman's wife.

Spirit: Greetings, my dear. This is your father.
My wife (German-born): *Guten Tag, Vater. Ich bin froh, dass Du hier bist. Ich hoffe, dass Du in Deinem neuen Leben glucklich bist.*
Spirit: Speak English, dear. I speak English now.[12]

The greatest detector of false mediums, for which many spiritualists have never forgiven him, was Harry Houdini. Houdini attended his first seance in 1891, at the age of seventeen, and was mightily impressed. Far from being the hardened sceptic spiritualists paint him, he believed, or at least hoped passionately, that it was true. His exposure of fakes came as a by-product of his lifelong search for the supernatural, a search which was intensified after his mother's death in 1913. He never stopped searching, right up to his own death in 1926.

Houdini, whose real name was Ehrich Weiss, met and married his wife Beatrice in the nineties; they toured the vaudeville circuits performing a mind-reading act until 1900. From then onwards, he was the Great Houdini, master escape artist and magician, daily performing wonders far more ambitious than anything the mediums could manage.

There is a double irony in his acquaintance with Arthur Conan Doyle. Houdini, who could perform public miracles, found no magic in private reality. Doyle, who could create the most observant and critical sceptic in fiction, was in life not capable of seeing through the most obvious frauds. They carried on a lively correspondence over the years, and Doyle wrote a book actually suggesting that Houdini performed some of his tricks by psychic means. It must have given the magician a few quiet laughs.

Houdini offered a substantial reward to any medium who could produce a single phenomenon which he, Houdini, could not duplicate. Hundreds tried to claim it; none succeeded. Before his death, he confided to Beatrice a message which, he said, would identify his spirit. He meant to escape, if possible, from even the prison of eternity.

After his unfortunate death, Beatrice offered $10,000 to anyone who could produce the secret message. The offer stood for two years. Again, hundreds of mediums became materialistic enough to try for it; again, none collected.

After the offer was withdrawn, Houdini's mother's spirit turned up at a seance held by Arthur Ford, saying she had a message which she ought to have delivered to her son: 'Forgive!' She also promised that he would be on the line at a later date.

Ford wrote to Beatrice Houdini of this, and she replied, saying that Harry would have liked to receive such a message from his mother. She believed it genuine, despite the late Mrs

Weiss's addressing her son as 'Harry' (she'd always called him
'Ehrich') and 'one or two other trivial inaccuracies'.

For some months, Ford tried contacting Houdini himself.
He finally received this message, which was taken down and
sent to Beatrice:

ROSABELLE**ANSWER**TELL**PRAY**ANSWER**
LOOK**TELL**ANSWER**ANSWER**TELL.

The widow was shaken by this message. The next step was
to invite her to a seance. Ford went into his trance, and soon
his 'control' spirit, Fletcher, began delivering a message:

> This man is coming now, the same who came the other
> night. He tells me to say 'Hello, Bess, sweetheart,' and he
> wants to repeat the message and finish it for you. He says
> the code is the one that you used to use in your secret mind-
> reading acts.[13]

Fletcher then repeated the cryptic message above, and asked
Mrs Houdini to take off her wedding ring and explain what
'Rosabelle' meant. She took off her ring and sang a short ditty
called 'Rosabelle'.

The code used by Harry and Beatrice in their act was:

A	Pray.	F	Speak.	K	Pray. Pray. (=AA)
B	Answer.	G	Please.	L	Pray. Answer. (= AB)
C	Say.	H	Quickly.		etc.
D	Now.	I	Look.		
E	Tell.	J	Be quick.		

A member of the audience would present some object for the
blinded Houdini to identify, and Beatrice would insert in her
patter the code words to spell the object's name. Beatrice had
sung 'Rosabelle' to open the act. Using this code, Ford's
message spelled out B-E-L-I-E-V-E.

> Mrs Houdini explained later that 'even though the stage-
> hands knew the words' she and her husband used as a
> code, 'no one but Houdini and myself knew the cipher, or
> its application.'[14]

While she was still overcome by emotion, Ford drew up and persuaded her to sign the following statement:

> Regardless of any statements made to the contrary, I wish to declare that the message, in its entirety, and in the agreed upon sequence, given to me by Arthur Ford, is the correct message prearranged between Mr Houdini and myself.[15]

Note the peculiar first clause. It is as if Ford's precognition enabled him to see that Mrs Houdini would later suspect a trick and recant, which she did. However, by that time, Ford's fame was assured, thanks to his inviting a wire service reporter to the seance.

Mrs Houdini may have recanted because it occurred to her that there were perfectly ordinary ways by which Ford could come by this message:

1 If 'the stagehands knew the words', all but the slowest of them must have cracked the code, which after all referred to simple objects like watches, rings and gloves, encoded in the same words night after night for years. Visiting professionals could have cracked it in one performance. Nor do we know that this code was the exclusive property of the Houdinis' act, since similar codes were common at the time.

2 When the two-year period for claiming the reward had ended, Mrs Houdini may well have revealed the message to some close acquaintances, since she'd given up hope of receiving it.

3 Beatrice Houdini came to the seance in a state of agitation and expectation. She'd already been given a letter with the 'Rosabelle' message, upon which she asked 'Did he say Rosabelle? My God! What else did he say?' The combination of hypnotic seance conditions, hope, and nostalgic references to their life together, could easily have brought Mrs Houdini to a state where she would sign anything. In such a case, Ford might indeed expect her to recant later.

Houdini's ghost was not even then allowed to rest. In the same year it was summoned by another medium to Conan Doyle's home, where, after complaining of the darkness, it said:

> 'It seems cruel that a man in my position should have

thrown dust in the eyes of people as I did. Since my passing, I have gone to many, many places (mediums), but the door is closed to me.... When I try to tell people of the real truth, they say I am not the one I claimed to be, because when I was on earth I did not talk that way. I ask you here to send me good thoughts to open the door, not to the spirit world – that cannot be yet – but to give me strength and power to undo what I denied [sic]. Why, oh why does my wife deny that I came? She is so changed.' (Here Dr Wickland suggested that pressure might have been brought to bear on her.) 'My wife has closed the door for me as well as for herself; but do not misjudge her, she has had a very hard time. In her heart my wife knows that I was there, talking through that fine young man, Mr Ford. She enjoyed it greatly at the time. I have done great harm to many, many mediums. How I wish I could go to every one of them and tell them that I did a false thing, that when they tried to work for the good of the cause, I tried to expose them as humbugs.' Asked about the *code* agreed between himself and his wife, he said that, in the predicament he was then in, he could not possibly recall what the code was.[16]

Thus the man who devoted his life to the cause of spiritualism, by trying to rid it of frauds who feed on grieving hearts, was made to mouth this childish, demented apology. If there is an afterlife, Houdini must be doing his best to pick its lock still, if only to come back and teach the frauds one final lesson. I hope he makes it.

Schubert's Finished Symphony
Most modern mediums scorn to put their powers to any kind of test. Many operate in such a way that no suitable test could be imagined. If Barbara Cartland simply insists that she has received a spirit message,[1] no one can dispute it. We're entitled to private doubts only.

But one basis for private doubt might be the extraordinary number of celebrity ghosts that turn up. Why have mediums been so successful with the famous? Judging from three issues of *Psychic News*, few second-rate spirits (other than spirit guides and close relatives) ever make it from the Other Side (see Table 17–1).

Table 17–1   Celebrity spirits
(Source: *Psychic News*)

Report date	Medium	Spirits
20-2-71	Rosemary Brown	Rachmaninoff, Schubert
	John Myers	Edgar Wallace (spirit photo)
	Canon W. S. Pakenham-Walsh	Henry VIII (concurrent with a TV series on Henry's wives)
13-2-71	Rosemary Brown	Liszt
	Edna Day	(prediction that all will go well with Dr Barnard's heart transplant team)
	Carl Jung	'Philemon', described as an 'ancient sage', probably Philomen
13-3-71	Rosemary Brown	Bach, Beethoven, Brahms, Chopin, Liszt, Debussy
	Geraldine Cummins	William Shakespeare (explaining how he stole his ideas from Francis Bacon, by reading his mind while he slept)
	Rose Gladden	Titanic victims
	Coral Polge	Dag Hammerskjöld (spirit photo). Also an article explaining that the Lady of Lourdes was a spirit guide.

Notice the shortage of famous names in the second column and the oversupply in the third. Rosemary Brown has of course achieved a kind of fame of her own, since being selected by the spirits of several composers to jot down the works they have composed since death, or haunting melodies. To critics who have listened to them, these works sound like clumsy pastiche, but this may be explained by aethereal interference and transcendental storms. Perhaps Miss Brown will be remembered best as having finished Schubert's Unfinished Symphony.

Spirit Gumshoes

There are certain persons who claim to be psychic 'sensitives', capable of picking up 'vibrations' of clairvoyant knowledge by touch. They are supposed to be able to speak of an unseen person or event simply by touching the person's belongings or visiting the scene of the event afterwards. Some are mediums, some have worked night-club acts, but those who make most headlines are the psychic sleuths.

Policemen are no less superstitious than the rest of us, and the need to solve a case can be, for various reasons, as great as the need of anyone who consults a fortune-teller – even greater, if we think of the cop who consulted Lady Wonder earlier.

Belief in this kind of ESP will die hard, if at all. Our attention is continually being directed to the number of times these sensitives have been called in by the police, and the number of successes they've had. Jess Stearn[2] lists Peter Hurkos as having solved 27 cases; Gerald Croiset, 4; Jeane Dixon, 2; a Georgia fortune-teller, 1; someone who has renamed herself Florence Psychic, several; and Josephine Pittman, 1. What might be more to the point are performance figures. How many attempts has each sensitive made which are complete failures? To what extent has his information really helped the police?

One of Jeane Dixon's solutions really amounts to astute character judgement. She told an executive that one of his vice-presidents was untrustworthy, and the man later embezzled, so it's said. Her other case is similar: she decided that a rich client was ripe for blackmail, and the client was subsequently blackmailed. I can't see what's especially psychic about these cases, since most of us have at one time or another, predicted how someone else would 'run true to form'.

Peter Hurkos, the most famous of several Dutch sensitives, received his psychic ability, like cinematic amnesia, through a blow on the head. Details of his 27 successes are hard to find and even harder to check, but we can check his performance on the Sharon Tate murders in 1969.

Friends of Jay Sebring, a hairdresser among the victims at the Polanski house, hired him to find the killers through what Ed Sanders calls a 'death-scan'. On 17 August 1969,

> Mr Hurkos crouched down in the blood-stained living room, picking up the vibes.... After his void-scan, Mr Hurkos announced that 'three men killed Sharon Tate and her four friends – and I know who they are. I have identified the killers to the police and told them them that these three men must be stopped soon. Otherwise, they will kill again.'[3]

Notice the discrepancies here: The killers were actually two women and one man, while a third woman stood lookout. Only three of the victims could possibly be called friends of Miss Tate's. The other was a boy visiting the caretaker, who had never seen her, and who was murdered only because he happened to be on the estate at the time. Hurkos's claim that he 'knew' who the killers were, and had 'identified' them to the police must be seen as an empty boast, for, at that very moment, they were all in Los Angeles county jail on another charge. If his identification had been positive, the police might easily have continued to hold them for this murder, or at least have kept them under surveillance.

The one particular in which Hurkos seems to have been right is in warning that they would 'kill again'; Manson's *ménage* had already continued the series. But even the least psychic policeman probably realizes that such ritual, or motiveless murders do tend to be repeated.

A case which Gerald Croiset 'solved' for the police in Holland may shed some light on how sensitives get their reputations. Stearn says:

> Once [Croiset] was asked to feel a hammer which a pretty girl had wrenched off the man who had battered her with

it, and run off. He described her assailant, whom she could
not identify in the darkness, as a 'tall dark man with a
disfigured left ear'. And when a man fitting this description
was picked up for another crime, police taxed him with the
hammer attack, and he confessed.[4]

Don't believe everything you read. C. E. M. Hansel read a
more detailed version of this story, substantially agreeing with
it, in *This Week* magazine (26 February 1961). He decided
to verify it by writing to the police of the town in question,
Wierden, Holland. Table 17–2 compares the *This Week*
article with the reply Hansel received from the head of the
local police.[5]

Table 17–2   Two versions of 'psychic crime-buster' story

This Week magazine	Burgomaster of Wierden
'A man leaped out from behind a stone storehouse, and assaulted her, hitting her on the neck and arms.'	There is no such storehouse in the neighbourhood of the crime. He hit her once (only) on the head.
'Police contacted Dr Tenhaeff [a parapsychologist] who came to the station, bringing Gerard Croiset.... He picked up the hammer, his large hand squeezing the handle as police watched ...'	Police were getting nowhere. The hammer was exhibited in a grocer's shop window, but no one recognized it. The girl's sister's employer asked the police to let him show the hammer to Croiset.
'Because the girl was in the hospital, Croiset didn't see her.'	The girl had not been admitted to the hospital, but taken home (since her injury was slight).
' "He is tall and dark, about 30 years old, and has a somewhat deformed left ear," said the paragnost. "But this hammer doesn't belong to him. Its owner was a man of about 55 whom the criminal visits often at a small white cottage ... near here. It is one of a group of three cottages, all the same." '	'About the performer of the assault, he told that he lived in a small house, rather similar to the houses of two neighbours, with a stone well behind it.... Further he told that it was a young person.... And the man would have a deformed left ear and a ring with a blue stone in it.'

This Week magazine	Burgomaster of Wierden
'The deformed left ear was a key clue. Several months later the police picked up a tall, dark 29-year-old man on another morals charge.'	'[Months later] Mr K. was arrested ... while committing the act of exhibitionism. He was tried for several hours by our police and at the end he confessed.'
'His badly scarred and swollen left ear led to questioning about the first attack. Finally, he admitted assaulting the girl with the hammer.'	'Mr K. had two normal ears.' If he owned a ring with a blue stone, 'he seemed never to wear it.'
'He said that he had borrowed [the hammer] from a friend, who, the police discovered, lived in a white cottage on the edge of town, with two others just like it on either side.'	'We don't even know yet who was the owner of the hammer. This morning [22 March 1961] one of my policemen asked him, but Mr K. refuses to tell us, so we suppose he has stolen it.'

Croiset seems to have been wrong about the ear, the ring, the owner of the hammer; while his popularizers compound the myth by changing his age (K. was twenty-six years old), adding details to the crime, pretending the police called him in, inventing the hammer's owner, and pretending that Croiset actually helped the police in any way. These mythic, or wishful, distortions will be seen again in chapter 24, in connection with other rumours.

The Dutch police inspector Dr F. Brink has investigated the techniques used by Dutch sensitives who attempt to help the police. He notices that their usual technique is to probe and interrogate, rather than to state their own opinions. Taking in hand an article of clothing or a weapon, they frame their discourse in subtle questions, as though testing the reactions of the policemen rather than establishing any vibratory truths. And since policemen may be expected to have already framed many reasonable hypotheses based on their experience, their replies can be illuminating.

Indeed, this is how sensitives work in general. Even if their clients suppress all verbal answers, their facial expressions and slight movements can provide readable clues, for those who know how to read them. The magician Carl Hertz mentions 'muscle reading' as a valuable aid to this kind of performance.

One of Hertz's tricks was to be locked in another room, while a pin was hidden by his clients. In one instance the pin was hidden by dropping it into one of the holes of a pepper-shaker so that it hung in the hole by its head. The shaker stood on the dining-table with other condiments. Told that it was a pin which had been hidden, Hertz took the hand of a woman present and asked her to concentrate on the location of the pin. He found it in less than two minutes.

For a repeat performance,

> The pin was hidden in a place where it seemed almost an utter impossibility for it to be found, even by the person who placed it there. On the sideboard stood a box of cigars. One of the cigars was taken from the box, and the pin pushed lengthways right into the middle of it, so that it could not be seen.... This cigar was then put back into the box, and the whole lot mixed up together. I am perfectly sure that no one present could tell in which cigar the pin had been placed.[6]

It took him five minutes to find it.

In 'muscle reading', the sensitive grasps the hand of a person who knows where the object is, and pulls him gently towards one part of the room, then another. The client unconsciously resists being pulled away from the object.

When it came to the cigars, Hertz picked up one at a time. Inserting the pin had disturbed the leaf on the target cigar, very slightly, and his client, perhaps unconsciously, recognized it when it was picked up. Hertz broke it open and produced the pin.

The sensitive often seems to use a similar method, if only unconsciously. Not only does he interrogate the person who presents him with the object, but his interrogation is aimed at producing 'My God! What else does he say?' reactions. If I hand a sensitive my grandmother's wedding ring and he immediately says, 'Your grandmother?' I might be taken aback by his accuracy. But this single statement could easily be deduced from its being an old-fashioned wedding ring. Similar

Sherlock Holmes deductions would produce the information that she is dead (I have the ring), that she lived a long time (it is worn), that she was a small woman (small ring) and so on. He may embroider these with as many imaginary details as he likes, for I am likely to correct his story unconsciously as it proceeds. If a detail is completely wrong, I steer him away from it by a change of expression, just as Hertz's client steers him away from wrong parts of the room.

A case of this kind is cited by H. J. Eysenck as first-class evidence for ESP, in his *Sense and Nonsense in Psychology*,[7] and I'm afraid he puts it with the former category. The reason seems to be that the medium, Mrs Piper, convinced a number of respected scientists and scholars, including William James, Dr Richard Hodgson and the physicist Sir Oliver Lodge.

Here Eysenck gives the heart of the investigation:

[Lodge] wrote to an uncle to ask for a relic of the uncle's twin brother who had died about twenty years previously. He was sent an old watch, which he gave to Mrs Piper while she was in a trance. She said, almost at once, that the watch belonged to an uncle, and after a lot of stumbling she produced the name of 'Jerry'. Lodge encouraged 'Uncle Jerry' to recall boyhood incidents that his surviving brother would remember. Several such incidents were mentioned, including the swimming of a creek, nearly being drowned, killing a cat in Smith's field, and possessing a long peculiar skin, like a snakeskin. The uncle with whom Lodge was in correspondence did not recollect all these points, but on writing to yet another brother, Frank, verification was received for every one of the items mentioned by Mrs Piper.[8]

These results sound even more convincing when we learn that Lodge himself did not know of these details, and so could not have tipped off Mrs Piper, and that he sent a private detective to Uncle Jerry's home town, to try to get the same information, and 'the result was almost nil'.

A spotless case for the psychic sensitive? Not quite. For one thing, Mrs Piper was staying at Lodge's house during the entire investigation. Lodge claimed that he had new servants who knew nothing of family history, and that he carefully locked away all photo albums and the family Bible. Mediums have been known to go much further than picking a lock to make their reputation, so this represents the first question mark. It might also have been possible for Mrs Piper to have had a look at the letter accompanying the watch. We further have no idea of the resourcefulness of Lodge's private detective: The son of an important family having a swimming accident might, for example, make the local paper. A fourth source of information might well have been papers, diaries, memoirs, clippings, etc., in Lodge's house, which he had not locked up either because he'd forgotten their existence, or because they were already stored away in trunks, etc. A fifth source might still be the servants, unless they were all hired at the same time, since old servants are perfectly free to hand on family anecdotes to their new co-workers. A sixth and most important source might be Sir Oliver himself, who is likely to have supplied his uncle's name and some details without realizing it, as in the usual sensitive's nightclub act. By means of these six hooked question marks, it seems at least possible that Mrs Piper could have dragged up every one of the details mentioned by Eysenck. A case with this many dubious features cannot be said to establish even the likelihood of psychic powers.

Eysenck does not question any aspects of this case, which might lead to a suspicion that his mind, far from being open on the subject, is given to uncritical belief. Nor does he mention that, on other occasions, Mrs Piper produced spirits who spoke nonsense, fished for clues, and knew next to nothing about their own lives on earth. These included a Frenchman who, curiously enough, could speak no more French than Mrs Piper had learned at school, which was very, very little.

A simple test of any psychic sensitive would settle any arguments: Let three people present him in turn with three objects, tape-recording his statements (questions) to keep the record clear. Person A gives him a control object bought from a pawnshop. Person B gives him something which belongs to the dead relative of someone he doesn't know, borrowed for the occasion. Person C gives him something belonging to a dead close friend or relative of his own. As a precaution against expression-reading, the three might wear masks, or hand the objects through a curtain. I feel fairly sure that, under these

simple conditions, the action of the aetheric vibrations would
be noticeably impaired.

Apportant Matter
Many mediums since D. D. Home have been taken to moving
solid objects about without touching them. The power has
been variously attributed to PK, to ghosts, and to ectoplasmic
extensions of the medium's body.

The medium Margery Crandon was one of those investigated by Houdini. At the time, she was trying for a $5,000
prize offered by *Scientific American* magazine for the genuine
production of psychic phenomena. Mrs Crandon had already
participated in some eighty sittings with scientists, who were
impressed. Houdini was also on the magazine's investigating
committee, but for some reason he hadn't been asked to witness
these early demonstrations.

When he finally did sit in, he found Crandon using a variety
of common spiritualist dodges, plus a few inventions of her
own. One was to give the investigator her right hand, in the
dark, telling him he had both hands; to give him her right
foot, telling him he had both feet. With her free limbs she
could then lever up and throw over a large cabinet violently.
During one routine she would pick up a megaphone from the
floor and put it on her head, dunce-cap fashion. She could
then really give both feet and hands to investigators to hold,
and still toss her head to fling the megaphone anywhere they
requested.

Houdini's 1924 investigations failed to convince all her
dupes. In 1925 the psychologist Hudson Hoagland tested her
again, finding her employing twenty different tricks.[9] The
American and British Societies for Psychical Research, still
not satisfied, conducted their own tests. Both groups found
her still using tricks, and one obtained her fingerprints from
an object she was supposedly apporting while her hands were
being held. This is one case where, I think it's safe to say,
there is 'something in' the idea that Mrs Crandon was a fake.

Believe it or not, some people still have faith in Margery
Crandon. Dr S. Ralph Harlow, a retired professor of religion
at Smith College, has written an article about her mentioning
none of the above exposures.[10] Instead, it concentrates on a
different test, said to demonstrate her remarkable powers in-

disputably, conducted by some unnamed 'MIT professors'. Other parts of the aricle indicate that Harlow was a close personal friend of Mrs Crandon and her husband which may partly explain his continued allegiance.

Another article of Dr Harlow in the same book[11] tells of other remarkable apports. The case of Leonard Stott, a Philadelphia steamfitter, sounds typical:

Stott produced the voices of two spirits, gruff Thunder Cloud, an Indian brave; and piping Barbara, a young girl. At the first session, Barbara announced she was bringing in a rose from 'a distant garden'. Thump. When the lights went on, there was a rose on the table 'its petals still damp with dew'. Harlow seems unable to entertain the thought that it might have been carried in in a test-tube of water, rather than whizzing in through the solid wall.

The second apport came several sessions later, when Thunder Cloud desposited a clod of earth with two weeds growing on it. The clod contained a two-pound stone axe, a 14-ounce stone mall, and two arrowheads. A research chemist present at the seance analysed the soil and had the artifacts examined by an expert. The soil was like that obtainable near Philadelphia, and the stone objects were valued at $50. Harlow seems convinced that they could not have been purchased and planted, because they were so dirty.

My guess is that Thunder Cloud, perhaps cleverly disguised as a steamfitter, bought or found the objects, rammed them into the soil, and planted or transplanted weeds on top, after watering and tamping down. Then he dug up the clod after a few weeks, brought it to Stott's house and hid it in the seance room.

The much-publicized apports connected with Bishop James A. Pike of California, and described in his book,[12] are quite another kind. In 1966, Bishop Pike's son committed suicide. Two weeks later the series of what came to be called psychic occurrences began: Two postcards were found lying at an angle of about 140°. Later, two safety pins and two paperback books were found lying at the same angle. Still later, the hands of the dead son's alarm clock were found standing at this angle, reading 8.19. The bishop took this to be the time of his son's death (though the actual time was never established). An editorial assistant who was staying at the bishop's house found her hair singed during the night. Crayon marks were noticed on the outside of the glass of the front door. The milk delivered one morning was sour.

Some of these are too ordinary to need explanation: Sour milk does get delivered. Children (and glaziers) make marks on glass. The culprit for the small pranks could well be the unconscious mind of Bishop Pike himself. He is reported to have talked in his sleep at length about 'using other people', 'getting them out of the way' and hurting them, to avoid being hurt. That same night the hair-singeing episode occurred. Men with far slighter burdens of grief have walked in their sleep, and played more bizarre tricks on themselves and those around them.

Science and Spiritualism

Thousands of mediums have been shown up as frauds, and this fact should carry some weight in making up our minds about spiritualism. Scientists cannot be expected to take time off from their normal work to set about disproving every claim of psychic phenomena, and it is by no means certain that some claims, even if fraudulent, could be disproved. The burden of proof, if there is to be one, must still be on those who support spiritualism. It is in their interests to detect and expose frauds, as (a) damaging to the profession, and (b) hopefully leaving behind a residue of genuine cases. The Society for Psychical Research seems to have been attempting such a clean-up for about a century, with little enough to show for it. The crudest kinds of deception are still being practised on bereaved people everywhere.

Simeon Edmunds tells of the celebrated medium William Roy, who practised in London in the 1940s and 1950s, fooling 'doctors, clergymen, journalists, Service chiefs, judges' of the highest reputation. Roy used a bewildering assortment of electronic devices, obtained inside information on his clients by modern spy techniques, and traded information with other mediums. In 1958 he publicly confessed, and explained all of his tricks in detail. Believers in spiritualism, far from feeling well rid of him, continued to try in the most pathetic fashion to make him genuine again.

Few students of the psychic would accept that a stage magician really saws a woman in half; that two witnesses giving different versions of the facts of a traffic accident can both be right; or that everyone who claims he is Julius Caesar is stating a fact. But take trickery off the stage, error out of the courtroom, or delusion out of the mental hospital, and such becomes the evidence of the Beyond.

Cesare Lombroso seems to be one of those lucky people who find the wonderful and unexplainable wherever they go. When he wasn't occupied with criminal physiognomy or the great Eusapia, Lombroso located a woman who,

> having lost the power of seeing with her eyes, saw as clearly as before with the aid of the tip of her nose and the lobe of her left ear.[1]

Another is Jules Romain, who, in addition to a hearty acceptance of ESP, has written *Eyeless Sight* to prove that we all have microscopic visual nerves, and indeed complete miniaturized optical equipment, all over our bodies. The skin can thus detect form and colour, which probably explains why blind people never have any trouble with traffic lights.

The Czech biochemist Milan Ryzl has discovered a subject, Pavel Stepánek, who claims a special kind of X-ray vision. Cards, black on one side and white on the other, are placed into envelopes by an experimenter. Stepánek can then tell which envelopes contain cards with the white side uppermost. just by handling the envelopes. Of course the only remarkable thing about this feat is the construction of the envelopes themselves. They're made of two pieces of card, stapled around the edges. By warping them slightly, Stepánek can peek at the cards inside. When a visiting psychologist tested him with special plastic cards which would make this impossible, Stepánek's vision returned to normal.

While we no longer hear stories of detectives taking photographs of murderers from the retina of their victims, other rumours continue to make the headlines. A recent American newspaper carried a wire service story headed BOY WITHOUT EYE SAID TO SEE WITH SOCKET, IN X-RAY VISION.[2] Chills kept being sent up the spine of the freelance photographer sent to cover the story for a popular tabloid, as this nine-year-old repeatedly saw things with his empty socket, and what's more, saw through them.

The boy had lost one eye three years earlier. When a patch was placed over his good eye, he was able to see clearly a flashbulb, a flashgun, a comb, and words written on a note pad. The X-ray vision demonstration came when he was shown the flashgun. He said he saw a battery. The reporter asked what kind it was. The boy spelled out *Ever Ready*, a brand so popular that most of us could hardly name another.

> I didn't even know what kind of batteries were in my flashgun so I opened it up and sure enough, it was an Ever[R]eady battery. It was weird.[3]

It was also claimed that the boy could read the label on the back of the refrigerator. X-ray vision is hardly the name for it, since no known radiation, X or otherwise, can both penetrate the metal of a refrigerator and stop at the ink on a label. What is needed here is an explanation. Not so much of why the boy can see through something, as of why the reporter can see through nothing.

Two quotations from the article give the kid's joke away:

> The boy has to have it (the object) at approximately the right distance, which is between 3 and 20 inches, and it has to be well lighted.
> [The boy] has to wiggle his head around to get a line on what he's trying to see ...

What he's doing is scanning the object through the crack between his face and the patch over his normal eye.

Slightly more sophisticated ruses have been used for some time by stage mentalists, who allow themselves to be thoroughly blinded and then try driving a car or shooting at a moving target. Their usual blindfold begins with a large ball of dough (in former times, a folded kid glove) pressed into the hollow of each eye. Over this an opaque bandage blindfold is tied securely, and over this goes a black hood, whose drawstrings tie around the neck.

According to Carl Hertz,[4] the first part of the trick comes in tying the bandage tightly. While this is being done, the performer contracts his brows to take the strain of this tight blindfold. Once the hood is on, he simply lifts his brows and the blindfold arrangement goes up with them, uncovering his eyes.

The hood is made of two layers of cloth. The outer layer is thin, transparent material, and the lining is thick. Thus any spectator could slip the hood over his own head and see that it was opaque. But when the drawstrings were pulled, the lining parts at the front seam, giving a clear view through the outer layer, *outwards*, while preventing by its blackness any spectator's seeing *in*.

I'm sorry to have spoiled this neat trick for a few magicians, but the fact is, it has been repeatedly abused by others over the last fifty years, in demonstrations of 'second sight'.

Spirit photography
This subject has been investigated by Simeon Edmunds, who comments:

> While there have been many 'mental' mediums of the highest integrity, and some 'physical' mediums who were never proved fraudulent, *not one* professional spirit photographer of any note ever escaped convincing exposure as fraudulent.[5]

The fad seems to have begun in 1862, when W. H. Mumler of Boston would take a portrait of some living person, and produce a final photograph showing him in the company of pale, ghostly figures. The trick, which was widely imitated in Europe and the US, was nothing but double exposure.

In Paris, Edouard Buguet soon began making spirit portraits of celebrities and the departed relatives of his many clients. He was caught in 1875, and confessed to fraud. Most of his pictures were fabricated by photographing cardboard cutouts, masks, etc. Many of Buguet's clients insisted that *their* photographs were genuine, even after the French police had proved them fakes.

Doubts were raised about the work of the British spirit photographer William Hope in 1908, when two of his clients each claimed that one of his ghostly 'extras' was their close relative. Hope continued to practise, though, and managed to con Conan Doyle and several prominent psychic researchers.

But he was caught by different groups of investigators in 1920, 1922 and in the early 1930s. His method was to obtain from the client a picture of his dead relative. Hope would then copy the picture on a plate which he would then mark, but not develop. When the client sat for a portrait, Hope would use the marked plate, producing the dead image hovering comfortably about the living.

One Armistice Day was celebrated by a Mrs Ada Emma Deane with a spirit photograph. It shows wreath-laying ceremonies, while the sky above is filled with tiny spirit faces, presumed soldiers. Some, however, proved to be the faces of football stars (alive and kicking) copied from news photos.

The last famous British spirit photographer was a dentist, John Myers, whose spirit guide (yet another Indian brave, named Blackfoot) told him in advance whose spirit face would appear in the finished picture. Myers was caught in 1932.

This brief list contains most of the spirit photography tricks that have been used in the past:

1 Trick plates with spirits exposed in advance.
2 Switching a prepared film for an unprepared one.
3 Double exposure.
4 Incorporating an image in the camera or lens.
5 Slipping a transparency into the film pack or plate.
6 Fogging film with light or other radiation.
7 A prepared background in which a flash can illuminate an image.
8 Introducing an image by means of a pinhole in the camera.
9 Double printing from two negatives.
10 Collages, retouched prints, etc.
11 Use of special film or filters with prepared backgrounds.
12 Scratching or retouching negatives.
13 Time exposure of moving lights, etc.
14 Imagination picking out chance background details and 'seeing' ghosts.

Most of these possibilities are listed in Major Tom Patterson's *100 Years of Spirit Photography*.[6] He seems to believe that some spirit photographs could not have been produced by any of these methods, and so must be genuine. This is over-optimistic, for two reasons. First, such methods can be used skilfully, or in combination, so as to elude detection by inexpert eyes. Second, the list is only partial; thousands of ways exist, and more are being discovered constantly, to produce odd photographic effects. (Quite recently two boys revealed that their excellent UFO photos, which apparently had fooled some experts, were made by painting the UFO on a pane of glass and photographing it with the sky as background.)

In any case, Patterson reproduces thirty-six photographs which spoil his case, since all could have been produced by tricks, and several are the proven frauds of people like Mumler, Hope, Mrs Deane and Myers. Patterson's figure 35, a quite ordinary double exposure, is captioned: 'The photograph which has been the subject of so much discussion could be no other than a spirit photograph.' In the text, he says:

> From the point of view of normal photography, Fig. 35 is clearly a double exposure, but from the point of view of spirit possibilities [!] it is clearly a super-normal manifestation.[7]

Polaroid Expedition

Finally, Ted Serios, the man with 'the uncanny ability to project his mental images directly on to photographic film', as the book jacket succinctly begs the question. The book inside is *The World of Ted Serios*, by Jule Eisenbud, MD, a psychiatrist.[8] The blurb goes on to speak of Dr Eisenbud's initial scepticism,* which was quickly disarmed by Serios's first pictures.

The sessions Eisenbud describes took place mainly in his colleagues' living rooms. Serios would begin the evening by some heavy drinking, chain-smoking and fiddling with his clothes. Cameras and film packs were supplied by observers. Serios preferred the room well-lighted, and the camera to be a Polaroid 95 with wink light. Sometimes the particular camera for a particular picture would be chosen from several, by random numbers. It would be set at infinity, or else have its lens turret removed. Control pictures were shot from time to

* Scepticism about Serios, but not about psychic phenomena, for Eisenbud had written many articles on the subject, and a book, *The Use of the Telepathy Hypothesis in Psychotherapy*, 1952.

time, to make sure Serios wasn't simply snapping details in the room.

His picture-taking technique varied. Sometimes he'd point the camera at his own head. Sometimes someone else held it, or tripped the shutter, or held their hand flat over the lens opening.

The first few tries were almost always 'blackies', i.e. unexposed. Whenever the lens opening was covered with masking tape, Serios produced 'whities' (diffused light pictures). These types aren't abnormal under these circumstances.

Serios liked to use something he called his 'gizmo', which invariably aroused suspicion. It was simply a short piece of tubing, or else an improvised paper collar. Some of his gizmos were closed at one end with clear cellophane, and at the other with blackened film. Others were simple open tubes. All gizmos were thoroughly checked by observers before, during and after sessions, and none seemed to have anything about it which could produce pictures. Serios claimed that they merely kept out stray light.

Serios not only seemed to think pictures on to film, he also aimed at specific targets. The first Eisenbud session, in a hotel room, is typical. Eisenbud supplied the camera and film, and he brought along, at someone's suggestion, pictures in an opaque envelope, as 'targets'.

For shot No. 1, Serios said he'd try for a fogged picture, or else a small dot and a large dot, or else a plus sign. It was a blackie. On No. 2 he tried for a concealed target of Eisenbud's (a snapshot of the Kremlin), which he guessed aloud to be 'An entrance, a driveway entrance or a walkway'. Blackie. No. 3, same target, he guessed 'A group of buildings with two people'. Blackie. No. 4 was a second concealed target, another Kremlin view. He guessed 'A white house, white boards, green roof'. Blackie. No. 5, same target, he guessed 'A white line, part of a building, white boards'. Blackie. Targets were then abandoned. No. 6 was fogged. No. 7 black. By now, everyone was getting bored except Serios, who was fairly drunk.

No. 8 astonished everyone. It was a blurred 'iris' circle containing a blurred but recognizable part of a tower. No. 9 was very dark, but showed a tiny corner of a square building, near the edge of the frame. No. 10 was fogged, No. 11 was very dark, but the dim outlines of an unmistakable building showed, including a sign: 'Stevens'.

Serios's 'thoughtography' seems remarkable, on this evidence. Here he produced three pictures on the camera and film of a man he'd never met. But, under many months of testing, other interesting aspects of his ability became noticeable:

1 *Serios was not clairvoyant enough to see through paper envelopes.* He was wrong about his guesses for the two concealed targets, though he knew they were buildings, and probed in six directions for the first, four for the second. Table 18–1 shows his performance on sessions using targets. Notice that Serios has two definite hits, each at a time when he knew the target. For one (No. 5), he chose the target himself. Eisenbud wasn't present for the other (No. 14), and we don't know the test conditions.

Table 18–1   Serios hits and misses

(@=concealed target)

Target	Result	Remarks
1 Statue on the Arc de Triomphe	Part of possible Arc de Triomphe	This the day after he'd produced shot of Arc de T., which was the day after *that* had been re-requested
2 Anything from the Olmec period, 800-400 BC	Part of modern door or window(?), unclear	
3 Ditto	(?)Unclear, a possible hit	
4 Etching of a medieval town with pitched roofs	Buildings with pitched roofs	Etching was room furnishing which Serios may have seen before
5 Scene in a certain Colorado town	HIT	Serios suggested target
6 @Versailles Hall of Mirrors	Round building with dome, columns	Serios sketched guesses of columned buildings, a sailboat
7 @Thai building	Edge of ordinary roof	Serios sketched guess of house with pitched roof, like the target

Target	Result	Remarks
8 @Piazza San Marco, Venice, showing the campanile	13 shots of parts of a windmill	
9 @Château Maintenon	(?)Bottle shape, possible manned orbital lab	Serios guessed 'something somewhere in France'
10 @Closeup of a pyramid	Trajan's column, Rome. Dome of a church in Rome	Serios guessed 'cobblestones' and both shots had them. Pyramid looks cobbled, so this is a marginal hit
11 @Scene in Charleston, NC	Blurry shot of possible pyramid	This target was really well-concealed
12 (unknown)	St Peter's Square, Rome	This was a target missed 3 days previously
13 University of Rome, a twin-towered church	Twin towers of Frauenkirche, Munich. A stone post	First try a partial hit, but target not necessarily concealed
14 Submarine *Thresher*	Parts of submarine *Nautilus*	Pictures produced were from a magazine in Serios's mother's home
15 Ditto	Elizabeth II, in her crown	These two shots were at the request of someone from *Fate* magazine (when the *Thresher* was missing). Conditions not specified. Eisenbud not present
16 Westminster Abbey	Blackie	Target selected by Serios
17 'a building'	Part of Westminster Abbey	Same session as No. 16. Again target selected by Serios
18 @Austrian church, with clock in tower	Blurry Big Ben	This after seven blackies, and after target revealed

2 *For known targets, Serios's thoughtography required a day or so to operate. In the table, this happens four times.*

3 *Serios was often able to produce something similar to the (known) target, from a limited photo vocabulary.*

4 *He often seemed to know what his own productions would look like, in advance.*

As time went on, other peculiarities emerged. In over forty living-room sessions, Serios produced from ten to forty pictures each. Nearly always, he was watched closely by observers, and film packs and cameras were carefully controlled, but other conditions were lax. Serios's power usually appeared late in the evening, when observers were bored, tired and inclined to be careless. A living room is also full of hiding places for secret apparatus (curtains, soft furniture), and Serios was continually fidgeting with his clothing (removing shoes and socks, emptying pockets, etc.). Only once was he stripped to the waist and searched.

By contrast, a public demonstration before the American Psychiatric Association's District Branch was more carefully supervised. Here Serios was strip-searched, given fresh underwear and sewn into a 'monkey suit' coverall garment. Sixty pictures were taken under these conditions. All but two were whities and blackies; the other two were faint round white blobs. Eisenbud enthusiastically identified these as breasts or crescents, but other psychiatrists were less easily impressed.

We can thus add two more points to the descriptive list:

5 *Serios's power worked well when observation may have been poor.*

6 *His power seemed to vanish entirely under strict conditions, including a strip-search.*

The character of Ted Serios is explored by Eisenbud at great length. He had stolen cars, shoplifted and jumped ship. He hinted at darker chapters in his life. He was an alcoholic (few alcoholics are completely truthful), a show-off, and an impostor (once, when arrested, he posed as Dr Eisenbud). He was mightily impressed by the serious scrutiny of psychiatrists, and thus motivated to keep the sessions going.

Finally, Eisenbud actually caught him in one minor fraud (tripping the camera shutter surreptitiously when he thought no one was looking) but still believed in him (as had Soal, in the Welsh boys). The next point, then:

7 *Serios was capable of fraud, had practised sleight-of-hand, lying and imposture, and was motivated to get results.*

Eisenbud's motivation was clearly to believe. First, he went to some trouble to go to Chicago to see him. Second, even before the first session was finished, he admits that the level of his own observation had dropped from careful scrutiny to this:

> I didn't note which end of the gizmo was up.... Again I didn't note (nor did Jon) which end of the gizmo was up (not that we could see that it should make any difference).[9]

This before any pictures had materialized.

Eisenbud also interpreted some misses as kindly as possible, 'reading in' verbal and pictorial puns. For example, take the pictures Serios produced when looking for the submarine *Thresher* (Table 18-1, Nos 14 and 15): Parts of a picture from a magazine his mother owned, and the head of Elizabeth II. Eisenbud's Freudian interpretation notes that Serios's mother's name was Esther, so he finds this name correspondence:

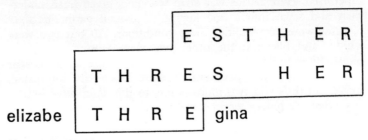

An elaborate hypothesis, when one considers a note written by the conscious Serios:

> Yes im a Drunk, Drifter Bum lo i.q. Steal but ... i say i do good Defend cats Dogs pigons Birds and small Kidds.[10]

If his unconscious is capable of elaborate codes, they ought to stand up to analysis, which the above doesn't. We may as well match up his mother's maiden name, MacNeil, his father's name, August, and the submarine *Nautilus*:

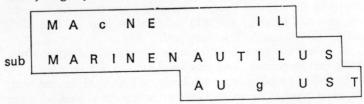

'August' of course also standing for the august monarch. He matches only four letters of Elizabeth's title with *Thresher*, but three can be matched from any royal prince or princess's title (HRH), and four from HRH Edward. (Can it be only coincidence that that prince's nickname was 'Ted'? Yes.)

By another contortion, Eisenbud equates the target, CHARleston, with the result, the pyramid at DaCHOUR. A similar equation might produce EiSENbud=SENility. Our final point then:

8 *Eisenbud was not a completely impartial observer or interpreter.*

All eight points of the list are consistent with fraud, namely the introduction of prepared pictures. The method alone is lacking.

Such a method is conceived by the British psychologist and lecturer on vision, W. A. H. Rushton. In an article,[11] Rushton examines the key question, 'Is it light that forms the Seriosphotos?' and finds that the answer is Yes. Serios's method works exactly like light in requiring a camera and film to make an image, in its effects on both the chemicals of film and the photo-emission of electrons from a TV camera, in being introduced through the lens opening, etc. Moreover, the image is introduced from the front, so that signs on buildings do not have mirror writing.

Rushton therefore supposes that Serios must generate a luminous body which hovers before the camera to project an image into it. A self-illuminated body would be noticeable, so he postulates that it uses the bright room lights that Serios always insists on having.

If the luminous picture occurs unnoticed it must be small and near the lens – probably in the 'gizmo' ... whose interior points to the camera but which is empty when examined before or after the performance.[12]

Finally, Rushton built versions of such a body himself. They are shown in Figure 18–1. This body is a glass hemisphere with a glass cylinder under it, in form (a), which has to be masked to exclude stray light. Form (b), which has been trimmed at a 45° angle, needs no masking. This gizmo is

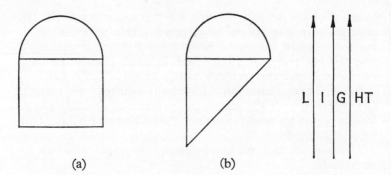

Fig. 18–1   A gizmo to produce 'thoughtographic' pictures

about $\frac{1}{8}$ inch long, or roughly the size of a grain of rice. With a square of microfilm taped to it, and plenty of light, it can project a clear image right through a lenseless camera on to its film.

Dr Rushton deliberately avoids scepticism about Serios. He merely points out that this gizmo is the way of achieving thoughtographic pictures. If Serios materializes something from the aether to make his pictures, the something must look like this.

Alternatively, Serios uses something like this, made of glass or plastic, for which he selects microfilm squares a day or so in advance. The observers may have been watching him closely, but how closely? This gizmo could be hidden under a collar, in a sock, or in his mouth, or scotch-taped to one finger. He could have exposed some films using it when no one was looking – as Eisenbud caught him doing. And he could have simply dropped the gizmo after use, picking it up off the floor later. Eisenbud noticed that his pictures in any one session were on 'two or three themes', indicating two or three of these grain-of-rice gizmos, each with its square of microfilm. Of course he could not perform after a strip-search.

It should now be easy for Eisenbud to arrange a genuine test to see whether Serios relies on a solid, or an aethereal, device of this type. My guess is that, as soon as such a test is arranged, this thoughtographic power will start going wrong, and that Eisenbud will then think of an explanation for its going wrong just then, and so on and on ...

Clay Feet

Those who complain about the inhumanity of scientists can't have met any scientists who are fools. Folly of any kind is so human a characteristic that, I feel sure, we'll always be able to detect humanoid robots by their lack of interest in circle-squaring and ouija boards. There will, I think, be no robot Marxists, no robot Nazis, no robot fools for Christ. If any machines are found getting into political arguments, believing advertising claims, building superbombs or calculating how many angels can dance on the head of a pin, we should know that they are not humanoid, but human.

Scientists, sad and glad to say, are committed to every human folly, from flying saucerism to inventing a universal language that will end all wars. I've met a physician who thinks copper bracelets cure arthritis; a psychologist who believes in spiritualism; and a physicist who heartily approved of the Hiroshima bomb, while heartily disapproving, on religious grounds, of *Playboy* nudes. More extreme examples follow.

Isaac Newton frittered away years on alchemy. Einstein was interested enough in telepathy to witness some shoddy examples of it at the home of Upton Sinclair. Thomas Edison was at work on an invention for communicating with spirits, right up to the moment he became one.

Then there's Michel Chasles, the eminent nineteenth-century astronomer and mathematician, member of the French Academy, who paid 140,000 francs for a large collection of important autographs. These included a letter from Pascal to Newton explaining gravitation, evidently establishing the French priority in Newton's discoveries. (Pascal died when Newton was nineteen.) But there were even more remarkable letters:

'Notre fils Cesarion va bien ...', wrote Cleopatra to Julius Caesar. There was a letter from Alexander the Great to Aristotle ('Mon ami ...'); from Lazarus to Saint Peter (concerning Druids); from Pontius Pilate to Tiberius; Judas's confession (to Mary Magdalene);[1]

and a letter from Castor, a Gallic doctor, to Jesus Christ. There were over twenty-seven thousand specimens in all – all written in French, and on paper watermarked with the fleur-de-lis. Chasles didn't suspect a thing, until others called certain discrepancies to his attention.

We've already seen how Sir William Crookes was taken in by mediums. Another famous and gullible scientist of the age was Alfred Russel Wallace, co-founder with Darwin of the theory of natural selection. Wallace believed implicitly in the medium William Eglington, a fraud who depended on false beards and muslin ectoplasm for his best effects. When the magician S. J. Davey duplicated these effects, Wallace began to suspect that Davey, too, had supernormal powers. Davey's effects, he said,

> are claimed to be *all* trick, and unless *all* can be so explained many of us will be confirmed in our belief that Mr Davey was really a medium as well as a conjuror.[2]

Wallace also practised phrenology.

Scientists can of course be fooled in their own fields. Often this happens to a man with a pet theory, a vision so powerful that it blinds him to the facts. In the 1720s, Johannes Beringer of Würzburg began finding confirmation for his theory that fossils were nothing but 'capricious fabrications of God', placed on earth to demonstrate His power and imagination. (The notion didn't sound so crazy at a time when other learned men were debating whether or not stones could copulate and reproduce.)

Two of Beringer's young assistants, having planted home-made fossils, helped him find them. These fossils were

> extremely realistic-looking figures: birds, lizards, frogs, fish, snails, crabs, worms, and flowers. Some of the frogs were coupling, one spider was in its web, another spider catching a fly. Gradually, more and more such 'figure stones' turned up: full moons and half moons, stars and comets, even Hebrew characters which spelled out the word Jehovah.[3]

Beringer, believing all of it, wrote a book on these curious

'Würzburg stones'. Others saw his folly therein: Beringer himself suspecting nothing until he found a stone with his name on it.

The story that he died of humiliation is more poetic than factual, for he outlived the chief hoaxer by several years. Besides, he regarded the forgeries as Wallace regarded the tricks of Davey: *Some* might be fakes, but the rest were without question the works of the Almighty.

A similar deception, practised on the Austrian biologist Paul Kammerer in the 1920s, led to his disgrace and suicide. Kammerer held to the Lamarckian view that evolution proceeds by the inheritance of acquired characteristics, rather than by natural selection. The two theories may be simplified as follows:

Lamarckian theory: A rabbit runs as fast as it can to avoid being caught and eaten. A small part of its running ability is inherited by its offspring, who then can run even faster. Over many generations the rabbit thus develops its long, strong hind legs and natural speed.

Natural selection: If a rabbit doesn't run fast, the chances are greater that it will be caught and eaten before it can produce many offspring. Chance mutations over many generations produce rabbits with slightly shorter or longer hind legs, but fewer of the former survive to reproduce.

Actually both theories are more complicated, and the two can overlap in some ways, but Lamarckianism is now widely believed to contribute little or nothing to evolution. Kammerer experimented with two races of midwife toad. One lived in water, and had as a consequence (by either theory) small black horny pads on its thumbs. The other lived on land, and did not. Kammerer tried to raise generations of the latter in water, in order to produce these pads. They appeared, and his reputation was made. Then someone discovered that the 'pads' were actually dots of India ink injected under the toads' skin. Whether Kammerer himself had done this, or a jealous assistant or one of his scientific opponents, Kammerer chose to shoot himself rather than face public humiliation.

Arthur Koestler has written an account of the Kammerer affair, *The Case of the Midwife Toad*. I rather suspect he sees the unfortunate biologist as a lone heretic, hunted to death by the mad dogs of a scientific Inquisition. This image seems to appeal to Koestler, for he returns to it in reference to flying saucers and ESP.

In *The Sleepwalkers*, his brief defence of flying saucers amounts to no more than a comparison of today's sceptical scientists with those who disbelieved Galileo.[4] The argument seems to be that the orthodox 'experts' are usually wrong, while the lone heretic is almost always right.

Oddly enough it is within esoteric circles that the harsher orthodoxy prevails. For ESP, we find Professor C. D. Broad (*Lectures on Psychical Research*) lashing out at C. E. M. Hansel for daring to suggest even the possibility of error in Soal's work. For UFOs, we've already seen the scorn ufologists heap on those who intimate that, just maybe, saucers aren't craft from another planet. For spiritualism, we've seen Houdini brought to trial posthumously.

The fact is, *any* heretic looks good in retrospect; every establishment treats its opponents badly. But moral posturing has no place in establishing the truth in such a case. Time will reveal the reality of UFOs and ESP, if they are real, but Koestler seems unwilling to leave it to time. Some of his friends, he says, accuse him

> of unscientific leanings towards preposterous subjects such as extra-sensory perception, which they include in the domain of the supernatural. However, it is comforting to know that the same accusations are levelled at an élite of scientists, who make excellent company in the dock.[5]

Once again, Koestler sees himself as a modern Galileo on trial. But paranoid references to accusations and the dock sound odd coming from a man so clearly identified with the establishment; most of our modern Galileos are being 'persecuted' for having trisected the angle or proved the concavity of the earth.

Left Science, Right Science

Galileo gave one of his new-fangled telescopes to the Venetian Senate, for use in detecting invading ships. The practice of buying scientists had begun long before, and governments are of course still dishing out research grants to men willing to swallow their consciences and work on weather control weapons and orbiting bombs.

On the other side are men like Dr Jerry Ravetz, who seem equally willing to let another kind of idealism override the truth. When his students asked what he would do if he came upon a potentially dangerous discovery, Ravetz

> shocked the class by saying that he would delay the discovery by deliberately lying. He would publish a paper which hopefully would discourage other scientists from pursuing the same line of research. A delay of five years might make all the difference to the survival of humanity. Of course he told the students that this is a rare and extreme situation; but it is an example of how *the old ethics of science, amounting to intellectual honesty, are no longer adequate for the new moral problems of science.*[6] (My italics.)

In fact the situation is so extreme that it's hard to think of any examples, short of a supernova bomb or a virus that kills everything. Every piece of truth carries some risk, of course (X-rays and penicillin have killed people), and it could be argued that all medical research contributes to over-population, hence global famine.

But the really disturbing part of Ravetz's view is the statement I have italicized. There are many ways in which a scientist can influence the course of research without lying about the facts. He may, for instance, refuse to work on weapons for the government himself. He may further try to persuade colleagues to do the same. He may pressure them professionally, socially, and through the mass media. If his conscience so dictates, he may resort to slander, coercion, sabotage, kidnapping and even murder. And he may lie about anything *but* scientific evidence.

But the instant a scientist lies about evidence, he ceases to be a scientist. The 'old ethics of science, amounting to intellectual honesty' are just and only what science is. Any tampering with that, for however noble a cause, allows science to collapse utterly into a tangle of gibberish and myth.

To see how far science can be politicized, we have only to look at the social sciences, where facts are few and disputable, and theories may be bent to any cause. Today we have Arthur Jensen's theory that intelligence is largely hereditary, hence racial, based on feeble deductions from genetic theories (neither his supporters nor his opponents have so far mustered very convincing evidence).[7] We have Robert Ardrey's polemic case that private property, social inequality and war are fundamentally tied to our instincts and cannot be eliminated, based on feeble deductions from the behaviour of the cicada-killer wasp. We have Arthur Koestler's suggestion that authority maintain itself by drugging the population, and B. F. Skinner's suggestion that it achieve the same end through behavioural conditioning. And all of these men probably think of themselves as liberal democratic idealists.

Aryan Science

Under the Nazis, science deteriorated rapidly into a propaganda medium for anti-semitism and 'Aryan' views.

Anti-semitism has of course an old history. The English celebrated the coronation of Richard the Lion-Hearted by a great massacre of Jews in several cities. The first influential German anti-semite was Martin Luther, who seemed to think it was a good idea to burn their homes.

The Nordic master race idea was first promoted in 1855, by the French Comte Joseph de Gobineau. Wagner was enthusiastic about the idea, and his son-in-law, the Englishman Houston Stewart Chamberlain, wrote the next influential book on Nordic superiority, *Foundations of the Nineteenth Century*, 1899. Chamberlain settled in Germany, became a close friend of Kaiser Wilhelm, and one of Hitler's early admirers.

Hitler derived his race notions from Chamberlain and from Lanz von Leibenfals, an ex-monk and crank socio-biologist. Von Leibenfals's major work is entitled *Theozoology, or the Accounts of the Apes of Sodom and the Divine Election – An Introduction into the Earliest and the Most Modern World Philosophy and a Justification for the Orders of Princes and the Aristocracy*.

Then there was Hans F. K. Günther, an anthropologist at the University of Jena, who explained German superiority in terms of its high proportion of 'pure Nordics'. He explained that Nordic characteristics included personal cleanliness, athletic abilities, bravery, modesty, chastity – all the virtues of Galahad. Nordic women, he took special care to note, sat on trams keeping their legs together modestly. The Nordic race was supposed to be practical and creative, to love honest hard work, natural beauty, children and animals.

By contrast, the Jews were supposed to be devious and calculating, dirty, cowardly, shiftless, given to vices and, according to Hitler, riddled with syphilis. Another Aryan authority said, in 1907, that the ancient Jews despised dogs.

> The attitude of the Jew to the dog is still the same nowadays.... Never can the dog have any emotional value to him, never can he devote himself unselfishly.... That only a German can do ...[8]

Mein Kampf sets out Hitler's ideas of Jews. They could not create, only imitate. Their apparent intelligence was all borrowed scraps from other peoples, and so on.

> To what extent the whole life of this people is based on a continuous lie is shown incomparably by the *Protocols of the Wise Men of Zion,* so infinitely hated by the Jews. They are based on a forgery, the *Frankfurter Zeitung* moans and screams once every week: the best proof that they are authentic.[9]

The *Protocols of the Elders of Zion* is of course a key sourcebook for anti-semitism. Though it has been shown a forgery again and again, it continued to find favour with anti-semites in Russia, Western Europe, and the United States (where its biggest booster was Henry Ford). The *Protocols* are supposed to be the minutes of a secret meeting of the Zionist Congress of 1897, revealing an international conspiracy of Jews, freemasons, socialists, anarchists and communists to overthrow all world governments! The instructions are to

> corrupt all the young generation by subversive education, dominate people through their vices, destroy family life, undermine respect for religion, encourage luxury, amuse people to prevent them from thinking, poison the spirit by destructive theories, weaken human bodies by inoculation with microbes[10]

and so on. It's no accident that this has the ring of satire; the *Protocols* have been plagiarized wholly from an 1865 satirical pamphlet attacking Napoleon III, entitled *Dialogues in the Underworld between Machiavelli and Montesquieu.*

When Aryanism came to power in Germany, all the sciences had to be purged of 'Jewish influences'. Anthropology was already a shambles. In physics, Einstein's theory of relativity had to be scrapped, because Jews can't think. The attack on 'Jewish physics' was led by two Nobel prizewinners, Phillip Lenard and Johannes Stark.

> Close to Nature, clear and full of common sense – this is how the Aryan saw the 'true depth' of Nature in this embarrassingly naïve picture. Abstract, high-faluting, 'formalistic', incomprehensible – this, on the other hand, is how 'Jews' and 'Bolsheviks' see only the surface of Nature.[11]

Said Lenard:

'... science, like every other human product, is racial and conditioned by blood.' Professor Rudolphe Tomaschek, director of the Institute of Physics at Dresden went further. 'Modern Physics,' he wrote, 'is an instrument of (world) Jewry for the destruction of Nordic science ... True physics is the creation of the German spirit.'[12]

Mathematics underwent a similar distortion, and concepts originated by Jews were suddenly found to be abstract, unclear and 'not from human experience'. Of course a few real scientists worked on, pretending to make no use of any theories with a non-Aryan taint. But most fled Germany.

Into the vacuum they left rushed pseudo-scientists. A Nazi veterinarian took over the University of Berlin and instituted 111 new courses: 25 in 'race science' and 86 in veterinary medicine. In chapter 1 we saw the German admiralty trying to photograph the British fleet by aiming cameras at the sky. Other German Naval officers were locating the enemy by other means:

> They used a map of the Atlantic on which they placed a miniature metal ship. A pendulum on a thin thread was suspended over that ship and when the pendulum moved it was supposed to indicate the whereabouts of an Allied convoy.[13]

Secret weapons of the day included an item bearing the code

name 'High pressure pump', which was to be used against London. This was a gun 100 yards long, with powder fed into it at various points along the barrel. Hitler liked this project so well, no one had the courage to tell him it wouldn't work.

One German Air Marshal's pet scheme, proposed by a scientist(?) named Schieboldt, was to use a high-voltage X-ray machine as an anti-aircraft death-ray. The hope was to fry Allied pilots in their cockpits. A similar project, code-named 'Hadubrand', would use two intersecting beams of infra-red light to fry Allied pilots, etc.

From the April 1933 issue of a popular astrological magazine, we learn that 'awareness of one's national heritage and blood ties with the Aryan race are indivisibly bound up with astrological science'.[14] A leader among early Nazi occultists was our old friend Lanz von Liebenfals, who cast Hitler's 'cabalistic horoscope' and founded the Ariosophical Movement.

Hitler's horoscope was cast many times, from his first emergence as a political leader. Elsbeth Ebertin did him in 1923:

> A man of action born on 20 April 1889, with Sun in 29° Aries ... can expose himself to personal danger by excessively uncautious action and could very likely trigger off an uncontrollable crisis. His constellations show that this man is to be taken very seriously indeed; he is destined to play a 'Führer-role' in future battles ...[15]

This is all sound astrology, for Aries is supposed to be a combative influence. The only trouble with it is, Hitler was actually born at 6.30 pm, when the sun had already passed out of Aries and into Taurus. Taurus is supposed to make us earthy, homely and docile.

Science can easily be geared to any political ideal, but the gearing often seems to warp it into pseudo-science. I might as easily have chosen the career of Trofim Lysenko in Soviet Russia. Lysenko, an ill-educated plant-breeder, rose through political connections to dominate Soviet biology. His opponents were purged, and Lysenko's word became biological law, despite his knowing nothing of plant genetics and practically nothing of plain gardening.

Or I might have chosen those fundamentalists whose only source of truth is the Bible, and who consequently see no harm in mutilating geology to fit their six-day creation theory. The principle is the same, whether science is made to tell lies for Hitler, Marx or Jehovah. If science is re-designed to tell lies, we cannot expect it to answer our questions with the truth.

Nor can the beauty of an ideal provide a kind of aesthetic justification for perverting the truth, for every ideal is beautiful. The capitalist wants to get rich and happy. The Nazi wants a world filled with beautiful Aryans. The Communist wants a world filled with laughing, lovely, peaceful peasants. The fundamentalist wants paradise. The dazzle in the distance can so easily blind us to the business at hand. It was a caricature, whip-carrying Nazi named Julius Streicher, a man who wrote sadistic pornographic fantasies about Jewish rapists and Aryan virgins, who said:

'Be beautiful, be natural, and be like God.'[16]

The men in this chapter are not important scientists who happen to have a cranky notion or two, nor are they obscure messiahs, propagating their visions by mimeographed tracts. Most are scientists, or men with some scientific training, who have become popular philosophers. Most have made but slight impressions on their colleagues. Yet, to outsiders, their words seem anointed with the sacred chrism of expertise. Though it should make no difference in judging their philosophies, admirers never fail to mention that Buckminster Fuller is an engineer, and Teilhard de Chardin a biologist.

Each seems to begin with a metaphor which he pursues so far that it becomes, not merely real, but the only reality. To take an example no longer in vogue, think of Marshall Mc-Luhan's slogans: 'The medium is the message', 'Media are the extensions of man' and 'The global electronic village'. McLuhan proceeded from these useful and interesting ideas to ridiculous and patently false statements. The Roman Empire became 'nothing but' a system of roads and written orders. Television was not a visual, but a tactile medium.

> Psychologists define hypnosis as the filling of the field of attention by one sense only.[1]

But they don't, as Jonathan Miller points out:

> If they did, biologists would go into a trance every time they looked down their microscopes and blind men become suggestible immediately they began running their hands over a page of braille.[2]

Inevitably, McLuhan's notions led him to see himself as the prophet of a New Age, and to explain why his ideas appeared, to conventional minds, so unintelligible.

> I am in the position of Louis Pasteur telling doctors that

their greatest enemy was quite invisible, and quite un-
recognized by them.[3]

Cyrus Teed, master of the concave earth, had a similar idea:

> The opposition to our work today is as unreasonable,
> absurd and idiotic as that manifested against the work of
> Harvey and Galileo.[4]

Again, compare McLuhan's warning with Billy Graham's:

> There are no remote and easy perspectives, either artistic
> or national. Everything is present in the foreground. That
> fact is stressed equally in our current physics, jazz, news-
> papers, and psychoanalysis. And it is not a question of taste.
> The flood has already immersed us.[5]

> Time is running out. The seconds are ticking away to-
> wards midnight. The human race is about to take the fatal
> plunge.[6]

Of course, McLuhan is only talking about juke boxes here,
but the ring of Noah's hammer is unmistakable.

Vibes
Pierre Teilhard de Chardin presents *The Phenomenon of
Man*[7] as a scientific paper, but I notice that booksellers tend
to shelve it in the 'Religion & Occult' departments; they know
their customers' heads. It's a difficult book to read, unless you
happen to vibrate on Teilhard's frequency, and even then the
information-to-noise ratio is very low. He seems to be saying
that:
  1 Consciousness exists not only in man, but in lower
animals, right on down to protozoa – and beyond, down to
even molecules. It's always been there, waiting to evolve.
  2 Ordinary scientists have not detected this consciousness,
because they're too objective, always looking at the surface of
things (like 'non-Aryan' scientists?).
  3 This invisible consciousness calls for an invisible form
of psychic energy which he names 'radial' energy. Science has
been wasting time looking at mere mechanical, or 'tangential'
energy, which only spins the wheels of living stuff, while
radial energy can make it evolve.

4 Evolution has a direction (greater consciousness) and an ultimate goal (supreme consciousness, which he calls 'Omega', alias God).

5 All our individual consciousnesses are already being assimilated by, or amalgamated into, Omega, by some obscure process (for a scientific paper, this is short on cause and effect).

Teilhard is usually advertised by followers as a scientific genius who realized the bankruptcy of science. But Sir Peter Medawar, who ought to know, describes him as practising

> an intellectually unexacting kind of science in which he attained a modest proficiency. He has no grasp of what makes a logical argument or of what makes for proof.[8]

Medawar also explains that 'the idea that evolution has a main track or privileged axis is unsupported by scientific evidence'.[9]

So much for the information. For noise, Teilhard uses the full arsenal of crank conceits. His aphorisms ('There are no summits without abysses' or 'The living unit is a centre of irresistible multiplication'), might have been uttered by a Rampa or a Cayce. His adjectives of excess (Medawar notes *astounding, colossal, endless, enormous, fantastic, giddy, immense, inexhaustible, infinite, innumerable, measureless* and seventeen more), have a Barnum ring. Then, like other occultists, Teilhard begins to lean on neologisms ('biota', which may be a unit of life; 'noosphere', that part of the animal kingdom where higher consciousness is at work (mankind?); 'radial energy' and so on).

He also borrows terms from other sciences, then uses them imprecisely. Thus tension, force, dimension and vibration are used, not in any recognizable scientific sense, but to mean (inexactly) what Teilhard wishes them to mean. Sometimes he manages to jumble these terms until it becomes impossible to follow his metaphor at all.

> By a tiny 'tangential' increase, the 'radial' was turned back on itself and so to speak took an infinite leap forward.[10]

So to speak.

There are parallels between the systems of Teilhard and McLuhan: The global village and the noosphere each have the intellects of all men soldered together somehow into a kind of universal think-tank. McLuhan has this come about through electronics; Teilhard is less specific about the method; but both see the process as inevitable. This idea, that man *must* be finally absorbed in God (or Universal Love), so far from being a statement about scientific law, is a traditional Roman Catholic idea, a favourite paradox iterated not only by these two Roman Catholics, but by Chesterton (in *The Man Who Was Thursday*) and by Francis Thompson in *The Hound of Heaven*:

> 'All which thy child's mistake
> Fancies as lost, I have stored for thee at home:'
> Rise, clasp My hand, and come!'

So Omega is waiting for us at the end of the evolution road. This is everywhere fascinating metaphysics, and nowhere good science. I have to keep reminding myself that Teilhard claims to speak as a scientist, especially when he proposes that molecules are conscious, and that atoms unite because they love one another.

God's Engineer

Imagine, if you can, a tribal technician sitting chipping flint arrowheads. Suddenly he stands up and begins uttering profundities: All the world's an arrowhead, he says; people are so many arrowheads; tribal history is a long chain of arrowheads pointing to the future; and God is simply the supreme Hard Flint.

This babbling technician may be seen by the tribe as mad or holy. Our industrial tribe so regards R. Buckminster Fuller, whose babbling has attracted quite a cult.

Nine Chains to the Moon is a collection of Fuller's essays, most written in the 1930s and 1940s. It is sometimes possible to separate from an essay's gush of wordy enthusiasm a central idea, but that idea too often turns out to be a simple aphorism. One essay says nothing more than that city life is a picture of hell. Another says that industry could do a better job at housing than architects are doing. Another says that if everyone were adequately housed, clothed and fed, using scientific principles and cheap mass production, war and crime would end. 'Dollar-ability' says that money can be considered a storage unit for human energy. 'The 2,000-Year Streamlining of Society' says that reason has enabled us to abolish slavery and use slave machines instead. With a garrulousness which would do credit to any bar-room philosopher, Fuller belabours these simple notions for hundreds and hundreds of pages.

One of his gods is mass production, and his hero is Henry Ford, the man who put a car in every garage. This is somewhat embarrassing in retrospect, since one of the reasons city life is a picture of hell is the mass-produced car. Los Angeles, for example, is one of the least crowded cities in the world, and one of the nastiest, mainly because of Ford's genius.

Fuller's excesses have led him to say a great many other silly things, such as:

'Static' abstractions like geometry have somehow bogged down mankind, because they fail to take into account dynamic things: time and radiation. Without facetiousness, he points to the Euclidean cube, which won't stand up because it has no diagonal braces.*

This metaphor carries Fuller far indeed. All cultures who happen to live in cube houses are backward, he claims. They stay in one place, think the earth is flat, and so on. But nomads are progressive: they travel a lot, and they use the triangle (in tents, sails, aeroplane wings and radio masts). And *northern* nomads – such as those he says we descended from, are especially okay.

> Populations originally existing in warm climes which dared to penetrate colder realms or higher altitudes have been abetted in their progressive 'thinking ability' by the abatement of the myriad of parasitical infections with which they were originally afflicted ...[11]

Maybe so. Unfortunately, few peoples actually fit into his

* Notice also that Euclidean circles have no spokes, and that many of our Arabic numerals are unstable. 8 has a way of rolling over to become ∞, and so on.

scheme. The Egyptians used the triangle in tombs and perhaps navigation, but their homes were cubes and their sails square, and they thought the universe was shaped like a shoebox. And how does Fuller account for the igloo?

> Very far north the simple hemispherical igloo is witness of an innate sense of the radiant universe amongst northerly people.[12]

Or perhaps an innate sense of the radiance of the fire or stove in the middle. The fact is, nomads and others have lived in houses of every simple shape, usually determined by the weather, building materials and tradition; so that by a suitable simplification, one can prove just about anything.

Fuller's flood of jargon-enriched prose rushes along in this and other books, occasionally cracking the sense-barrier:

> – BUT that finity COULD, by its essential language, mathematics, be discovered and its limits ramified in the terms of itself, RELATIVITY (or imperfection) as a time-calculus POSTULATE, and PROBABILITY reduction to POSSIBILITY and thereby REAL-I-ZATION thereafter to become STATISTICS of 'IT HAS HAPPENED [']; and its (Time's) (Finity's) ERROR, and therefore, its 'ALL' (for Time is – is an error illusion) eliminated by its successful pronouncement, thus inevitably isolating infinity, by elimination of all error – by the comprehension of the latter.[13]

> These hierarchies of constellar configurations disclose in turn a hierarchy of dynamically symmetrical constellation phases and their respective maxima-minima, asymmetric and complementary, accommodative transformabilities which are not apparently permitted within an omnirational, omnidirectional, omniequieconomic, energy-accounting, co-ordinate system of universe.[14]

Talks good, don't he? Anybody still listenin'? Hit 'em again, Buck.

> Omniscience is greater than omnipotence and the difference is two. Omnipotence plus two equals omniscience. $META = 2$.[15]

W.R. Finds a Ray

Roentgen really started something. Not eight years after he discovered X-rays, Prosper Blondlot at the University of Nancy thought he'd found an 'N' ray. But when the American physicist R. W. Wood witnessed a demonstration at Blondlot's lab, he found that it was possible to remove an important part of the apparatus secretly, without affecting the 'pictures' Blondlot saw.

Blondlot was deceiving only himself, but it was otherwise with Shearer. A medical orderly in World War I, Shearer claimed to have found a new ray that could photograph the softer tissues of the body, as the X-ray did bones. As a result, he was given a lab and assistants, promoted to captain, and visited by generals. Shearergraphs were used in at least one case to plan surgery; the wily orderly hinted that they might also make a good death-ray. To some, his pictures looked suspiciously like photos of line drawings of the organs, but the British Army was otherwise uncritically enthusiastic.

Shearer demonstrated that his device could also take pictures of the outsides of buildings.

Then someone said that as wireless stations were sending out radiation, 'surely you should be able to get pictures of them.' Thus Shearer made his fatal error, by producing a picture of the wireless station at Teneriffe, which was the frontispiece of that month's *Wireless*. That finally shook his two experts and they began removing parts of his apparatus, just as R. W. Wood had done with Blondlot's, without affecting the result.[16]

This should serve to introduce the most famous finder of rays of our time, Wilhelm Reich.

Reich began studying law in Vienna in 1918, switched to medicine, and within a year was practising psychoanalysis, under the supervision of Sigmund Freud. Reich made significant contributions to Freudian theory during his first few years, but his attempt to reconcile it with Marxism was displeasing to both sides; he was expelled from both the Communist Party and the International Psychoanalytical Association.

Reich emigrated from Nazi Germany to Scandinavia, and later, to the United States. His theories developed further, and diverged further from those of his mentor.

There has never been general agreement, in or out of the profession, on the value of Reich's later work. He developed the notion of 'character armour', boxing up the individual's 'instinctual energies', resulting in muscular tensions of the face and body, and preventing orgasm. In Reich's 'vegeto-therapy', the analyst works directly on these tensions, trying to relieve them by persuasion, massage and deep breathing, until the patient reports having involuntary movements of the pelvis.

Reich postulated a kind of energy discharge during orgasm, and he named it 'orgone energy'. It was blue. He claimed that it could be seen under a microscope, and detected by Geiger counters, thermometers and electroscopes. At the same time, orgone was altogether different from light, heat, electricity or radio-activity, which these instruments are made to detect. Only Reich and his disciples ever managed to observe and measure orgone energy by any method.

When two beams of orgone radiation, or OR, travelled to-wards one another (in spiral paths) they embraced like lovers, giving birth to an elemental particle called a 'bion'. When a dizzy person sees spots before his eyes, Reich reasoned, he's really seeing bions.

The orgone energy accumulator (better known as the orgone box) is a kind of upright coffin made of alternative layers of metal and insulation. Sitting inside it is supposed to charge up a person's orgone batteries, resulting in cures of such disorders as anaemia, colds, arthritis, ulcers, wounds, and the early stages of cancer.

Reich saw cancer as merely the breaking away of cells from the body to function independently as protozoa. Protozoa could also be formed, he said, by the clumping together of bions, and bions could be formed by the disintegration of matter, as well as by embracing rays.

Reich felt sure that OR could be used to combat harmful atomic radiation. This formed the basis of his disastrous ORANUR experiment, here described by his wife, Ilse Ollen-dorf Reich:

It was Reich's idea to help eradicate the terrible effects of the atom bomb through a three-fold attack: by using orgone energy to heal radiation sickness, to neutralize the effects of an atom bomb, and, eventually, to immunize mankind against radiation.[17]

He accordingly obtained radioactive material and a number of lab mice. Within two months, his assistants had noticed Geiger counters running wild, but of course they put it down to excesses of orgone energy. Forty test animals died in one day, having all the symptoms of radiation poisoning. Then lab assistants began coming down with the same symptoms. Ilse became seriously affected and required surgery. Reich, whose scientific training was slight, never seemed to catch on.

He extended his researches to weather research, on the theory that since OR is blue, the sky must derive its blue colour from it. But when clouds 'threatened', and birds stopped singing, the culprit must be a powerful evil force, which he named destructive OR, or DOR.

The only thing to do with DOR clouds was to shoot them down. Reich's 'cloudbuster' experiments used a battery of hollow pipes on an anti-aircraft turntable. The pipes were connected to a running stream. Thus he could draw DOR out of the clouds and into the water, where it could only make the fish neurotic.*

DOR came in handy when the flying saucer craze hit. Reich decided that saucers were powered by orgone motors, which meant that they must be giving off dangerous DOR exhaust. In 1954 he used a cloudbuster to disintegrate some of these saucers, which he called Ea (probably another of his acronyms).

Sex-economics, weather control, a cancer cure, 'orgonometric equations', a mysterious ray, a new theory of matter, flying saucers – almost no crank tradition remained untouched by Reich's erratic genius. He even built an orgone motor drawing power from a non-physical source, qualifying him for the perpetual motion club.

* Nothing is easier than dispersing clouds at will. The main requirement seems to be a lively imagination. Rolf Alexander, in *The Power of the Mind*, 1956, claims to be able to do it just by gazing steadily at a cloud and concentrating. His book shows a series of photographs of a small cloud disintegrating under his influence. The cloud is blown out in wisps, as though by a psychic wind. So are all the other clouds, on which he isn't concentrating.

Reich was intensely paranoid in later years, partly because he really was being persecuted, by the US Food and Drug Authority. Their reason (that orgone boxes were being distributed as cancer cures) was sound, but their methods seem copied from the KGB. The attorney who prosecuted Reich had previously been his lawyer. The FDA exceeded the court order (to destroy advertising literature for the boxes) and burned Reich's political and psychological writings. Finally, Reich, aged sixty, with a severe heart condition and pretty clearly deranged, was imprisoned for disobeying a court order. He died after eight months.

Reich never understood what was going on. He remained convinced to the end that the Rockefellers and the communists were out to get him, that President Eisenhower and the Air Force were protecting him, and that the Air Force sent out planes to watch over him like guardian angels.

Reich's ideas cannot of course be judged by the baseness of his opponents in the FDA. He himself was inclined to be authoritarian and intolerant: Insanely jealous of his wife while having affairs himself, a pathological hater of homosexuals (he said he would never accept 'such swine' for treatment) and a pathetic paranoid who identified himself with Christ.

L. Ron Hubbard Makes His Pile

Lafayette Ronald Hubbard was born in 1911 in Texas. Other biographical information on him is harder to come by. He claims to have a BS from George Washington University Engineering School and a PhD from Sequoia University, and calls himself a nuclear physicist. The truth is more modest: He flunked physics at the first university and left after a year. Sequoia (formerly known as the College of Drugless Healing) mails out doctorates to anyone, for a fee. Hubbard's only degree, Bachelor of Scientology, has been conferred by himself.

Up to 1948 he travelled, wrote science fiction, radio scripts, movie scripts. Then he invented his own brand of psychotherapy, *dianetics*.

To understand dianetics, we must first dip into Hubbard's private jargon:

engram: A kind of repressed memory of some traumatic

experience. This may have occurred earlier in life, in the womb, right on back to conception. More than a buried memory, the engram is said to be somehow printed right on the protoplasm. This explains how it can affect an embryo before it has a nervous system.

audit: A therapy session, wherein the patient is encouraged to recall, and thus erase, his engrams. The analyst is an *auditor*.

clear: A person whose engrams have been erased.

analytic mind: The ego, which, we're told, works like a computer.

reactive mind: The unconscious mind, or id, usually packed with bad engrams.

thetan: Seems to correspond to the super-ego, conscience, or soul. If the mind and body are a machine, the thetan is in the driver's seat. It has no mass, energy, space or time (MEST), and so is capable of astral travel.

Hubbard's idea of neurosis is simple engineering: The thetan is just doing his job, driving the machine. The analytic mind is computing away, working on the data given it. But the reactive mind is providing 'false data', that is, engrams, so everything goes wrong. The only solution is to erase the engrams. Dianetic terminology is full of quasi-cybernetic words like 'straight wire' (recalling an engram quickly), 'key-in' (asking the right questions to produce the engram), 'circuit', 'line charge' and 'processing'.

The typical engram seems to go like this: A man's mother, while pregnant with him, was beaten by her husband, who also shouted at her 'You're no good!' The poor foetus heard this, and thought it applied to him. He was born and grew up believing himself basically no good.

Foetuses, according to Hubbard, have a hard life. Their fathers are usually beating their mothers and kicking them in the belly, or else the mothers are attempting abortion with knitting needles:

'Twenty or thirty abortion attempts are not uncommon in the aberee,' Hubbard writes, 'and in every attempt the child could have been pierced through the body or brain.'[18]

Moreover, the mother's constipation can lead to crushing

strains, her indigestion can cause painful gurgles, and even her sneeze can knock the kid out.

Anything said at the time seems to compound the engram. Foetuses not only have keen ears, they're fond of Freudian puns. If someone strikes the pregnant mother, saying 'Take that!' the child is liable to grow up to be a kleptomaniac. Someone made the mistake of offering one American mother an aspirin, which profoundly affected her foetal daughter. The daughter grew up to have an unaccountable rash on her bottom, having believed she was offered an 'ass-burn'. (Presumably this wouldn't apply to an English foetus, for whom the offer of 'aspirins' could only set off an uncontrollable urge to rinse out small snakes.)

But engrams need not be confined to foetal life. Hubbard believes in reincarnation, estimating that our 'real' lives are about 75 million years. One patient traced his persistent headache back to a blow he'd received as a Roman centurion in 215 BC. Chronic condition, I suppose.

Martin Gardner gives extracts from a couple of auditing sessions.[19] These plainly show the auditor asking leading questions of his patient, helping him to construct a fantasy past. Neither patient nor auditor seems to know what the hell he is doing. One man described a womb memory of his parents sitting and talking in their bedroom. Despite his poor vantage point, he had no difficulty in telling exactly how the room looked.

To boost the cybernetic image, Hubbard sells a gadget called the electropsychometer, or E-meter, supposed to work as a lie detector. It's a pair of tin cans wired to a cheap galvanometer. The patient, or 'preclear', holds the two cans during the audit, and, in theory, lying will make his hands perspire, which will show up on the meter. In practice the device is all but useless.

After dianetic's first popular success, a change came over the movement. Hubbard probably discovered that churches pay no taxes in America. Behold the coming of the Church of Scientology, or dianetics without taxes. This may be a good point to look at the finances of Hubbard's group. In order to become clear, a member must pay for a series of six courses, beginning at £311 ($750) for the first, and totalling £1,923 ($4,625). To achieve the higher *Operating Thetan VIII* costs another £1,185 ($2,850), but then Operating Thetans can use astral travel to perhaps save on fares in getting to work.

The system runs on a sound financial basis of cheap labour. Since most members can't possibly afford prices like the above, they can, for much less, become auditors. Then they work off debts by auditing others, office duties, etc. They also get a ten per cent commission (in credit) on anything spent by anyone they can drag into the sideshow. Every regional organization passes on tithes to the master, and is also expected to buy £4,000 worth of his books, and £1,700 worth of other equipment, including E-meters and pictures of Hubbard.

Those who get involved with Scientology and then find they can't pay are in serious trouble. One man who refused to pay for his son's auditing received a letter:

> ... I am an expert at harassment, try me and find out ... one more word out of you and I'll have you investigated ... I'll just start my people on you and before long you will be broke, and out of a job, and broken in health ...[20]

Anything learned in someone's auditing may be used against him. Not only does no confessional seal or code of ethics prevail in therapy sessions, but auditors exchange details, and particularly lurid items are sent to the head office. Besides, members may be periodically given a 'security check', using the E-meter and asking them if they've ever been

> insane, a communist, a spy, or had a police record, raped anyone or been raped, had an abortion or performed one, practised cannibalism, adultery, sex with animals, exhibitionism, incest, miscegenation, pederasty, prostitution, voyeurism, masturbation ...[21]

A truthful answer of Yes to any of these (from a person who believes his lies are being detected) would certainly be tempting to a blackmailer. And since it is an alleged policy to hire kids off the street as auditors, giving them as little as twenty minutes' training, blackmail does not seem an altogether remote possibility.

Hubbard's third wife divorced him in 1951, charging that he was a 'paranoid schizophrenic' and that he tortured her while she was pregnant, by beating, strangling and denying her sleep. He was last rumoured to be cruising the Mediterranean in a well-guarded yacht. Scientology-dianetics stands as a twisted monument to his megalomania, where members pay £2.50 a copy for his picture, and number the years 'After Dianetics'.

Some of this sounds familiar: A nosey establishment which screens and controls the lives of its members. A cybernetic bias. Paranoia in the ranks, and a leader who exacts the last ounce of loyalty. An organization built on the hardest sell. Either deliberately or by accident, Hubbard has aped the achievement of Thomas John Watson: Scientology is the pseudo-scientists' IBM.

Figures in a Landscape

There are great differences between the above cult figures, but what they have in common is an unshakable faith in their own systems and a determined indifference to everything else. Each proposes to tell us what lies over the horizon, but all are blind to what lies right in front of them. Like Giambattisto Vico, whose theory of the cycles of history allowed him to 'turn every hypothetical conjunction into a certainty', they force the facts to fit their Procrustean bed. They cannot for the life of them see why a Truth which applies always and everywhere also has to apply here and now.

Eureka!

To begin with, a bouquet of strange physicists.[1]

Valentino Herz has proved that the earth rotates from east to west. Osborne Reynolds discovered that 'empty space' is really crammed with tiny solid spheres, tightly packed, and that so-called matter is 'simply bubbles of nothing, moving about in this dense, elastic, granular medium'.[2] Someone signing his pamphlet 'The Longitude' showed that the moon's no solid body, but simply the well-focused image of the earth. Another stranger explained that comets are nothing more than volcanos, rocketing around the sky under their own power; yet another proved that planets, like the circulation of the blood, are driven by light.

The earth doesn't move, wrote Captain Woodley, RN, in 1834:

> The fact is, nothing can be more certain than that the stars have not changed their declinations or latitudes *one degree* in the last $71\frac{3}{4}$ years.[3]

Thomas H. Graydon of California is equally certain that gravity is not a pull, but push that emanates from the sun. Alexander Wilfred Hall, writing in unrhymed verse, argues that sound is a substance made up of solid atoms. Charles Palmer shows the sun to be ice: Specifically, it is an ice lens that doesn't give off light, but focuses the radiance of God in the manner of a burning-glass.

Then there's the unique biophysical theory of Peter D. Ouspensky, that animals are symmetrical because they have been folded in half in the fourth dimension, so that they come out like Rorschach ink blots. And if anyone's been wondering just why Einstein was wrong, let him ask George Francis Gillette, who says: 'Each ultimote is simultaneously an integral part of zillions of otherplane units . . .'[4] If that's not too clear, it's because you don't understand that an ultimote is the Nth sub-universe plane, while 'Gravitation is the kicked back nut of the screwing bolt of radiation'.[5]

According to a privately-printed book by John Fenn Smith, gravity is the 'respiration' of energy particles normally hidden inside atoms. From these breathing atoms he deduces that lasers are anti-gravity devices, and that 'time does not exist'.[6] But, according to Alfred William Lawson, there are no tedious forces or pieces of matter; the cosmos is instead filled with stuffs of heavier or lighter density, and all phenomena accounted for by Suction and Pressure. Light is sucked into the eye, we are sucked towards the earth, iron is sucked towards magnets and males are sucked towards females, until we all reach 'Equaeverpois'.

'I'm no scientist ...' Roger Babson once said, and went on to prove it by founding the Gravity Research Foundation, whose original aim was to search for a 'gravity shield'. This old science fiction prop is a platform made of some special alloy which, when you stand on it, makes you weightless. If Einstein is right, gravity is not a kind of radiation that can be screened off in this manner, but that hasn't stopped Babson from looking for the 'right alloy'. Since there are millions on millions to be tried, the search resembles that for the Philosopher's stone, and has met with similar success.

Babson's really keen on gravity. The foundation studies its effects on personality (change your mood by squatting down), on elections and so on. In 1951 he marketed an 'anti-gravity' pill, said to be good for the circulation, and he thinks it is noticeably easier to climb stairs during high tide, with the help of the moon's gravity. (Actually, it would take over 100 moons directly overhead at the time, to make the stair-climber weigh about an ounce less.)

Perpetual Motion Machines

It's common knowledge that a machine cannot be built which will run continuously without outside energy being put into it. Nevertheless, so many patent applications for perpetual motion machines found their way to the US Patent Office in the last century, that its officials had to cut back the flood by requiring every such application to be accompanied by a working model.

All perpetual motion machines to date seem to fit into John Phin's categories of Absurdities, Fallacies and Frauds.[7] Absurdities are not possible even in principle; Fallacies seem possible but contain hidden violations of physical laws; and Frauds are of course the only type of which working models are actually built.

Figure 21–1 shows two versions of an early (13th C.) absurdity which has dominated schoolboy attempts over many centuries.

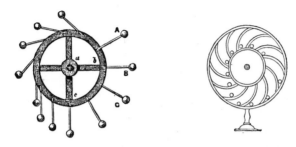

Fig. 21–1 Early Perpetual motion machines

Balls, weights, or drops of mercury are swung around by the motion of the wheel, and they swing or roll outwards so as to keep it unbalanced, hence turning. What's wrong can be seen by drawing a vertical line across each wheel, and counting the weights on the ascending and descending sides. In the first wheel, $4\frac{1}{2}$ descending weights are expected to lift $7\frac{1}{2}$ ascending. That they 'swing out farther' makes no difference, since

Fig. 21–2 Perpetual motion goblet

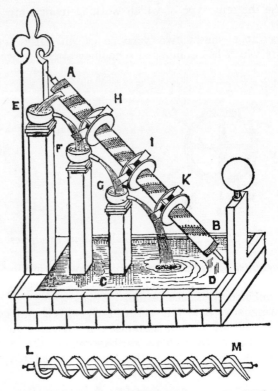

Fig. 21-3(a)   Perpetual motion water wheels

they are expected to impart enough energy to make the $7\frac{1}{2}$ swing out just as far.

A perpetual motion goblet is shown in Figure 21–2. Here the idea is that the weight of the water in the large part will push the water up the small tube until it overflows back into the large part. Straightening the tube might be expected to produce puddles on the ceiling.

Water wheels are an old favourite with p.m. inventors; being coupled to various devices for returning the water upstream (Figure 21–3). But unless they return *more* water upstream, they obviously cannot overcome their own friction.

Capillary action seems to raise water in fine tubes in defiance of gravity, so it seems a natural for p.m. Two devices using it

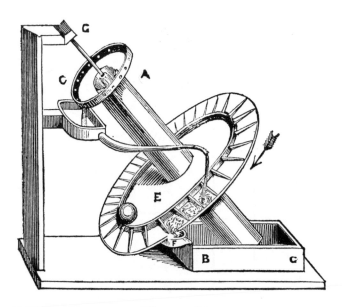

Fig. 21–3(b)

are shown in Figure 21–4. Type (a) assumes that the water will be drawn up the tube, flow out the hole in its side, and back down again. But since capillary action is only the attraction of the surface of the water to the sides of the tube, it clearly can't rise above the bottom edge of the hole. Type (b) shows an endless belt of sponge, with attached weights, running over three pulleys (and through shallow water). Capillary action draws water up into the sponge on side AB, dragging it down. Pulley C squeezes the sponge dry. Of course it also exerts tremendous forces of friction on the system, which the minute weight of water drawn up can never overcome.

A final absurdity is the magnet-powered p.m. shown in Figure 21–5. The magnet draws the steel ball up the inclined plane to B, where it drops through a hole and rolls down the curved plane to A, where it emerges to be pulled up again.

Perhaps the most ingenious p.m. fallacy ever proposed was that of the physicist James Clark Maxwell, a device known for a century as Maxwell's Demon. As proposed in his *Theory of Heat*, 1871, it seemed perfectly sound in theory, and yet

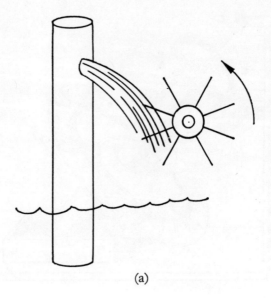

(a)

Fig. 21–4 Perpetual capillary action
(a) Simple tube with hole

it violated the Second Law of Thermodynamics, the law of increased entropy.*

Maxwell imagined a box divided into two compartments, both filled with air. In the wall between the two is a tiny door, just big enough, when open, to let through a single molecule of air. At this door is posted a tiny creature who can open the door, when he chooses, to allow a molecule to pass through.

Now, suppose this demon opens the door whenever a molecule approaches in compartment A, allowing it to pass through to compartment B, but he never allows a molecule from B to

---

* Entropy is loosely defined as disorder. By 'an increase in entropy', scientists refer to what happens when you put an ice cube into a glass of water, or drop an egg on a hard floor. If you lived in a universe where entropy *decreased*, you might expect plain water to separate into ice cubes and warm water, or the broken egg to unite its pieces and splashes into a whole egg, which would rise from the floor to your hand, as in a reversed movie film.

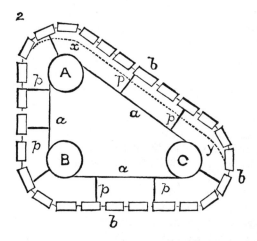

Fig. 21-4 (b) Sponge belt and weights on pulleys

return to A. (Maxwell's example was slightly more complicated, but on the same principle.) Eventually compartment B will become crammed with air, compressed to a high pressure, while A will be partly evacuated. The air in B could then be used to power a compressed-air engine, and the exhaust returned to A, to start over again. The demon and his door are so tiny that the energy they might require could more than be supplied by the engine.

Physicists from 1871 to 1951 argued about Maxwell's Demon. For a time it was thought that the animate intelligence of the demon (in deciding when to open and shut the door) was itself a violation of entropy, and Lord Kelvin proposed that human intelligence, too, violates entropy. But by now few biologists (aside from Teilhard) believe that humans are in any way exempt from the increasing disorder that affects, so far as we know, the rest of the universe.

Finally Maxwell's Demon was defeated by rather sophisticated arguments involving information theory, by Leon Brillouin in 1951. An explanation of his arguments may be found in a *Scientific American* offprints.[8]

If alchemists ever find the Philosopher's stone, its ability to turn lead into gold at a touch might be used in a perpetual motion machine. The stone could be located at the bottom of a large wheel studded with lead knobs, arranged so that each knob would brush over it, becoming gold. Since gold is lighter than lead, the descending lead knobs would raise the gold knobs to the top. There a sceptic might be posted, to tell the gold knobs that they're violating the Law of Conservation of Matter, whereupon they would turn back to lead for their descent.

Chaucer noticed that alchemists seemed much better at getting gold from their patrons than from their experiments. This type of alchemy seems to be practised by our third type of inventor, the perpetual motion fraud.

Run Your Car on Water!

Phin mentions a nineteenth-century inventor named Adams, who exhibited his p.m. machine in England for large fees. One day two onlookers decided to try lifting the machine from its base. Immediately there came from the base the sound of a clockspring running down. When the sound had ceased, they replaced the machine and offered the owner £50 if he could set it going again. He didn't. Concealed clockwork seems to explain the wheel devised by 'Orffyreus' (Jean Ernest Elie-Bessler), said to have rotated for forty days in a locked room.

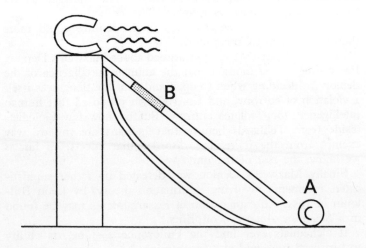

Fig. 21-5 Perpetual magnetic motion

Later inventors fraudulent never called their gadgets 'perpetual motion machines'. John E. W. Keely called his a 'vibratory generator with a hydro-pneumatic pulsating engine', but it became better known as Keely's motor.

He demonstrated it first in Philadelphia in 1874, in his home laboratory. The machine certainly ran, though seemingly connected to no power source. One Keelyite explained that it obeyed the 'laws of aetheric force', drawing its power from the source of all knowledge, and likened it to 'caloric and electricity'.

Keely said that, with nothing more than air, water and his motor, he could produce a

> vaporic substance ... having an elastic energy of 10,000 pounds to the square inch.... It is lighter than hydrogen and more powerful than steam or any explosives known.... I once drove an engine 800 revolutions a minute of forty horse power with less than a thimbleful of water and kept it running fifteen days with the same water.[9]

From time to time investors in the Keely Motor Company began to wonder if they were wasting their money. Keely always persuaded them to waste a bit more.

Demonstrations always took place in Keely's home, where the motor tore ropes apart and twisted iron bars, while its gauges showed enormous pressures – all from a pint of water. Committees of scientists and engineers were invited to see his demonstrations, but not to inspect the motor. They did so, however, after his death in 1898, and found in the cellar the compressed-air equipment that really ran it. Long, long afterwards, one of the trustees of Babson's Gravity Research Foundation, having evidently just heard of the Keely motor, thought there just might be something in it. Frank Edwards, in 1959, went much further, asserting that 'The secret of Keely's mystery motor died with him. Scientists could never agree on how it had operated.'[10]

The fable of an engine running on cheap water still fascinates the public. It turned up briefly in the 1930s, when the London *Daily Telegraph* reported that an Italian was running his car 'by decomposing water and using hydrogen in the cylinder in place of petrol'.[11] This confidence swindle has been played in the US for years. The 'inventor' pulls into a gas station, fills his gas tank conspicuously with water, drops in a pill and starts the engine. Then of course he tells the rubes all about it. The engine, needless to say, runs on ordinary fuel from a second, hidden tank.

Old cons are always good for another try. This column appeared in the London *Sunday Times* for 7 February 1971:

> Last Sunday I told of the £10 Spanish engine which could enable a car to do up to 540 miles on a gallon of water, and people began to shake their heads sadly.... Not so the South Africans. Last week two engineers, Tullio Stermin and Giovanni Zabbia, gave a demonstration in Cape Town of a 250 cc petrol engine which ran five miles on hydrogen gas liberated, by a simple chemical process, from ordinary tap water. They heard of the almost identical Spanish invention and hurriedly took out provisional options on world patent rights.
>
> The device can easily be adapted to a car, the inventors claim ... The car would be fitted with a water reservoir, a pressure tank and a magazine which will automatically drop tablets – containing a common metal and an ordinary household chemical – into the pressure tank when the gas level falls. As Senor [sic] Zabbia pointed out shyly water *is* cheaper than petrol. If these inventions are genuine we can open book on which of the oil companies comes galloping in first to buy them out.[12]

Note the last line, a standard feature of miracle invention myths. That the promised miracle never comes to pass is always put down to 'industrial interests' who buy up the patent and suppress it. In this case, the oil barons would have not only to buy up the patent, but to buy off the considerable interest of many governments. For example, the US and USSR might be expected to show some enthusiasm for the idea of running their vast submarine fleets beneath seas of free fuel, while the French might have a mind to go to the moon on a pint of Perrier.

Dowsing for Fun and Profit
The dowsing rod is a forked stick, usually of hazel, peach or willow. By no known laws of physics it is supposed to enable the dowser (water diviner or water witch) to locate underground sources of water, minerals or even oil. When he walks over the right spot, it dips. Despite hundreds of books on the subject, no comprehensive theory of dowsing has emerged. Four tentative hypotheses are:

1 The rod is moved unconsciously by the dowser, who is really sensing the water by clairvoyance.

2 The rod is drawn down by electromagnetic vibrations.

3 Vibrations affect the brain of the dowser, who dips the rod.

4 The dowser is, like many mediums, either a self-deluded crank or a fraud, or a bit of both.

In 1897 the physicist Sir William Barrett made a massive study of two hundred cases of apparently successful dowsing.

> A number of cases ... were found, upon geological observation of the spot, to be capable of explanation by the rapid detection of surface indications of underground water by the dowser.[13]

In 1927, *Nature* reported that

> The question has been investigated by the officers of the US Geological Survey, who found that the successes of the dowsers were less numerous than the laws of chance would have led us to expect.[14]

In one such experiment, the dowser failed, although the chances were 10 to 1 in his favour.

A series of tests reported in the *Journal of the Royal Society of Arts*[15] showed dowsers troublesome about accepting any test conditions except the obviously expensive one of drilling a well for each finding (even then they could always claim the drilling had not gone deep enough). Of three who did cooperate: Dowsers A and B were asked to locate a hidden well inside a room. They tried three times each, but only one of their six guesses was within ten feet of the well (nineteen feet was as far away as a guess could be, without running into a wall). Dowser C tried guessing when water was flowing in a pipe, and when it was still, under conditions of his own choosing. Figure 21–6 shows the result. C was right about the state of the water for only 17 minutes out of 60. If he'd simply flipped a coin, he'd have been right for 30 minutes out of 60. Finally, dowser B was asked to locate gold coins hidden under two of eight cushions. He failed on all attempts.

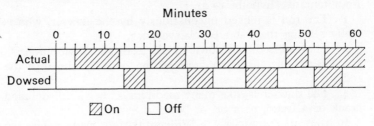

Fig. 21–6 Dowsing for running water in a pipe

In another test in 1911, the theory that dowsers locate water by visual geological clues was examined by leading a dowser over the grounds of an estate and letting him dowse water in 11 places, which were marked. He was then blindfolded and led over the same route, but starting from a different point. Again he dowsed 11 places, but none was close to any of the original 11.

In 1913 a committee of scientists, some of whom believed in dowsing, tested seven dowsers in three areas. The believers were converted to scepticism by the poor performance of the seven, who failed to find (among other things) sewers, a large underground reservoir, and a spring yielding fifty thousand gallons per hour.[16]

Ackermann cites dozens of such tests, which would certainly indicate that dowsing has had a fair trial, and that whenever test conditions are scrupulously fair, dowsers do very poorly. Yet there are probably more believers now in *radiesthesia* (dowsing and divining by pendulum) than ever.

Pendulums have been used to find metals and water, to find out the sex of unborn children, and to diagnose illness. Like dowsing, they have also been used to hunt for wanted criminals, which caused one investigator to wonder how a clever dowser can tell whether his rod is pointing to a running crook or a running brook.

A sensational book by Kenneth Roberts[17] tells of the divining successes of Henry Gross, using both twigs and pendulums. Gross easily finds water in the local area where he's been a game warden for years, and which he knows as well as a palmist knows his own hand. Roberts also subjected him to a number of tests, but somehow his repeated failures only served to convince the novelist of his powers. He failed to tell jars of water from jars of sand, to detect coins in certain envelopes; he wrongly diagnosed the sex of nine out of sixteen unborn children; he failed a water pipe test; and he found gold in an ore sample containing none. Roberts's faith never wavered.

What is known about radiesthesia is that:

1 The movements of the rod are caused by the dowser (this also applies to the pendulum, the ouija planchette, and the pencil in automatic writing).[18]

2 No known type of radiation has been shown to operate on either the dowser or rod.[19]

3 There are a few successful dowsers, such as Major C. A. Pogmore of Bombay, who scored as high as 47 wells out of 49 tries, and in difficult areas. Such persons probably depend on surface indications of water (e.g. soil colour and dampness, plant growth and distribution, temperature or even smell), of which they may themselves be imperfectly aware.[20]

4 The great majority of self-proclaimed dowsers show no such special abilities; they aren't genuine dowsers. These simply ignore failures and play up successes, or else they dowse in areas where water is plentiful. If a well goes deep enough, it can strike some water virtually anywhere.

The chances of hiring a good dowser seem slim. One engineer, after a long experience, reports that he knows no instance in which a diviner located water under conditions that would have surprised a hydrologist.[21]

Medical Machinery

Brian Inglis defends medical radiesthesia on the ground that no one in the nineteenth century would have believed in TV, either, not understanding its invisible waves. But in the nineteenth century, many intelligent scientists did believe in the

invisible healing vibrations of radiesthesia. It is because it
failed their tests that it declined from a diagnostic method to
an occult toy.

Some pendulum diagnosticians suspend their bobs over the
patient, some over his photograph or blood sample, and some
over a special ouija board, where it can swing towards the correct disease. Others simply question the bob, letting it swing,
say, in a circle for Yes, back-and-forth for No. That it works
just as well for any of these, or other systems, raises one question about the pendulum's cleverness: How does it know
which system is being used?

Pendulum methods have by now penetrated other occult
fields. Homeopaths may prescribe by dangling it over various
compounds and asking its professional opinion. Ufologists
dangle it over flying saucer photos to detect signs of life. Meanwhile, medical radiesthesia has undergone a curious transformation. The vibes are now electrical.

Electrical and magnetic cures have been popular for about
two centuries. In 1780, a Londoner had only to spend one night
in Dr Graham's Celestial Bed (electrified) to restore lost
virility and have guaranteed beautiful children. At that time
in Paris, F. A. Mesmer was using magnets, mysterious passes,
a giant battery and incidental hypnotism to effect marvellous
cures. And in America, Dr Elisha Perkins's 'metallic tractors',
pairs of metal rods, when stroked over the skin, drew disease
out of the body of a patient with ineluctable magnetic
force.

There were snags. Mesmer learned that magnets played no
real part in his cures. He then ascribed them to 'animal magnetism' flowing from his fingertips, an idea which caught on well.*
As for Perkins's tractors, wooden dummies of them were found
to work quite as well – provided the patient thought they were
metal.

Nevertheless, the public liked the basic ideas of 'drawing
out disease' and 'restoring vital force' so well that they con-

* Nearly a century after Mesmer, Mary Baker Eddy suspected
that her husband had been murdered by 'mesmeric poison', by
some unnamed enemies of her Christian Science movement. When
travelling by train, Mrs Eddy ordered an extra engine to precede
her train, to drive 'malicious animal magnetism' off the tracks.

tinued buying electropathic belts, harnesses and the like until the close of the nineteenth century (restoring their v.f.) and buy magnetic bracelets still (drawing out arthritis).

Inevitably, such crazes were synthesized with the mysterious vibrations of medical pendulums. Dr Albert Abrams, in 1910, discovered that lack of v.f. could be diagnosed by electrically detecting vibrations with his 'dynamizer'.

> It was a box containing an insane jungle of wires. One wire ran to an electrical source, and another was attached to the forehead of a *healthy* person. A drop of blood was obtained from the patient, on a piece of filter paper, and placed inside the box. Abrams would then percuss (tap) the .abdomen . of a healthy person who was ... facing *west.*[22]

By this method he could not only diagnose, but determine the age, sex and religion of the patient, from a blood sample sent through the mail.

The American Medical Association sent Abrams a drop of blood from a healthy male guinea pig, given as from a 'Miss Bell'. Abrams reported cancer, sinusitus and an infection of the left fallopian tube. Later he found a rooster to have cancer, malaria, diabetes and clap.

Abrams's successor* was Ruth B. Drown, a Los Angeles osteopath, who claimed to broadcast healing vibrations to patients anywhere in the world, using similar blood-sample techniques. In 1950 'Drown Radio Therapy' was put to a test by University of Chicago scientists. Rather than try any subterfuge, they gave her blood samples from ten patients with real diseases. Drown did so badly on the first three that she gave up. Nor were her vibrations effective in stopping the bleeding of an anaesthetized lab animal, though she kept trying for an unbearably long time.

Martin Gardner lists a variety of quack gadgets, all emitting healing radiations, including: Robert T. Nelson's 'vrilium' cylinders, worn by the patient to banish pain (they turned out

---

* Omitting several vibe-detectors like the oscilloclast, the reflexophone, the pathoclast and the emanometer.

to be filled with rat poison);* Dr Fred Urbuteit's Sinuthermic
Machine which cures everyone's arthritis but his; the Auto-
motrone of 'Professor' William Estep, which shines coloured
light on plain water to turn it into potent medicine; and
Colonel D. P. F. Ghadiali, who once advised a diabetic to eat
plenty of starches and brown sugar, to bathe in yellow and
magenta light, and to stop taking insulin (the patient lived
three more weeks).[23]

Brian Inglis remains unsceptical about such systems, and
manages to find fault with the medical profession when quacks
like Ghadiali kill people:

> Part of the blame must be put on the profession for its
> refusal to consider that there may be something in radies-
> thesia that orthodoxy lacks – thereby leaving the field open
> to charlatans.[24]

Similar blame no doubt attaches to the physicists for not considering that there may be 'something in' perpetual motion,
perhaps conferring physics doctorates upon all p.m. inventors
who are not outright frauds.

The something Inglis finds in Abrams's box seems to be
that it was given a test in 1924 by a committee chaired by Sir
Thomas (later Lord) Horder. But Inglis forgets to say what
actual tests were performed, or how the box fared. Only
two points are clear. First, incredibly, the test seems to have
been performed *on* members of the committee. Second, Horder
and one other member emphasized feeling 'an alteration in
their abdominal muscles' at the appropriate moment. On the
face of it, such a test sounds unpromising. Later, Lord Horder
said he felt that radiesthesia 'warranted no further study'.[25]

Backyard Inventor Baffles Science!
For the thirty-four years he edited a prominent science fiction
magazine, the late John W. Campbell seems never to have
stopped looking for the kind of backyard genius who could

---

* Vril, or *wril*, was a power invented by Bulwer-Lytton in a
science fiction story of 1871. Madame Blavatsky claimed her
Atlanteans used it, and that it was the secret of the Keely motor.
In the nineteenth century, vril's rival was Odyle ('odic force'),
the aetheric power invented by the physicist Baron von Reichen-
bach.

tinker with a few old parts and stumble on some earth-shaking discovery. His editorials are filled with references to Galileo's fight with orthodoxy, the Wright brothers' amateur status, Edison's lack of education. The scientific method is seen as stultifying and unimaginative, bounded by outmoded Aristotelian logic, while alternative trial-and-error methods have given us curare, opium and digitalis. Campbell devoted much space in his magazine to two inventions which, his hunches told him, just might be the next backyard breakthrough: The Hieronymous machine and the Dean drive.

Figure 21–7 shows the Hieronymous machine and its circuit diagram. Invented by Thomas G. Hieronymous, it is supposed to detect 'eloptic radiation' from minerals. On top of the box is a dial and a plastic plate. A piece of metal is presented to the detector, and a person twiddles the dial with one hand while feeling the plastic plate with the other. When the vibes are right, the plate begins to feel sticky. This happens in spite of the fact that the machine makes no more electrical sense than an Abrams box. Martin Gardner comments:

> Among electronic engineers, Hieronymous' patent (No. (2,482,773) is passed around for laughs, and considered in a class with Socrates Scholfield's famous patent of 1914 (No. 1,087,186), consisting of two intertwined helices [in fact, springs] for demonstrating the existence of God.[26]

From the patent specifications, Campbell built a Hieronymous machine. He writes:

> Of the first dozen people who tried the device, nine got reaction, varying from 'weak but definite' to one young woman who was decidedly scared by having her fingers become, seemingly, almost immovably stuck to the plate.[27]

He called it a psychic-electronic, or 'psionic' machine, akin to the ouija board and Drown Therapy box. According to the inventor, it worked just as well on photographs of minerals as on the real things. Campbell found that it worked when not plugged into an electrical supply – but not when any of its electronic parts failed.

To test it, Campbell allowed his ten-year-old daughter to try the gadget, carefully not telling her that the plastic would feel sticky. She found it felt 'sort of like tar' at a reading of

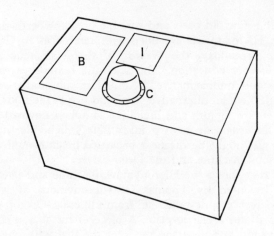

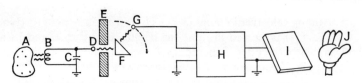

Fig. 21–7 Hieronymous machine detecting a gold potato. Rays from the potato (A) hit detector coil (B). Knob (C) adjusts things. Bit (D) seems to send something through slit (E) and prism (F) to other bit (G). Amplifier (H) does something else to plastic plate (I), felt by hand (J). The three Xmas trees at the bottom are unessential, and the things that look like smells are supposed to be eloptic radiation. The experimenter's imagination is not shown.

'about 42 to 46 on the dial' which is calibrated from 0 to 50. Then he asked her to try it again, screening the dial from her sight. Amazingly, 'she was able to return to the same dial reading, plus or minus about 2 divisions.'[28] This is about as unusual as rolling a 7 with a pair of dice.

What is unusual, however, is the construction of Campbell's second model of the Hieronymous machine. Someone had suggested that he perform the Blondlot test – remove or alter essential parts. He went further, and built a model which contained no electrical parts at all, but instead, an ink-drawn circuit diagram. When this model continued to produce sticky feelings, he didn't jump to Adrian Hope's conclusion that they are

> more likely due to the laws of friction than radiation magic. Try it yourself by stroking any smooth surface repeatedly (with or without the Hieronymous circuitry) and you will find the drag changing.[29]

On the contrary, Campbell saw that the machine really operated via 'relationship-in-itself', so that imaginary circuits worked just as well as real. If this is so, it should be possible to prove it by imaginary experiments, which might be imagined as already performed by ink drawings of scientists ...[30]

In 1961, Campbell came up with the Dean drive, the invention of non-scientist Norman L. Dean. The drive as patented (No. 2,886,976) consists of little more than two rotating vanes and a jerking solenoid. The idea is that when the weighted vanes reach the position shown in Figure 21–8, the solenoid gives a tremendous jerk and lifts the frame on which they are

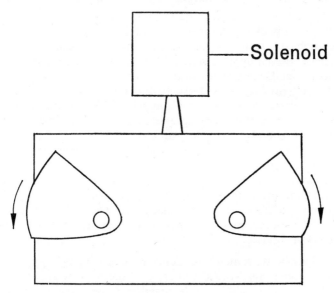

Fig. 21–8   The Dean drive

mounted. The result, thought Dean and Campbell, was anti-gravity.

> The Dean drive is simply a device that generates a one-way force; it lifts [itself] if you point up, but it pushes in any desired direction, without need of something to take the reaction. There isn't any.[31]

From this he predicted space drives, wingless airplanes, flying submarines and turning the family car into a moonship.

Campbell and Dean seemed to think that, at the critical point in their rotation, the two vanes became weightless. Then it would be a simple matter for the solenoid (a magnetic plunger) to pull them off the ground. On the next revolution, it would pull them (and itself) higher, and so on.

So much for theory. In practice, Dean's models never did anything but chatter around on tabletops, though they vibrated his test apparatus – a bathroom scale – enough to make him believe they were losing a little weight. And when he tried more sophisticated test equipment, he alone managed to see any significant results. All Campbell ever saw were these non-flying models and photographs of flying models which Dean, alas, had already 'tested to destruction'. In his columns, Campbell kept attacking government and industry for not paying attention. In fact, several organizations did examine Dean's models, test equipment and fallacious mathematics, and concluded that Dean was a crank.

I don't pretend to understand the Dean drive, and since it doesn't work, I suspect that Campbell and Dean didn't understand it either. But a device expected to pull against itself to lift itself sounds very like an electric motor that drives a dynamo to supply itself with power, or a water wheel that pumps water upstream to power itself, or a wheel swinging with weights so that, in the words of one inventor, 'the right side of the machine is always higher than the left'.

Campbell never stopped looking for that backyard genius. Mistaken though his dream may have been, it must have been a pleasant reverie.

> Somebody, somewhere along the line is going to come up with some bread-board contraption that negates gravity. And someone else will bumble together some haywire rig that does clairvoyance – with control knobs.[32]

The ubiquity of number superstitions says something about man's confidence in his own reason. We may believe that mysterious forces seek to harm us, but we trust that we can outwit them by simple formulae. Bad luck is allowed to work only in threes, or through the agency of the number 13. Naturally this white magic is ours alone; we don't normally expect a computer which breaks a mirror to endure a binary 111 years of bad luck.

Both scientists and magicians sift the number patterns they find in nature, trying to make sense of them. But while scientists are obliged to test their findings now and then, occult mathematicians are under no such obligation. For them, any coincidence is meaningful.

In *The Roots of Coincidence*, Arthur Koestler describes Paul Kammerer's search for some pattern behind chance events. We've all experienced some of the kinds of coincidences he studied: thinking about someone when their letter arrives, two persons saying the same word together, two friends having the same birthday, etc. In his *Das Gesetz der Serie* (The Law of Seriality), Kammerer lists 100 strange coincidences, such as: A concert-goer finds that he has seat No. 9 and cloakroom ticket No. 9. Next night, at a different concert, he receives both seat and cloakroom ticket No. 21.

Two soldiers admitted to the same hospital are both nineteen years old, both born in Silesia, and both named Franz Richter.

In a doctor's waiting room, someone is reading a magazine in which are reproductions of a painter named Schwalbach. At that moment, the receptionist opens the door and calls for Frau Schwalbach.

Kammerer saw these coincidences as governed by some mysterious law outside the laws of physical causality. Koestler, too, thinks there must be *some* meaning in these great meaningless improbabilities (other than the aesthetic interest they might hold for a Ripley or a Fort).

Whether such coincidences are all that improbable is another question. The concert-goer's problem looks banal. It's true that, to guarantee such an event, he might have to attend between thirty thousand and a million pairs of concerts. But millions of people do regularly attend concerts, so it seems likely that others must have encountered his coincidence. At any given concert, if there are as many seats as cloakroom tickets, the odds are about two to one that someone gets duplicates.

There is a better than even chance that, in any group of 23 persons, two will have the same birthday. With 35 persons, the odds rise to 5 : 1 in favour of a duplication. Testing this on a list of celebrities in an old almanac, I found the first birthday twins (Larry Adler and Dame Judith Anderson) in the first 24 names; the first 64 names contained four pairs.

Other kinds of coincidence, such as the two soldiers from Silesia, are difficult to determine. In his *Scientific American* column, Martin Gardner mentions a US experiment testing the 'small world problem'. The problem is, how distant is anyone in acquaintance from anyone else? The psychologist Stanley Milgrams selected total strangers in distant American cities as targets, and sent them letters via chains of acquaintances. That is, he sent each letter to a friend, who forwarded it to a friend, and so on, each selecting the friend most likely to lead to the target. For Milgram's test, the entire chain never needed more than ten links![1]

Life seems to be crammed with coincidences, perhaps because we all tend to see patterns in the most trivial juxtapositions. Two anthropologists who work together, named Lionel Tiger and Robin Fox, first met at a zoo. The actress Lily Langtry died at the age of 77 (her initials upside-down) and the two *y*s ending her names can be mirror-reflected to give two Greek *lambdas*, or LL again. Not long ago, during the investigation of a crime, two suspects were found to have 'identical' fingerprints (actually very similar, but identical by the usual classification methods).

Statistics on US presidents provide a few Eurekas. John Adams and Thomas Jefferson both died on 4 July 1826, exactly fifty years after Independence Day. Since 1840, every president elected in a year ending in 0 (in 1840, 1860, 1880, 1900, 1920, 1940 and 1960) has died in office. Moreover, they are the only presidents who died in office, except for Zachary Taylor, who died in a year ending in 0.

Numerology

Gematria was the Greek and Hebrew system of assigning a number to each letter of the alphabet, then adding up words to find hidden correspondences. Thus in the Kabbalah, *Achad* (unity) equalled *Ahebah* (love), because:

A	Ch	D		A	H	B	H
1 + 8 + 4 = 13				1 + 5 + 2 + 5 = 13			

Gematria has since deteriorated into a form of clumsy fortune-telling called numerology, which 'can help you learn about the real you, hidden in the numbers you've used all your life', meaning the numbers 1 to 9.

According to the former bandleader Vincent Lopez, it works like this: Letters of the alphabet are numbered 1 to 26. The client's name is added up and reduced to a single digit, which is then looked up in Lopez's book to disclose a personality. Thus DONALD DUCK=89, 8+9=17 and 1+7=8. An 'eight' personality is characterized by 'Honour, prestige, conservatism, wealth, business acumen and financial genius'.[2]

Like everyone else, Lopez has predicted the assassination of President Kennedy. He probably did so from his name, plus his 'Path of Destiny' (the number obtained from his birth date). But since millions of people must be guided by identical numbers (anyone called 'Bill Jones' or 'Eric Brown' for instance), there must have been quite a murder rate that day.

Lopez lists, among other successful predictions: That Hitler *wouldn't* die in 1940; that World War Two would end someday, and so on. Bullseye after bullseye.

Circle-squarers and Golden Rectangles

The ancient problem was: Given a circle, construct a square of the same area, using only a straightedge and compasses. As mathematicians now can prove, it's impossible.

That hasn't stopped amateur circle-squarers from trying. For years they've laboured over it, mistakenly believing that (a) some government offers a huge reward for the solution;

(b) it is a major mathematical problem; and (c) the answer is really something quite simple, like a circle drawn inside a square.

One seventeenth-century man squared the circle in a way which would, he said, convert all Jews and infidels. Then Henry Sullamar squared it by using the number of the Beast of Revelations, 666.

> In 1753, M. de Causans ... cut a circular piece of turf, squared it, and deduced original sin and the Trinity.... He offered a reward for the detection of any error.[3]

In the next century, circle-squaring became a universal pastime. One Frenchman tried to sue the French government for not rewarding his solution, and a Jesuit missionary sailed from South America to England, hoping to collect his reward.

Any attempted solution will produce a value for the circular ratio, *pi* (3.14159 ...). This is an irrational number, i.e. it cannot be expressed as a fraction (computers have now worked it out as far as 100,000 decimal places). Amateur solutions have invariably produced fractional values for *pi*, such as $3\frac{9}{64}$, $3\frac{1}{7}$, $3\frac{1}{21}$, even $2\frac{7}{9}$. James Smith of Liverpool defended his value of $3\frac{1}{8}$ with an endless stream of bombastic pamphlets and books, most of which dwelled on the stupidity of orthodox mathematicians. In 1897 the Indiana state legislature tried to pass a bill officially fixing *pi* once and for all at a sensible $3\frac{1}{5}$.[4]

Another irrational number that continues to fascinate like-minded people is *phi*, the so-called golden ratio or golden section. It is obtained by dividing a line two lengths, a and b, so that $\dfrac{a}{b} = \dfrac{a+b}{a}$. This gives a value of 1.61803 ...

Phi turns up in various geometrical constructions, and in natural forms such as the spiral shell of the chambered nautilus and the space of plant leaves along a stalk. From this, and from its use in Greek sculpture and architecture, occultists have exalted *phi* to a place of universal mystical significance. This campaign opened in 1884 with the publication of Adolphe Zeising's *Der Goldene Schnitt*. Zeising decided that the most pleasing possible rectangle was that whose sides have the ratio *phi* (the 'golden rectangle') and that the number provided a

key to art, architecture, music and human anatomy. Fortean
Frank A. Lonc of New York

> has confirmed one of Zeising's pet theories by measuring
> the heights of 65 women and comparing these figures to
> the heights of their navels, finding the ratio to average
> 1.618+.[5]

Phi-ologists evidently feel that 65 New York women represent
a statistically significant sample of the 1,500 million women
elsewhere.

Le Corbusier based his *Modulor* system of architecture on
golden rectangles whose lengths derive from an 'average man'
six feet tall (!), whose navel is of course at a suitable *phi*
height. At first he settled for an average man of five feet nine
inches, until a friend reminded him that this was a rather
French height:

> 'Have you noticed that in English detective novels, the
> good-looking men, such as the policemen, are always six
> feet tall?'[6]

The eminent architect promptly re-scaled his system, setting
his magnificent buildings in proportion to the heights of the
navels of fictional bobbies.

Cycle Searchers
Giambattista Vico imagined that he saw history revolving
through four ages in a never-ending cycle: the age of gods,
the age of heroes, the age of men, and disintegration to chaos
(out of which emerged new gods). Unfortunately his theory,
however noble in outline, was defective in detail. Benedetto
Croce wrote:

> Vico was in a state similar to that of drunkenness; con-
> fusing categories with facts, he felt absolutely certain *a priori*
> of what the facts would say; instead of letting them speak
> for themselves he put his own words into their mouth. A
> common illusion with him was to see connections between
> things where there were none.[7]

This could serve as a description of almost any eccentric

scientist, but it applies with peculiar force to the cycle-makers. Oswald Spengler saw Western civilization at the end of its thousand-year decline, and his *Decline of the West* explains in great detail how philosophy, art and science were all dying.

> It is enough for the moment that for us the time of the *great* mathematicians is past. Our tasks today are those of preserving, rounding off, refining, selection – in place of the big dynamic creation ... [8]

Yet stubbornly, the West's mathematics, philosophy, art and science have refused to lie down and die; indeed, physics and biology seem to have undergone their rebirths several centuries ahead of schedule.

More modest, but funnier, theories of historic cycles are with us still. The Foundation for the Study of Cycles, of Pittsburgh, Pennsylvania, churns out its monthly reports, plus books and pamphlets, explaining that nearly everything is (or will be, as soon as they work it out) cyclic.

A seminal work is Edward R. Dewey's *Cycles: Mysterious Forces That Trigger Events*,[9] which argues from the existence of known cycles (heartbeat, menstruation, tides) to the existence of unknown cycles affecting stock market prices, war, and the abundance of tent caterpillars in New Jersey. Moreover, there is a determined attempt to *keep* mysterious cycles mysterious, by avoiding any explanation of lesser magnitude than sunspots and 'cosmic forces'.

Dewey and colleagues have diligently scraped up nearly every phenomenon which can possibly vary with time. They've found that the abundance of fox (four varieties), lynx, wolf, marten, mink, coyote, hawk and owl in Canada increases every 9.6 to 9.7 years to a maximum, then drops off again. As isolated facts, these might seem inexplicable, except that we're also told that the incidence of a certain disease in North American humans follows the same cycle. The disease is tuleremia, or rabbit fever. Hm. Sure enough, the rabbit abundance follows the same cycle. Obvious cause-effect relationships between rabbits, rabbit-connected disease, and rabbit predators come to mind.

Our cyclomaniacs would point out that we don't know why rabbits should be controlled by a 9.6-year cycle. But there are any number of possible factors influencing the abundance of any species: food, predators, weather, disease ... even the effects of crowding may operate as a self-regulating mechanism (leading to perhaps increased stillbirths, fighting, disease and starvation). If the Cycle Foundation are to insist that rabbit abundance cycles *must* be mysterious, then they ought to be able to find the same mystery in the yearly abundance of Christmas cards and in the mails. Conversely, if they had the slightest interest in the causes of any of the phenomena they've found, they would finance research into those causes.

That the weather is dependent on celestial influences, namely gravity and electromagnetic radiation, is not disputed. But while meteorologists would like to know how much influence, and by what chain of cause-and-effect it is felt, Dewey's group is content to speak of already-well-documented cycles and point to the sky.

Other 9.6 to 9.7 year cycles include barometric pressure in Paris, ozone content of London's air, incidence of heart disease in New England and growth of tree rings in Arizona. All four might easily be weather-connected phenomena. The 'incidence of heart disease' is probably only the incidence of heart attacks. In a precipitous winter, men shovel more snow – a prominent producer of heart attacks in New England.

Weather seems able to account for nearly all the 9.6 to 9.7 year cycles mentioned in *Cycles*: Wheat acreage, cotton prices, bird and insect abundance, etc. Two it does not at all explain are financial crises and war. And since Dewey devotes an entire chapter each to economic cycles and war cycles, they deserve closer study.

Economics, especially in relation to finance, seems to be the winding-key of the Foundation. Among its directors are six bankers, three company directors and three men associated with investment. Dewey was himself the former chief economics analyst for the US Department of Commerce.

The overall picture of market price fluctuations is even harder to get at than that of animal ecology or weather. We might expect that, with enough information, weather forecasts would become reasonably certain, but stock markets are affected by rumours and other psychological factors which no amount of information can take into account. If the abundance of foxes were dependent on the *rumoured* merger of fur companies, predicting it would cease to be a science and become a poker game.

Dewey plunged in, however, in 1944, making a ten-year forecast of the movements of the (Standard & Poor's Combined) market price index. Dewey's forecast looks reasonably good, as Figure 22–1 shows. In fact, he claims it would have made speculators $185 for every $1 they invested.

Yet, notice that the actual market shows no evidence of

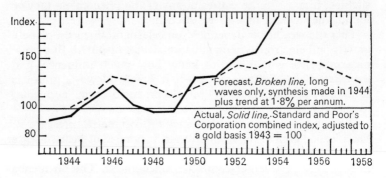

Figure 22–1   Dewey's cyclic stock market forecast
(Source: *Cycles*)

a cycle, rhythmically rising and falling. So how did he do so well?

First, he allowed for an upward trend of 1.8 per cent. Next, his system involves no more than plotting 11 points (the midpoints of each year) and connecting them by a line.

How does his forecast compare with a random effort? If we allow for an upward trend of a round 2 per cent, then let the market rise or fall by a round 10 points each year (flipping a coin to decide whether it rises or falls), we generate one of 2,048 possible random curves. 95 of these are better than Dewey's at matching the 'actual' curve. In other words, if 22 coin-flipping monkeys set out to make this ten-year forecast, one of them would almost certainly have beaten Dewey's result.

This neither confirms nor denies that markets are subject to periodic fluctuation. Dewey's presumption is in insisting that he's cracked the code, without being certain that there is a code to crack.

His claimed payoff of 185 to 1 is not for me to question, but if he's that good, he must be one of the richest men alive. Had he repeated the trick for subsequent decades, he would now have over 6 million dollars for every dollar he had in 1944. In fact, beginning with a modest $1,000, he could have, by 1984, enough to pay off the US national debt, and a few billion left over to play with. And so would one of our monkeys.

This is monkey-business of course. The movements of any large amounts of money distort the market, just as they affect the odds at a racetrack. Which means that any market forecasting system must, in the long run, defeat itself. If a worthwhile cycle is found, thousands of investors will flock to that successful system, until the combined force of their trading cancels the cycle. The idea of a successful long-term cycle is as paradoxical as thinking the next thought you're about to think, before you think it.

How about a short-term 'killing' before the cycle changes? Well, that too is a system which, if successful, must attract investors and so defeat itself. Thus the idea of a mathematical, continuing method of beating the market thus recedes before the tipsters like a mirage. Not surprisingly, Dewey has the approval of that old mirage-hunter, Roger ('anti-gravity') Babson, whom Dewey in turn describes as 'one of America's great geniuses in the field of investment'.

Dewey's chapter on war cycles is based on the work of Professor Raymond H. Wheeler, formerly of the University of Kansas. Wheeler has worked out a Viconian system relating history to weather. Both, he claims, move in 400-year cycles, with four phases of 100 years each:

cold-dry   period=anarchy and weak governments
warm-dry period=governments stronger and more organized
cold-wet   period=dictatorships, economy declining
warm-wet period=states dissolve, trend is 'back to Nature'

Notice that these are medieval categories, corresponding to the four alchemical elements.[10] Dark stuff indeed, and most mysterious: Wheeler seems to have access to weather reports from as far back as the sixteenth century, at least.

Wheeler also prepared a mammoth wall chart of all recorded 'international battles' from 600 BC to 1952 AD, allotting each a Wheeler severity score (a mild battle gets one point; a medium, two; a heavy, three). *Cycles* doesn't explain:

1 Why he chose only international battles. Surely the civil wars in England, America and Spain count for something.

2 What allowance he might make for historical errors or missing records.

3 What determines the severity of a battle? Could it be the number of troops or ships involved? Casualties? Duration? Strategic importance? Cost? Or some combination of any of these?

4 What meaning the scores could have. In what sense is a mild skirmish 'worth' exactly one-third of a battle of Gettysburg?

Dickens said that 'a man who never read or wrote either' can call his back parlour a 'study'; I suppose Wheeler is likewise entitled to call his wall-chart a study of war; but there is more mystery about it than he intends.

Dewey makes this data even more suspect by withholding part of it. He shows cycles occurring from 1050 AD to 1915 AD, leaving out 1,687 years which fail to fit these cycles. He also applies a peculiar cycle-hunter's law here: If you don't find *one* cycle in the data, try to find *more than one*. Thus he works and reworks Wheeler's chart to find at least eight different cycles (of 5.98, 17.31, 17.71, 11.241, 21.98, 57, 142 and 163.5 years), all arbitrary. The method is to remove a long cycle and then inspect the fluctuations that are left for shorter cycles, and so on, until the line on the graph straightens out. The result has about as much meaning as the number of warts on faces in the clouds.

The cyclomaniac can always blame failed predictions on 'trends', 'random factors' or still more undiscovered cycles. One of Dewey's battle-cycle charts shows distinct lumps at 1804, 1861 and 1918. It stops abruptly at 1930, however, and just in time: If continued, it would show the years 1940-44 to be one of the most peaceful periods in history.

UFO Geometer

Beginning with the reasonable assumption that if a saucer flies, it flies from place to place, the French journalist Aimé Michel began plotting UFO sightings on a map of France. He found them to make a pattern of straight lines, with as many as five

UFO sightings (out of twenty-nine) lying on one line. *What could this mean?*

One thing it didn't mean was that UFOs fly in straight lines, since

> the appearance of the UFOs in these various reports along a line may look quite different.... Moreover, the times of seeing the UFOs do not occur in the order of displacement along a line[11]

as they would if a solid object were travelling along that line. To this cold water from the Condon Report, ufologists reply that the *pattern* of sightings still must mean something, because it looks so geometrical.

> This network is astonishing, not simply because of the presence of those straight lines marked out by as many as seven sightings, but because of the convergence of these straight lines in star formations. That chance or coincidence should explain these convergences is extremely unlikely...[12]

Michel seems unaware that:

1 He wasn't plotting the locations of UFOs, but of those who see them. If the UFOs were, say meteors, they might be ten miles away.

2 Interesting 'star formations' can be generated by any set of random dots. For any 29 dots there are 712 possible connecting lines.

3 He used a map roughly a yard (representing 600 miles) square. On that scale, each 'dot' is really a circle $1\frac{1}{4}$ inches across. With 29 of such circles, it becomes extremely likely that 5 or more can lie on a straight line.

Small wonder that Michel's system (which he calls 'ortho-teny') has been rejected by even some ufologists, among them a mathematician.[13]

Other seekers of UFO patterns have turned to Dewey's methods. John A. Keel has made elaborate charts plotting sightings vs time-of-day and day-of-week, evidently on the theory that saucer pilots synchronize their watches and have Tuesdays off.[14]

Damon Knight has drawn up charts of yearly 'UFO activity',

as reported by the Air Force, and of monthly mysteries, as reported by Charles Fort.[15] In the former, it is the *absence* of a pattern that Knight finds meaningful. He feels that the number of 'unidentified' UFO sightings ought to fluctuate from year to year in accordance with the number of 'explained' sightings. I can think of no reason why they should follow any pattern whatever.

The Fortean data include strange happenings (rains of frogs, etc.) during the years 1802-1931. Knight charted these and scrutinized the resulting jagged line to see which planet might be influencing it. For sixteen years of the data (1877-92), Mars seemed to be the culprit, with maybe some help from Venus. In this part of the chart, many peaks lay close to the times when Mars was in one of four key positions.[16] So closely did the rains of coffee beans, turtles, etc., fit the planet cycles that

> chance ... would not be expected to bring about this result more often than once in a hundred times – meaning, in this case, once in sixteen hundred years.[17]

As it happens, once in a hundred times is enough. Notice that Knight has selected only one stretch of 16 years out of 130 years of data. This selection can be made in 115 ways, which seems to bring his uncanny result well within the reach of pure chance.[18]

The I Ching and Other Mysteries

In essence, the *I Ching*, or *Book of Changes*, is a compendium of proverbs indexed, and with an elaborate random access system. Its present popularity in the Western world seems to have three roots: That it is old and Chinese recommends it to users who are neither. That it is mathematical excites number mystics. That its pronouncements are often uncannily appropriate makes it irresistible to anyone.

It certainly is old, but perhaps not as exclusively 'Chinese' as many think. Originally the *I Ching* was possibly a simple list of omens, of the kind every society develops (e.g. 'Black cats are unlucky', 'When your ears burn, someone's talking about you', 'Red sky in the morning, sailors' warning'). Arthur Waley[19] divides such omens into three classes: Those involving plants and animals; those involving involuntary feelings, sneezes, stumbles, etc.; and those involving weather and natural phenomena. He quotes a set of warnings from Babylonian omen tablets of 2000 BC:

When a dog runs in front of you,
A great battle will follow.
When a dog halts in front of you,
You will lose the fight.
When a dog obstructs your path,
The fall of the city is certain.
When a dog mounts a bitch in your house,
Your house will be destroyed.[20]

He compares it to this set from the *I Ching*:

When the thunder comes crash, crash,
There will be laughter and talk, ho, ho.
When thunder wakes people a hundred leagues away,
You shall not lose ladle or spoon.
When the thunder comes sharply,
In your counting you shall lose a cowry.[21]

Much later, such prophecies were fleshed out with specific divination formulae, e.g. 'Good fortune', 'Perseverance is favourable', and 'Be not sad'. Over the centuries the book was rearranged several times, ending up as 64 prophecies. Using either sticks (yarrow stalks) or coins, the questioner obtains a set of random numbers which, after a tedious ritual calculation, refer him to a specific prophecy. The calculations also tell him whether the prophecy remains stable or changes into one of the other 63. Thus the total number of possible readings of the *I Ching* is 4,096. Despite its size, however, this system appears to hold no number mysteries of interest. It is of the same mathematical genus as another frequently consulted oracle, the petals of the daisy.

The uncanny appropriateness of its message seems to depend largely on interpretation by the user. The inert text, often murky in translation,[22] may act as a kind of Rorschach ink blot pattern, which the user invests with the answer he desires or fears. The best evidence of this is that, when people by mistake or miscalculation read the wrong prophecy, they seem to derive just as much meaning from it as otherwise. This is not to deny that the *I Ching* may be of real help to indecisive people, or for critical decisions. Let those who will, use it.

On the other hand, there is no need to drag in occult arguments involving space and time to 'explain' its workings, as Jung does. While aware of the psychological effects of projection and selection in its operation, he nevertheless seeks to tie the *I Ching* in to his theory of 'synchronicity'.[23] 'Synchronicity' is synonymous with Kammerer's 'seriality'; it is a vague attempt to assign meanings to coincidences. The Chinese, he explains, have no problem understanding how the *I Ching* provides the right answer to the right problem at the right time.

> It is only we who are puzzled, because we trip time and again over our prejudice, viz., the notion of causality.[24]

So we never learn by our mistakes? But if causality were really only a prejudice, how could we?

Some believers in meaningful coincidences find number manipulation a satisfying way of proving it. C. Sklaire of New York explains that pulsars and quasars (signals picked up by radiotelescopes which have not yet been accounted for as stars) are superior extraterrestials trying to contact us. He begins, 'I have discovered Mind in the Universe!'[25] and goes on to show that pulsars and quasars are cleverly encoded radio messages. He alone has cracked the code.

> Numerology is the key that identifies the pieces of the puzzle and places them correctly in the Grand Design.[26]

These messages are broadcast

> from an advanced super-civilization on a megacycle frequency corresponding to the number for the Holy Trinity, 111.[27]

Most of his numerology depends on the pulse's repeating every 1·3372795 seconds.

> Assigning atomic numbers to each successive two-digit number in the ... rate leads to this fascinating observation: 13 = Aluminium, 37 = Rubidium, 27 = Cobalt and 95 = Americium or in other words, the Red, White and Blue of

America. And the message to America? Joining the first two digits 1 and 3 yields B, and what is America to Be? 37 times 27 equals 999; America is to be BENIGN.[28]

Perhaps Mr Sklaire has this upside down. Surely America can be identified with the number of the Beast, 666, obtainable by multiplying the 6 white stripes in its flag by magic 111. Or has he noticed that America's birthdate, 1776, minus 666, gives 1,110? Anyway:

The number 727 represents the spiritual forces in perfect balance. This truth is confirmed on a physical level through the reality of the huge Jet Boeing 727's ... Aleph, the symbol for the Cosmic Force, adds to 111 in Hebrew. The Air Force's F111a profanes that symbol ...[29]

A London newspaper, writing of a recent plane crash, seems to have Sklaire's idea in mind, for they speak of the accident's happening 'only a mile from the start of the runway for which the Being was believed to be making'.

As we've just seen, juggling a set of figures to arrive at some desired answer isn't difficult. All it takes are a lively interest in finding patterns, a belief in the authority of calculation, and of course perseverance. The same qualities enable the pseudo-cryptanalyst to find and solve ciphers where none exist, usually to 'prove' his pet theory.

There are fashions in pet theories. Just as pyramidologists keep finding History in the corridor, as sham archaeologists keep finding UFOs in Mayan pictures, and as radiesthesists keep finding vibrations in everything, so do the pseudo-cipher men keep finding Francis Bacon's ghostly hand in Shakespeare's plays. These are their premises:

1 Francis Bacon did invent and use ciphers.
2 Shakespeare is a relatively obscure figure.
3 We have no draft of any play in Shakespeare's hand.

Ignatius Donnelly, the populist politician, Atlantean, and student of comet catastrophes, worked from these premises to the grand conclusion of *The Great Cryptogram*, published in 1888.

> He had begun by misapprehending Bacon's cipher. Based upon this, he had sought an interrelationship of numbers that would locate the words of the hidden message in the open message of the plays by their serial position on the page or in an act.[1]

Donnelly went through a complicated calculation for each page of the First Folio edition to arrive at a number indicating the position of some word on that page.* For page 75, he

* He used five arbitrary 'root numbers', 505, 506, 513, 516 and 523. Selecting one of these, he subtracted from it an arbitrary 'modifier'. From the result he subtracted the number of italicized words on the page, then added the number of bracketed or hyphenated words, to arrive at his key number. This number might indicate the position of a word in the first column or the second, or the position counting backwards from the end of the page, or else the position in the scene or act.

arrived at 'Shak't', the first line of a cipher message: 'Shak't spur never writ a word of them,' meaning the plays. Elsewhere he came up with the names of prominent Elizabethans: 'seassill' (Cecil) and 'More-low' (Marlowe).

Donnelly deceived only himself, for the critics showed instant unkindness. Joseph Gilpin Pyle wrote *The Little Cryptogram*, using Donnelly's methods to produce lines like 'Don nill he [Donnelly], the author, politician and mountebanke, will worke out the secret of this play ...'[2] The Reverend A. Nicholson used Donnelly's system exactly, including his beloved 'root numbers', to get 'Master Will I am Shak't spurre writ the play and was engaged at the Curtain.'[3] Moreover, he produced this text five times, from the very pages Donnelly had used.

Of course a cipher with this much ambiguity is no cipher at all. As L. Sprague and Catherine de Camp say, we may as well decide that Shakespeare wrote the Forty-Sixth Psalm, for the forty-sixth word from the beginning of it is 'shake', and the forty-sixth word from the end is 'spear'.[4]

Baconology dies hard. Orville Ward Owen, MD, of Detroit has 'proved' that Bacon wrote all the works of Shakespeare, Marlowe, Spenser, Robert Greene and George Peele, plus Burton's *Anatomy of Melancholy*. Why? Simply to conceal a cipher showing himself to be the illegitimate son of Queen Elizabeth and the Earl of Leicester.[5] (This theory is disputed by another MD, Timothy Healey, who maintains that Elizabeth *was* Shakespeare, a secret transvestite.[6]) Owen's system uses the key words 'fortune', 'honour', 'nature' and 'reputation'. His method is to scan the above works for any of the thousands of occurrences of one of these key words, then seize upon any nearby text that seems to help his theory. Enigmatic Bacon thus led Dr Owen to dig up the grounds of Chepstow Castle in a vain attempt to recover the original MSS.: One day the 'cipher' named one spot, and another day – when no treasure turned up – it directed him to another.

Among many who have found the name 'Bacon' concealed in Shakespeare's plays is Walter Conrad Arensburg. He found it in *Hamlet* I. iii, lines 70-73, which begin with the words *Costly, But, For* and *And*. From these he took the letters *Co, B, F* and *An*, which he anagrammed to *F. Bacon*.

In *The Shakespeare Ciphers Examined*,[7] two professional

cryptologists, William and Elizabeth Friedman, inspect all of the supposed Bacon ciphers up to 1950, applying two simple tests of validity:

1   Does the message make sense?
2   Is it a unique solution?

For Arensburg's find, they counted

the initial letters of 20,000 lines of the First Folio. They calculated that chance would assemble the letters *b*, *a*, *c*, *o* and *n* in that order only 0·0244 times in the approximately 100,000 lines of the First Folio. Significantly, Arensburg did not find any such straight acrostic. Instead, he had to widen his field to include second letters, such variants as 'Baco' and 'F. Baco', and anagrammed forms of these. This promptly brought the pure-chance probabilities well within range of the First Folio.[8]

In general, allowing anagrams greatly increases the ambiguity of the supposed cipher. For example, *aemt* could be read as *meat, mate, meta, team* or *tame*. How is one to determine which is the intended cipher message? Jonathan Swift put it like this:

If I should say in a letter to a friend, *Our Brother Tom has just got the piles*, a skilful decipherer would discover, that the same letters which compose that sentence, may be analysed into the following words: *Resist, a plot is brought home; The tour.*[9]

Baconologists are often trapped into this kind of 'decipher-ment'. Taking the longest word in Shakespeare, *honorificabili-tudinitatibus*, Sir Edwin During-Lawrence readjusted it to *Hi ludi F. Baconis nati tuiti orbi* (These plays, F. Bacon's offspring, are preserved for the world). The Friedmans showed by an equally convincing Latin anagram of the word that Dante's ghost was the real author. Or why stick to Latin? With a little fudging, we can get: *I, B. Johnson III, writ a lift'd batch.*[10]

Pseudo-ciphers can often be recognized by their high level of ambiguity. A case in point is Col. Churchward's analysis of linguistic evidence for Mu. Table 23–1 shows part of his com-parison of the Greek alphabet with what he supposes to be the

Mayan alphabet. The Greek letters are supposed to be formed
from the serial words of a Mayan epic about the destruction
of Mu:

Table 23–1   Greek and 'Mayan' (Churchward)

Greek	'Mayan'	Literal translation
alpha	*al*, heavy; *páa*, break; *ha*, water.	Heavily break the waters
beta	*be*, walk; *ta*, where, place, plain.	extending over the plains.
gamma	*kam*, receive; *ma*, mother, earth.	They cover the lands
delta	*tel*, deep, bottom; *ta*, where, place, plain.	in low places, where
epsilon	*ep*, obstruct; *zil*, make edges; *onom*, whirlwind.	there are obstructions, shores form and whirlpools ...
★★★★	★★★★	★★★★
upsilon	*u*, abyss; *pa*, tank; *zi*, cold; *le*, place; *on*, circular.	... now abysses, cold depths. In circular places ...

Notice that epsilon and upsilon are broken in completely
different way, to derive different messages. Elsewhere our
forgetful Muvians-Mayans change the word for 'place' from
ta to *le*; for 'obstructions' from *ep* to *ka*, and re-define *ka* again
as 'volcanic sediments' (as they change the meaning of *zi* from
cold to vapour). Of course all true languages are full of
ambiguities, but we would not normally expect to find so many
crowded together in this 52-word treatise. The English equivalent might be 'She bears each cross patiently. Time flies like
an arrow.'

A few linguists, including Benjamin Lee Whorf, have followed Diego de Landa's stumbling lead in trying to establish
a phonetic Mayan alphabet. Russian linguists have tackled it
with computers, but so far have produced only texts closely
resembling computer verse ('The young maize god fires pottery
from white clay'; 'The woman's burden is the god of war').[11]
Pseudo-linguists have gone much further, and Peter Kolosimo
mentions a theory that Christ's words on the cross (*Eli, Eli,
lama sabachthani?*, or 'My God, my God, why hast Thou
deserted me?') were really Mayan (*Hele, Hele, lamah sabac*

ta ni, or 'Now I feel weak and my face is hid in the darkness').[12]
Such bad puns on (what may be pseudo-)Mayan are as ambiguous as anagrams; a naturopath might with the same justification argue for 'Ailing, ailing, lemme see botany', a call for
herbal cures. To accept Kolosimo's version is to accept that the
painter Constable really was, in Frank Muir's famous pun,
'later promoted to Sargent'.

Most scholars believe that Mayan writing is pictographic,
having no phonetic alphabet. I. J. Gelb writes:

> The best proof that the Maya writing is not a phonetic
> system results from the plain fact that it is still undeciphered.
> This conclusion is inescapable if we remember the most
> important principle in the theory of decipherment: *A
> phonetic system can and ultimately must be deciphered if
> the underlying language is known.* Since the languages of
> the Mayas are still used today, and therefore well known,
> our inability ... means that it does not represent phonetic
> writing.[13]

Gelb also describes one common error in deriving etymologies
which crops up again and again in Atlantis-Mu theories: The
assumption that, because two writings have several symbols
in common, they are close relatives. He takes eight languages
which have no proven relationship and compares them as in
the first eight columns of Figure 23-1. The ninth column
clinches his argument, for it shows symbols from a 'secret
language' invented by a German schoolboy. In the tenth
column I have included symbols from the alphabet of Mu,
as imagined by Col. Churchward. Other of Churchward's
Muvic symbols seem to come straight from Hebrew and from
Egyptian hieroglyphs, without the slightest modification.

H. S. Bellamy, the undisputed authority on Hörbiger's ice
theory, has invented a curious etymology for the cross and
swastika. Beginning with Hörbiger's (and Chicken Little's)
assumption that the sky was falling, he deduces ways in which
the ancients must have tried to prop it up. The cross's

> extreme ends are the four cardinal points, and they are
> connected by a system of girders [fastened to the tops of
> upright poles] giving greater strength. The upright props

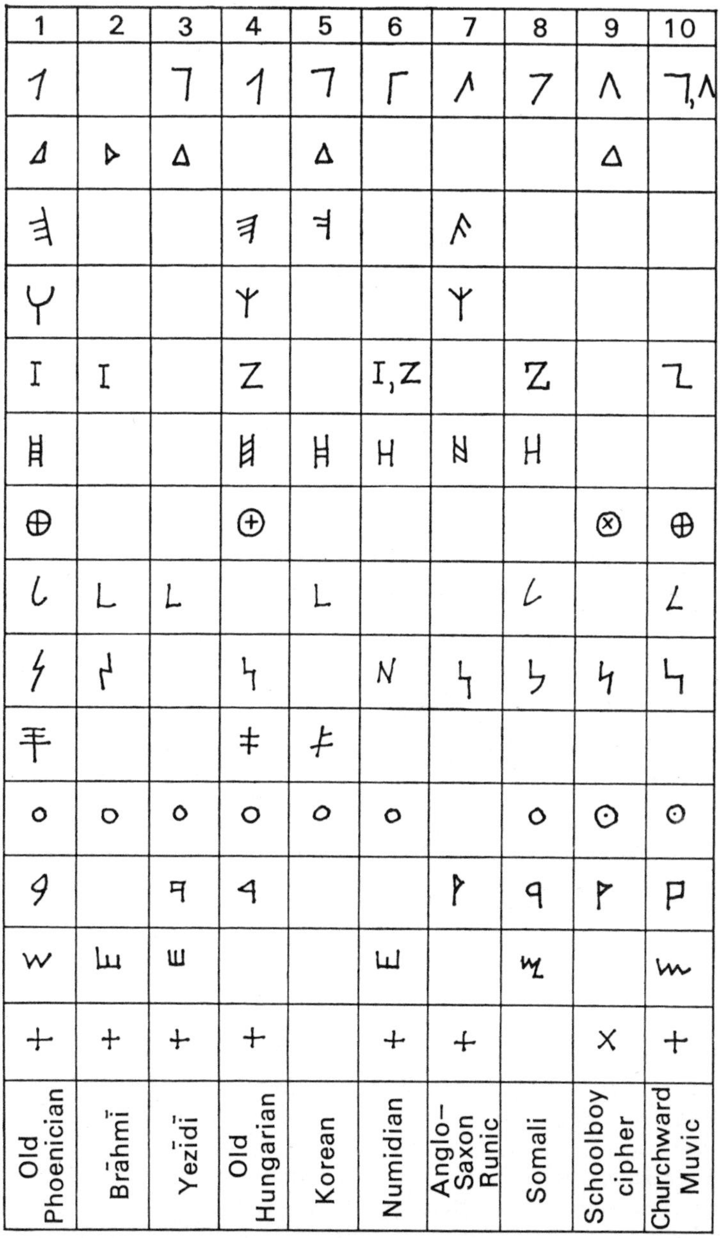

1	2	3	4	5	6	7	8	9	10
Old Phoenician	Brāhmī	Yezīdī	Old Hungarian	Korean	Numidian	Anglo-Saxon Runic	Somali	Schoolboy cipher	Churchward Muvic

Figure 23-1 Comparison of symbols from ten unrelated
languages (after Gelb)

are understood; while in the swastika or gammadion, they are depicted, in a primitive attempt at perspective.[14]

One imagines some future Bellamy working a similar decipherment upon our copyright symbol: © can only be a primitive moon-on-sun sign, warding off the dreaded eclipse.

Real Ciphers, Unreal Solutions

The Voynich manuscript, named after the American bookdealer Wilfred Voynich who bought it in 1912, first came to light in Prague in 1666. It consists of 204 pages written in a unique script and illuminated with drawings of astrological, botanical and medical subjects. Some show tiny women like *Playboy* 'femlins' in the works. One such creature stands in half a scrotum, like a miniature rowboat, and shoves something down the tube. Sperm? The life force? Gonorrhea? No one knows, because no one has yet deciphered a word of the manuscript.

The task has been tried not only by expert cryptanalysts, but by historians, botanists, astronomers and biologists – but in vain. Their failure affirms Professor Gelb's statement, for the language of the Voynich manuscript is unknown.

Naturally pseudo-cryptanalysts have had their way with the mysterious document, too. Occultist William Romaine Newbold announced in 1919 that it was an arcane work of the thirteenth-century monk, Roger Bacon. Bacon, it seemed, had anticipated many modern discoveries, including the microscope and telescope.

Newbold learned this by finding what he thought were 'shorthand symbols', tiny threadlike forms surrounding the letters of the text. These he put through a bewildering five-stage system of analysis, which included changing letters to their phonetic equivalents (e.g. *d* becomes *t*), anagramming, and an elaborate arrangement of interlocking letter pairs which no one really understood (not even Newbold).

His results were questioned on three counts:

1 Bacon, genius that he was, could not have used this complex system. To encipher a text using interlocking letter pairs is all but impossible; to anagram risks losing the message

2 Newbold could not, as he admitted himself, decipher altogether.

the same portion of text twice and get the same message.[15]

3   Most damning of all, what he supposed were 'shorthand symbols' turned out to be nothing but the spreading of ink on the rough fibres of the vellum.

In 1943 a New York lawyer came up with an even sillier solution in Latin. A translated portion of it reads:

> The feminated, having been feminated, press on the fore-bound; those pressing on are moistened; they are vein-laden; they will be broken up; they are lessened.[16]

This may make sense to readers of the *Occult Gazette*, but not much to others. The Voynich remains a mystery.

Two facts about it should intrigue ufologists of the von Däniken school of conjecture. It may well be written in an artificial language, and botanists have said that the plants it depicts are imaginary. Before long, I suspect, we'll have breathless announcements that it can only be the work of spacemen.

The composer Edward Elgar, who was fond of ciphers, has left behind him a few puzzles which are still unsolved. The best known is his *Variations on an Original Theme*, music in which the original theme never appears. This theme is sup-posed to be a musical cipher, whose 'dark saying', according to Elgar, 'must be left unguessed'.

Elgar also enciphered a note to his friend Dora Penny in 1897, which neither she nor anyone else has been able to decipher. A tracing of the note is reproduced in Figure 23-2. An attempt upon it appears in *The Musical Times*, February 1970, by Eric Sams. Sams's solution is the somewhat uncon-vincing message:

STARTS: LARKS! IT'S CHAOTIC BUT A CLOAK OBSCURES MY NEW LETTERS, A, B, BELOW: I OWN THE DARKNESS MAKES E.E. SIGH WHEN YOU ARE TOO LONG GONE(T).

Fig. 23-2   Elgar's note to Dora Penny

Yet, it isn't until we examine Sams's key that the solution begins to look improbable. He has combined alphabetic and phonetic substitutions, allowing some symbols to stand for several sounds and letters each. For example, the same symbol stands for *E*, *V*, *Z* and the sounds *nu*, *ch* and *rs*. Likewise a single symbol triples for short *I*, *O* and *U*. Indeed, using Sams's rules exactly, I was able to turn message No. 1 below into Elgaric symbols, and decipher it as message No. 2.

1 Do we make the(e) sing, poacher? Twang a rude 'A' of coarse delight: Zoo ear resounds either with a seal's bark or bone chip as some raven dines.

2 Do we make the composer too angry? We are of course delighted. Eerie sounds: Zither with, as chalk bars, our bones. It takes on grave nuance.

Sams's own message fares no better, since his *larks* can be *locks*, his *letters* may become *lepers* if they aren't a *levee*, his *cloak* can be *clothes* or *close*, and so on. It's hard to believe that a skilful encipherer like Elgar could have wished *composer* scrambled to *sing, poacher* or even *King Poker*; or a *rose* to be known by the decidedly less sweet names of *roe, arose, arrows, roars, rove* and *roach*.

Pseudo-cryptanalysis is a close cousin of pseudo-science. In each, the practitioner deceives himself that his solution must be right, because he has devoted so much time, skill and ingenuity to it. But a genuine solution – to a cipher or a scientific question – needs no such special justification. It wins acceptance by being the simplest possible solution that makes the most sense at the time.

The End

Rumour, or information generated by hysteria, in its milder forms amounts to no more than weighting facts with emotional ballast. Further up the scale, facts are considerably distorted, until stories begin to resemble dreams (or nightmares). At rumour's worst, or lynch-mob stage, hallucinations and delusions take over from facts.

The facts of an incident are almost completely irrelevant to their interpretation, at any stage. UFO experiences were variously interpreted as hostile invaders from space, friendly aliens protecting us from our own atomic monster, dangerous demons from inside the hollow earth, Russians, secret Air Force weapons, robot bombs.

A dietary fanatic in Chicago believed the saucers were hallucinations brought on by bad dietary practices. He thought the skies would clear if Americans would only eat fifty dandelion blooms every day.[1]

One of the longest-running rumours ever is the idea that the Egyptians were powerful magicians. From the time of Plotinus down to the decipherment of the Rosetta stone (sixteen centuries) the hieroglyphs were universally supposed to be powerful spells or keys to universal knowledge. A sixteenth-century Jesuit read one symbol group as 'The life of things, after the defeat of Tryphon, the moisture of Nature, through the vigilance of Anubis.' Actually it meant only 'Osiris says'.

With the discovery that hieroglyphics might be used for prayers, proclamations or only laundry bills, some of the mystery wore off – for scientists. The public continued to nurse its belief, and, a full century after the Rosetta stone, we had the curse of Tutankhamun.

The tomb of this boy king was opened in 1922 by Howard Carter and Lord Carnarvon. The excitement of this great find of tomb treasures communicated itself to the public, inspiring novelists, dress designers, architects and film makers. Lord Carnarvon died the following year of pneumonia and possible malaria, and the Curse was born. Edgar Wallace wrote how, on the day the tomb was opened, a cobra ate the pet canary belonging to one of the expedition, portending doom. A hieroglyphic curse was said to promise death to violators of Tutankhamun's grave.

The story still circulates, revived by the 1972 exhibition of the Tutankhamun treasures in London. In vain did Dr I. E. S. Edwards, Keeper of the Egyptian Antiquities at the British Museum, try to exorcize the rumour in a radio interview. He said that, first, he had himself read all of the inscriptions on the tomb, finding no such curse. Second, the story was originally started as a journalistic hoax. Third, the lifespans of all members of the expedition who had so far died had been compared to life expectancies from actuarial tables – expedition members appeared to live longer than most of us.

This seems to be one of the cases where a big news story, because it is big, acquires a rumour and seems to substantiate it. A remarkable number of Everest climbers have seen yetis; round-the-world sailors are inevitably asked if they've spotted any sea monsters; and astronauts who see UFOs seem to become, for no particular reason, unimpeachable witnesses.

The appeal to private prejudice is too obviously a part of many rumours. The racist takes up the story of a Negro rapist as eagerly as the radical takes up a police brutality story. Italian-Americans are interested in disproving Lief Erikson as much as fundamentalists are in disproving evolution. None of us is, or could be, exempt from this kind of thinking. If a scientist studies the relationship between race and IQ, he does so out of a conviction that this particular 'information gap' is critical. He may be further led to rush preliminary findings into print, generating hysteria on both sides of the question. Newspapers and popularizers take over and build a rumour from the slightest evidence, on any such delicate issue. To name recent examples, issues like race and IQ, 'test-tube babies' and urban environment have become riddled with rumours of 'scientific proofs' of all the popular clichés: 'Negroes are stupid', 'You can't tamper with Nature', and 'We'll all be dead by the year 2000'.

Information gaps

In times of disaster, the demand for news outruns the capabilities of news services. Gordon W. Allport and Leo Postman[2] report that, after the San Francisco earthquake of 1906, four rumours circulated:

1 That a tidal wave had engulfed New York simultaneously.
2 That Chicago had slid into Lake Michigan.
3 That the quake had broken open the zoo, and that animals were devouring people in the park.
4 That men were found with women's fingers in their pockets, having cut them from corpses to steal the rings.

The disaster need not be real, as the 1938 broadcast of a dramatization of H. G. Wells's *War of the Worlds* showed. Listeners who tuned in late heard dance music interrupted by an ever more electrifying series of news flashes, describing an invasion from Mars. Mobile units were rushed to the landing sites; one announcer was killed by the invaders; a professor of astronomy was called in to explain the invasion. Such touches of realism overrode assurances that it was all a play, and panic broke out over the whole United States. New York police switchboards were jammed. Los Angeleans fled to the hills. In the South, people gathered in the streets to pray. Twenty families in New Jersey believed they were under a gas attack, and came down with appropriate choking symptoms. New Yorkers claimed to hear battle sounds; others saw the flames of a holocaust, heard bombing and felt the swish of landing Martian craft.

For some people the rumour changed course. Hitler was marching on the United States. Enormous meteorites had devastated Eastern cities. An enormous number of people phoned the authorities to ask if it were really the end of the world. There was enough violence, looting and evacuation to make some parts of the country look as if the Martians *had* landed.

J. P. Chaplin gives three reasons for the spread of this rumour. First, the news everywhere was unsettling. It was one of the worst years of the Depression; Hitler had begun his conquest of Europe. Second, many listeners actually did tune in late, missing the introduction to the play. Third, Orson Welles had taken great pains to make the play as realistic as possible, partly because producers had insisted that science fiction was too far-fetched for adult audiences.

Marshall McLuhan further feels that the medium of radio itself may have had a profound effect ('The subliminal depths

of radio are charged with the resonating echoes of tribal horns
and antique drums ...'). But his feeling that it could not
happen on 'cool' TV has less to do with imagery than with the
difficulty of faking realistic visual effects. There is no apparent
reason why TV audiences are less suggestible than radio
audiences (Suppose *The War Game* had been presented on
BBC at the height of the 1969 Russian invasion of Czechoslovakia ...).

Obituaries

The sudden death of a celebrity constitutes a first-class news
crisis; the media simply can't keep up with the rumours. Two
books came out of Lincoln's assassination; one claiming that
Booth had not been caught;[3] one claiming Booth committed
suicide (like Judas).[4] Lincoln was killed on the orders of his
cabinet, by a Roman Catholic group, by southerners, etc., etc.

The hysteria generated by Valentino's death provoked a
riot in New York, involving sixty thousand people. He was
said to be interred in a 1.5 ton bronze coffin, to be engaged
to Pola Negri, to be a fascist ... and of course, to be alive.

After Valentino was alive, Amelia Earhart had to be alive*
as did Glenn Miller, Hitler, James Dean (alive but horribly
disfigured); then a long list of pop singers didn't really die
in their car accidents, plane crashes, or drowning accidents.

Bob Dylan, who did stay alive, was of course said to have
died, and an elaborate mystique enveloped the rumoured
death of Paul McCartney: A message about his death was
said to be recorded on the end groove of one record; the
mourning scene on the cover of *Abbey Road* was genuine;
various songs had hidden meanings; the word 'BEATLES' on
one album could be read as a 7-digit telephone number where
the Truth could be learned; on one album McCartney was
photographed sitting behind a sign saying 'I WAS'; and many,
many more.

President Kennedy's death set off a rumour cycle that will
probably run for years to come. The Warren Commission
Report attempted to lay the ghosts of most of the grandest
conspiracy theories (the commission even investigated the

---

* As late as 1970, the aviatrix was said to be a Mrs Irene Bolham,
in *Amelia Earhart Lives*. Mrs Bolham brought suit against the
authors. (Source: London *Evening Standard*, 30 August 1971.)

FBI, using agents from the Internal Revenue and other government services), but it left a number of questions and answered others in an unsatisfactory manner. This is of course to be expected in any such complex situation, but the *need to know* continued to set off new rumours of multiple bullets, multiple assassins, secret connections between Oswald and the FBI, between Ruby and the Dallas police, etc. And each item became the basis of some amateur sleuth's theory: [5]

1 Mark Lane's *Rush to Judgement* makes much of how one eyewitness testified to seeing something, near a wooden fence at Dealey Plaza, 'that I could not define precisely'. He also tried to get a witness (to the killing of Patrolman J. D. Tippit) who picked Oswald from a lineup, to change her mind. Apparently Lane completely fabricated the testimony of a third witness – all to prove that a great conspiracy existed, involving Lyndon Johnson, the FBI, and Supreme Court Justice Earl Warren.

2 Penn Jones, Jr, a newspaper editor and publisher, printed his own book *Forgive My Grief*, trying to relate several other deaths to that of Kennedy. He claimed that, of five people who met with Jack Ruby's roommate on the day Ruby killed Oswald, two were later murdered and a third 'died under strange circumstances'. The meeting was actually a press conference, attended by Ruby's two lawyers, one detective, and a number of reporters. The 'suspicious death' was a heart attack; it happened to a man who wasn't actually at the conference. One of the reporters was murdered later, possibly by a hater of homosexuals. The policeman was accidentally shot by a colleague two years later. But the editor-publisher's death hunt carries him further and further into paranoid fantasy:

> Jones actually believes that the power failure which crippled New York City ... following Miss Kilgallen's [gossip columnist who interviewed Ruby] death [by barbiturate poisoning] was a thinly disguised ruse to shove her story off newspaper front pages.[6]

3 Edward J. Epstein's *Inquest* attacks the Commission's famous 'single bullet' theory, stating that X-rays of the President's body weren't examined by the Commission. Of course non-medical men are not likely to make anything out of looking

at X-ray plates; the Commission relied instead on expert opinion (as they would for fingerprint or ballistics data).

4 Harold Weisburg's *Whitewash* contends that the FBI, or somebody, destroyed four critical frames of a movie of the assassination. Len Deighton has picked up this rumour and puts it as an 'unanswered question' in his 'Jackdaw' file, *The Assassination of President Kennedy*:

> Examination of other frames, however, appeared to indicate that the missing frames might have recorded the piercing of a traffic sign alongside Elm Street by a bullet.[7]

This looks like a classic rumour on the wing, in the supposition that an unseen bullet is depicted in unseen film footage. The missing four frames were not actually suppressed by the FBI or anyone else: The amateur who took the film sold the original to *Life* magazine and gave copies to the FBI and Secret Service. In the rush to process pictures, someone at *Life* broke the film (diagonally, across these frames) and someone else spliced it, discarding them. The Warren Commission examined this film and also the official copies containing the four frames. It decided to publish the *Life* version, merely because it was a clearer print.

5 A few wilder theories are that there were really two assassins (Oswald and someone who impersonated him, leaving false clues); that it was all the plot of a Texas oil millionaire; that Oswald was framed; that a 'missing' tree on a nearby knoll shows that an artificial tree had been installed, to camouflage the real sniper; that blowups of photos of the area show a host of snipers lurking in shrubbery; that the assassination bullet was planted where it was finally found (on the hospital stretcher of Governor Connally); and of course that Kennedy is alive.

6 The wildest of all is that of George C. Thompson:

> Five people were killed in Dealey Plaza. There were at least twenty-two bullets fired. The suspect is Lyndon B. Johnson. An automatic weapon equipped with a silencer was used. Kennedy was not killed. He was impersonated in the Presidential limousine by Officer J. D. Tippit.[8]

Propaganda and Self-Deception

The fulminations of World War I propaganda are often singled out as shameful manipulations of public opinion. Yet, even when the press is not deliberately 'managed', it can provide its own rumour system. Consider this sequence of news stories from World War I papers, following the fall of Antwerp to the Germans:

When the fall of Antwerp became known, the church bells were rung [meaning in Cologne]. – *Kölnische Zeitung*.

According to the *Kölnische Zeitung*, the clergy of Antwerp were compelled to ring the church bells when the fortress was taken. – *Le Matin*.

According to what *Le Matin* has heard from Cologne, the Belgian priests who refused to ring the church bells when Antwerp was taken have been driven away from their positions. – *The* (London) *Times*.

According to what *The Times* has heard from Cologne via Paris, the unfortunate priests who refused to ring the church bells when Antwerp was taken have been sentenced to hard labour. – *Corriere della Sera*.

According to information to the *Corriere della Sera* from Cologne via London, it is confirmed that the barbaric conquerors of Antwerp punished the unfortunate Belgian priests for their heroic refusal to ring the church bells by hanging them as living clappers to the bells with their heads down. – *Le Matin*.

Here we can see that the misreading of a single sentence began the chain-reaction, and an atmosphere of anti-German hate propaganda provided everything necessary to keep the reaction building up.

American political party propaganda, often crude, hit a new low of crudity in the 1930s:

In addition to the whispers regarding the physical and mental health of President Roosevelt, the 1936 campaign evoked the rumour that he was actually a Jew named Rosenfeldt.... A story was printed prominently by the Chicago *Daily Tribune* that American Communists had been instructed to vote for Mr Roosevelt.[9]

And of course Nazi propagandists made considerable use of these rumours after America entered the war.

E. H. Gombrich offers certain insights into the Nazi management of propaganda,[10] contrasting Roosevelt's method, in which the President pretended to be dropping into people's living rooms for a 'fireside chat', with that of Goebbels, in which the living room was itself transported to the *Sportspalast* for a huge and stirring rally. News was delivered as an oration, special victory announcements were introduced with fanfares, and even music programmes

> were all planned to make the listener feel that he or she was living through great times and stirring events, and that the radio provided him with a privilege of witnessing history in the making.[11]

Gombrich stresses the importance, for the propagandists, of creating such a world-view, a false inner model of reality which the individual can carry around with him and apply to every experience. Being integrated with his personality, this model is a logic-tight structure. Facts can never penetrate it; they can only be arranged around it, in conformance to the basic structure:

England will never come to France's defence, because the English are a Teutonic race. But England does come to France's defence. Very well, this only shows how England is in the grip of Communists and Jewish bankers. When Germany wins a battle, it demonstrates that History is but an extension of Cosmic Evolution – that the Aryans are fitter to survive. When Germany loses a battle, it demonstrates the fanatic barbarity of the other side, driven by their slave masters: the commissar puppet-masters in the East, the degenerate aristocracy of England, or 'Rosenfeldt'.

The internal contradictions of such a model are apparent – to those who don't make use of it. On a test of anti-Semitic beliefs in the US,[12] the same people evidently strongly agreed with *all* of the following, obviously contradictory statements:

> One general fault of Jews is their overaggressiveness, a strong tendency to display their Jewish looks, manners and breeding.
>
> Jews go too far in hiding their Jewishness, especially such extremes as changing their names, straightening their noses, and imitating Christian manners and customs.

The Jews should give up their un-Christian religion with all its strange customs ... and participate actively and sincerely in the Christian religion.

The Jews should not pry so much into Christian activities and organizations nor seek so much recognition and prestige from Christians.[13]

In Britain at the moment, similar sentiments are being expressed concerning the Asians, who, on the one hand are castigated for not giving up their foreign diet, language and dress and 'trying to fit in with the British way of life'; and on the other hand are said to be scheming to take over Britishers' jobs, houses, social and health benefits, women. And here too, there are newspapers and politicians playing upon these irrational fears.

But the frightening aspect of propaganda is not the slanted news item, the scare headline or the ranting orator, but the strong appeal of such tricks to mental stereotypes of reality. Like it or not, we all have and use such stereotypes, and that means that we can all be moved by propaganda, insofar as we fail to recognize our own inner propaganda machines.

Rumour Analysis

J. P. Chaplin believes that rumours appeal to five kinds of basic needs:

1 Animal needs. People deprived of food, sleep, warmth, etc., begin to show psychotic behaviour. When deprivation is irritating but not extreme, they are inclined to either blame someone else for their condition, or to project their frustrated desires on to others. This famine story comes from Berlin, in 1946: A blind man with cane, dark glasses, etc., bumped into a woman on the street. She asked if she could help him, and he asked to be directed to the address on an envelope he carried. She explained that the place was some distance away, and finally agreed to deliver the letter for him. They parted.

She had gone twenty or thirty yards when she happened to glance back to see if the blind man was making out all right. He was indeed making out all right: he was walking rapidly along the sidewalk with his cane under his arm. There was no mistaking [his distinctive clothes]. Instead of delivering the letter, the woman took it to the police station and told how it had come into her possession. The police went to the apartment the envelope was addressed to and found there two men and a woman and a quantity of meat that, upon inspection, was declared by a doctor to be human flesh. The letter in the envelope consisted of a single statement: 'This is the last one I am sending you today.'[14]

2 The need for safety and security. Chaplin devotes an entire chapter to the Mattoon, Illinois 'Gasser' of 1944. The gasser seemed to be a fiend who liked to sneak up at night on some house where a woman was alone (there must have been many in that terrible year) and spray a sickening-smelling gas in through the window. The woman would begin fainting, vomiting, swelling about the lips, gasping for breath. Often someone would run after the gasser, but all they ever saw (in dozens of such attacks) was the occasional glimpse of a tall figure in a black skull-cap. Local and state police set trap after trap; the FBI looked in on the case, and the news went from local to national headlines. Every lead was investigated, every crank and chemist questioned. Finally the police announced that they considered it a wave of attacks, not of gas, but of hysteria. Then the attacks tapered off and vanished as mysteriously as they had come.

Two clues point to the action of hysteria and rumour: The victims' symptoms were characteristic of hysterical seizures, and, after the very first attack, the local paper printed this headline:

'ANAESTHETIC PROWLER' ON THE LOOSE
Mrs Corbin and Daughter First Victims

Chaplin comments:

Perhaps the editor was displaying unusual prescience, or he may have been guilty of wishful thinking.... After all, an 'anaesthetic prowler' can scarcely be expected to come the way of a city editor more than once in his journalistic career.[15]

3 The need to belong. The obvious factor in all racial, political and other 'Us-Them' rumours.

4 The need for power and prestige. The amateur detectives

who 'solved' the Kennedy murder (and earlier, the Lindbergh baby kidnapping) were out to beat the experts at their own game.

5 The need for self-expression. During the *War of the Worlds* rumour, many people really came to life for the first time. Some organized prayer meetings, some offered their services to the police for evacuation traffic control, some looted gun shops and barricaded themselves in their homes, preparing to make a last heroic stand.

Allport and Postman succeeded in creating controlled rumours for study, by showing one subject a picture (often one with emotional overtones), asking him to describe it unseen to a second person, asking that person to repeat the description to a third, and so on, up to around fifteen repetitions. The types of distortions the stories underwent bore a remarkable resemblance to the distortions of dreams and other fantasies. Sometimes a fact would be reversed (in one picture a white man holding a razor is talking to a black; in later versions they are arguing or even fighting, and it is the black man who has the razor). There were distortions of names, dates, numbers and time; elaboration (as in the 'bells of Antwerp' case); projection (as in the Berlin case); verbal misunderstandings (ditto); a shift of theme (as when 'San Francisco earthquake' is coupled to 'New York flood'); an economical and simplified explanation; changes of label and locale; levelling-out; closure; concretization and personalization; and other forms of dream work.

We've already seen this processing in earlier chapters. A man watching a bright planet setting on the horizon elaborates a vision of a spacecraft with flames and portholes. The story of a psychic sensitive's 'helping' the police undergoes distortions and accrues imaginary details in later versions. Faith healing cures of a questionable nature are completely refashioned by the press into dreams come true. Among the pseudo-archaeologists and others, scraps of story, unverified anecdotes and completely fictional items are picked up, traded, and reinterpreted; stories like Byland Abbey (page 56) and the Book of Dyzan (page 67) have become almost standard myths.

Before we look at this dream work, there remains one more class of myth to be examined: prophecies of the end of the world.

Jorge Luis Borges says of dreams:

> We see the image of a sphinx and the image of a drugstore,
> and then we invent a drugstore that is changed into a
> sphinx. We put the mouth of a face that looked at us the
> night before last on the man that we shall meet tomorrow.[1]

He is commenting upon J. W. Dunne's theory that dreams are
a kind of time-travel, but his remarks seem curiously applicable
to prophecies. By no coincidence, prophecy, that most familiar
form of time-travel, often reads like the transcription of a
dream.

A prophecy can only fail if it is specific and prosaic, like a
weather forecast. Most, on the contrary, are written in veiled
dream language; they are no more intelligible than the riddle
of the drugstore.

> Triumphant Death rides London through,
> And men on tops of houses go.

It has been suggested that this couplet of Mother Shipton's
refers to the Great Plague and Great Fire of London. In this
case, the dream work seems not to have been done by Goody
Shipton herself, but by someone who lived after the publication
of Pepys' Diary. But more ambiguous visions of the Great
Fire may be found in Nostradamus:

> The blood of the just will make a complaint to London,
> Burnt by lightning in twenty-three the sixes;
> The antique lady will fall from the high place,
> Of the same sect many will be destroyed.

The antique lady may be the spire of old St Paul's, an old

woman jumping from a burning roof, or both. Certainly few of any sect actually lost their lives in the Great Fire. Alas, Nostradamus' Great Fire seems to take place in 2366 AD, which can only be reconciled with reality by subtracting a magical 7 centuries. Like Mother Shipton's version, it seems intelligible only after the fact, if at all.

Mother Shipton (1488–1561)
On the cover of a pamphlet called *The Life and Prophecies of Ursula Sontheil, better known as MOTHER SHIPTON,*[2] is a drawing of the old hag herself, after an inn sign painted some two hundred years after her death. It shows her as a Hallowe'en witch: chin and nose meeting, a cloak over her hunchback, a broad-brimmed hat, besom and black cat. According to the pamphlet (written ca. 1900) she was born in 1488 at Dropping Well Estate, Knaresborough, Yorkshire, to an orphan girl who claimed the father was a handsome spirit. The mother was accused of witchcraft, but acquitted. Her ugly, deformed child was sent to school, learned to read and write, and soon acquired a reputation for casting spells.

At the age of twenty-four, Ursula married Toby Shipton and settled down to housework and fortune-telling. Her reputation grew, and she prophesied for the nobility. She died in 1561, having of course foreseen her death to the day and hour.

The predictions ascribed to Mother Shipton include Henry VIII's marriage to Anne Boleyn; the arrest of Cardinal Wolsey at York; the birth of Edward VI by caesarian delivery; the reign of Bloody Mary; the long reign of maiden Elizabeth; Drake's defeat of the Armada; the accession of James I; the Gunpowder Plot; the Civil War and death of Charles I by violence; the interregnum; the Restoration; Raleigh's introduction of the potato and tobacco into England; horseless carriages; men under water and in the air; iron boats; electric-speed communications; the steam engine; the Crystal Palace; war in Turkey; the end of the world in 1991.

Curiously, though her powers were highly esteemed during her lifetime and for some two or three centuries afterwards, there is no record of anyone's having believed in *and profited by* a single of these predictions. Having seen how successful she was with earlier predictions, it is almost unbelievable that anyone could have failed to see the significance of:

> And the Western monarch's wooden horses
> Shall be destroyed by Drake's forces,

least of all the Western monarch himself. That monarchs did pay considerable attention to soothsayers is evident from the pathetic story of Ursula's rival, the Nun of Kent.

Elizabeth Barton, a girl who lived near Canterbury, began falling into trances and uttering prophecies. Apparently she was used by the local convent, who made her a nun and then tried to convince the public that her prophecies were divinely inspired. She said that, if Henry VIII divorced Catherine of Aragon and married Anne Boleyn, he'd be dead within a month. The King came to have a talk with the girl, and took her prophecy seriously enough to have her executed for treason, along with her 'helpers'.

Mother Shipton's helper was her maid, who extorted large sums of money from callers in addition to the small sums the seer asked, and who was not above manufacturing a prophecy herself when Ursula baulked.

Many of her prophecies, like dreams, are less 'true' than capable of true interpretation:

> The world upside down shall be
> And gold found at the root of a tree.
> Through hills men shall ride
> And no horse or ass be by their side,
> Under water, men shall walk,
> Shall ride, shall sleep, and talk;
> In the air men shall be seen,
> In white, in black, and in green.

Others are unquestionably true:

> Eighteen hundred and thirty-five,
> Which of us shall be alive?
> Many a king shall end his reign
> Many a knave his end shall gain.

At any rate, some of her prophecies seem to have been so

adjustable as to keep believers at least hoping for confirmation:

> The world then to an end shall come
> In Nineteen Hundred and Ninety-one.

This particular prophecy used to read (at least in 1872, when Augustus de Morgan mentioned it) 'in *Eighteen* Hundred and *Eighty*-one'. If it keeps sliding to new dates, it has at least one chance in a hundred of perfectly predicting the end.

Nostradamus (1503–1566)

L. Sprague de Camp evidently performed an exhaustive analysis of Nostradamus's predictions. According to Bergen Evans, he found two reasons for non-amazement: First, there were twenty Nostradamuses in all, 'the name having become a generic term for prophet'. (Likewise, at the 1972 Epsom Derby, there appeared twenty fortune-tellers, each claiming to be 'the original Gipsy Lee'.)

Second, much of Nostradamus's stuff was too garbled to read as predictions, but of the 449 de Camp found, 18 have proved definitely false, 41 have been fulfilled (but many were worded so as to have an even chance of fulfilment), and 390

> cannot be identified with anything that has happened. They may be verified someday, but for the first three hundred years, Nostradamus's rate of success as a prophet is considerably below what he would have obtained by flipping a coin.[3]

Evans compares this kind of prophecy to that of business newsletters (like the market tips of Edward R. Dewey) which, analysis shows, are right less than half the time. For myself, I don't think coin-flipping analogies can really apply to Nostradamus's prophecies, if only because, out of 449 tosses, 390 times the coin seems to have rolled down a crack in the floor. In other words, it's too often impossible to tell whether a prediction has come true or not. Each age has seen its own face reflected in the dark mirror of these quatrains, and the same lines that 'foretold' the French Revolution later 'foretold' the Second World War. Ellic Howe[4] mentions one quatrain, 3.57, which kept on being interpreted and reinterpreted until it came partially true in 1939, when Germany invaded Poland and England went to war. Frau Dr Goebbels made much of it at the time, but only by ignoring other parts of the quatrain which were patently untrue.

Stewart Robb identifies the following quatrain with the Montgolfier balloon:

> Istra de mont Gaulfier et Aventin,
> Qui par le trou advertira l'armee.
> Entre deux rocs sera prins le butin,
> De Sext. mansol faillir la renommee.

> There will go from Mount Gaulfier and Aventine
> One who from the hole will warn the army.
> The booty will be taken from between two rocks,
> The renown of Sextus the corner-stone will fail.[5]

Robb finds it 'beyond the batting-average of chance' that this refers to the Montgolfier hot-air balloon, invented about 1785. Balloons have holes, they can be used for warning the army, and the 'Sext.' is said by Robb to refer to Pope Pius VI, who reigned in Montgolfier's day.

> And note this: from the time of the prophet [early 16th C.] until the present [1961] there has not been another Pope in the Holy Sea [sic] with that number attached to his name.[6]

Not until Pope Paul VI, anyway. Ultimately the clearness of this particular vision rests upon the equation

$$\text{mont Gaulfier} = \text{Montgolfier}$$

But there is no reason to suppose that the Montgolfier family name might not have come from the name of a mountain or place, which might also have been known to one of the Nostra-damuses. But to show how easy it is to link up such a prophecy to some chosen modern event, let us pretend that it refers to the US Open Golf Championship of 1927. Played at Oak-mont course, it was won by Oakmont golfer Tommy Armour, whose first and last names have both been connected with armies. His last name has six letters (to this day there has not been another six-letter champion at Oakmont). The warning from the *trou* can also mean 'from the mouth', namely 'Fore!' The booty (*butin*) is first prize, and 'one from the hole' could also mean a hole-in-one.

Hister

Since the 1930s, one great tradition in Nostradamus-reading has been equating his references to 'Hister' with Hitler. Robb is no exception, although he knows perfectly well that 'Hister' was the old name for the Danube river.

> Now *Hister* with one letter changed will give *Hitler*. The change of one letter was permissible in anagram writing.... What other word could serve better than *Hister* to specify both the name, and the place of origin of [Hitler]?[7]

The river of Hitler's origin was not the Danube, but the Inn. As for that remarkable anagram, the change of one letter can produce so many names from *Hister*. *Lister*, for instance, or even *Christ* (also born near an inn).

Here are the three quatrains referring to Hister. Make of them what you will:

Liberty will not be recovered,
A bold, black, base-born, iniquitous man will occupy it,
When the material of the bridge is completed,
The Republic of Venice will be annoyed by Hister.

In place quite near, but far from Venus,
The two greatest of Asia, and Africa
It will be said that they are from the Rhine and Hister,
Cries, tears at Malta, and Ligurian coast.

Animals fierce with hunger to swim rivers:
Greater part of the camp will be against Hister,
It will have the great man carried in an iron cage,
When the German child watches the Rhine.

Robb seems to ignore the way all three stubbornly keep talking about rivers: The first refers to Hitler's invasion of Bulgaria (probably a Robbian anagram from *Venice*); the second puzzles even him. But in the third (which does, at least, mention Germany) Robb brings all his crank scholarship to bear, and deduces that the 'great man' (Hitler) has been carried away in an 'iron cage' (submarine) to South America. As evidence, he quotes a pulp magazine article entitled 'Positive Proof Hitler in Argentina'.

Able Was I Ere I Saw Bale

Inevitably the Provençal seer has prophesied Napoleon.

> *Pau.nay.loron plus feu qu'a sang sera*
> *Laude nager, fuir grand aux surez,*
> *Les agassas entree refusera,*
> *Pampon Durance, les tiendra enserrez.*

Pau.nay.loron will be more fire than blood,
To swim in praise, the great one to flee on the confluence of waters,
He will refuse the agassas entry,
Great bridge Durance he will hold them imprisoned.

Again, the main strength of Robb's interpretation is an anagram with letters removed.

> Pau.nay.loron (note the periods) is an anagram. Separate from it *roy*, which leaves Pau.na.lon, then reverse, and you have
>
> Na.pau.lon
>
> ... the odds against such a possibility are practically incalculable. The reader may judge of this for himself by experiment. Let him take down a book from his shelf, open it at the beginning, pencil mark off the text into groups of eleven letters apiece, and continue doing so till he finds a combination re-arrangeable to Napaulon roy.[8]

The invitation being too 'paulite' to decline, I took down Isaac D'Israeli's *Curiosities of Literature*. On page 1, line 15 were the words 'perennial repositories'. I pencilled off the 11 letters 'ennial repos'. From this I removed *res* (which represents the Republic as *roy* represents the King), leaving:

                nnial epo
      Anagram: Napolien.

Other Uses of Nostradamus
During the Second World War, a few more 'Hister' quatrains
turned up in Germany, including:

> Hister, who in his warlike struggles
> Has borne more victories than was good for him;
> Six will murder him in the night,
> Naked, without armour, he will succumb.[9]

These were collected in a booklet entitled *Nostradamus pro-
phezeit den Kriegsverlauf* (Nostradamus prophesies the course
of the war). It was a fake, produced by British Intelligence and
smuggled into Germany in hopes of shaking the people's faith
in their leader. Earlier (1939) German Intelligence had tried
a similar trick on the French.

> There were the Germans industriously planning to under-
> mine French morale with material culled from [Nostra-
> damus], while the French authorities, on their side, were
> subsequently busy banning Nostradamania in order not to
> give offence to the Occupying Power.[10]

Similarly the Allies and Axis planned great occult propaganda
campaigns against each other, each side being under the impression that the other was likely, as Goebbels said, to 'fall
easily for that type of thing'.

But it is not until we look at Stewart Robb's commentary
on Nostradamus that we find someone wholly committed to
'that type of thing'. A quatrain on the millennium:

> A great king of terror will descend from the skies,
> The year 1999, seventh month,
> To resuscitate the great king of Angolmois,
> Around this time Mars will reign for the good cause.

Robb feels this may refer to an invasion from Mars in 1999,
and he links it to a Great Pyramid prophecy setting the end

of the world in 2000 or 2001. Other predictions for the future
include: An Anglo-American federation; Anthony Eden's
return to the office of Prime Minister; 'a world of increasing
Moslem might'; the Golden Age, beginning about 1963; Armageddon, in 1973 (for twenty-four years); a thousand years of
peace.

Robb of course believes the Anglo-Saxon-Celtic peoples to
be the Lost Tribes of Israel. The Great Seal of the United
States, he notes, has a star of David; the British coat-of-arms,
a harp of David. The jacket of Robb's book describes him as
a 'noted scholar on the Bacon-Shakespeare controversy' and a
lecturer on psychic phenomena. It should be clear, therefore,
whence come the cryptic revelations, the half-predictions badly
sewn to half-facts, misshapen creatures lurching out of the
mists of Nostradamus's prose.

Later Prophets
The turbulent times of the late eighteenth century seemed to
turn up quite a few amazing prophets. Richard Brothers (1757-
1824), founder of the Anglo-Israel movement, wrote a sensational letter to George III asking him to hand over his crown
and acknowledge Brothers as world leader. He signed it
'Richard Brothers, Nephew of God'.

After Brothers had prophesied accurately the violent deaths
of the kings of France and Sweden, he was locked away in a
lunatic asylum before he could pay George the same com-
pliment. Oddly enough, he had by this time a powerful friend
in Nathaniel B. Halhed, MP, who obtained his release. Halhed
later lost interest in God's nephew and went over to the movement of Joanna Southcott. The Anglo-Israelites marched on
for many years, however, perhaps now and then singing their
leader's hymn to himself, which begins:

> Jerusalem! Jerusalem! shall be built again!
> More rich, more grand than ever;
> And through it shall Jordan flow![!]
> My people's favourite river.

Joanna Southcott began to prophesy in 1792, at the age of
forty-two. Evidently she was correct in predicting the Spanish
Revolution of 1820, and the fall of other monarchs. In those

frightening and exhilarating days, it was fairly safe to predict a revolution anywhere.

Her forecast that the Messiah would land in England found great favour with Anglo-Israelites (and still does). At Joanna's death in 1814, some of her writings were sealed up in a box, to be opened only by the convened bishops of the Church of England, in public and 'in time of national danger'. The Panacea Society is still trying to get the bishops to comply. One of their pamphlets also promises

> Slow but Sure Deliverance ... from Nerves, Rheumatism, Eye, Ear and Throat Troubles, Mental Anxiety, Business Worries, Faults of Disposition, and in the Tribulations and Perplexity that will precede the Coming of the Lord.[11]

The society has crossed out from this list 'Consumption, Epilepsy, Paralysis'.

Before the seals on Joanna's box were cold, American prophets were setting up in business. Lady Hester Stanhope, a niece of William Pitt, calculated that the Second Coming was less than a horselife away; she kept two Arabian stallions at her Pennsylvania home (one for her and one for the Saviour). Harriet Livermore addressed Congress four times, urging them to transport the Indians, who were the Lost Tribes, to Jerusalem before it was too late. In 1831 William Miller, an ex-soldier, reluctantly allowed God to talk him into preaching Apocalypse.

The End would come in 1833. This Miller had calculated, by five different formulas, from the books of Daniel and Revelations. There would be signs in the heavens and the earth would open to give up its dead. This would certainly take place by 1834, at the latest.

1833 passed, with a spectacular meteor shower (the Leonids). 1834 passed. Miller recalculated, setting the new Second Coming for April 1843. That Spring, a huge comet appeared, so brilliant that it could be seen in broad daylight. The latest possible date, Miller assured his (by now fifty thousand) converts, was 21 March 1844. He preached to hundreds of camp meetings, and established a Tabernacle in Boston. (A cruel rumour had it that the Tabernacle was insured for seven years.) As the *final* final date approached, Millerites neglected their farms, sold houses and goods, and made themselves lovely Ascension robes.

When the appointed hour had passed without any signs in the heavens other than a few pranksters' fireworks, the Millerites split into several groups. Miller's own group became the Seventh Day Adventists.[12]

Prophetic cults like the Millerites are still very much with us. An inside look at one such is given in *When Prophecy Fails*.[13] It is written by three social psychologists who infiltrated observers into the group to study it before, during, and after the Day of Wrath.

They describe how the leader, Mrs 'Marian Keech' (all names in the book have been disguised) earlier dabbled in dianetics and the occult I AM movement. She developed an interest in flying saucers in the early 1950s, and at last began receiving messages, by automatic writing, from inhabitants of the planet Clarion. Gradually she attracted a small group, including a physician and his wife, who felt there might be some connection between saucers and the rising of Atlantis and Mu, with the simultaneous sinking of North America. As the group grew, it became clear that they held other strong beliefs, such as reincarnation (Mrs Keech had been the Virgin Mary); their central belief, however, was millennarian: The world would be flooded on 21 December 195–, and flying saucers would rescue the elect at the last moment.

Similarly the Aetherius Society claims communication with the 'cosmic masters' (who really control our planet) through the brain of their leader, Dr George King. The cosmic masters recently planned a series of earthquakes, designed to knock the earth several degrees off its axis of spin, but Dr King managed to talk them out of it. Thus California has 'miraculously escaped seeming catastrophe', but King cannot promise to hold off the wrath of the CMs for much longer, unless the US stops its nuclear tests and moonwalks. In this case, it would seem as though the cosmic masters had been reading up on the San Andreas fault, which is expected by earthly geologists to generate earthquakes before long.

Herbert W. Armstrong, who publishes the fundamentalist *The Plain Truth*, finds his best prophecies in the Bible, especially in the words of Christ ('the world's greatest NEWS-CASTER'). The Good Book seems to give him details of a coming world government, even the names of its leaders. It will begin with the Common Market, perhaps joined by the United States, since

the United States, the British Commonwealth and some of the countries of Northwestern Europe are indeed the descendants of the lost tribes of Israel.[14]

The Common Market seems to be the Beast of Revelations. Armstrong's other articles favour questioning titles, the answers to which can be given in a word or two: 'Where Will the Millennium Be Spent?' (Here on earth); 'Is This the Time of THE END?' (Yes); 'Century 21 – What Will It Be Like?' (An earthly paradise for Herbert W. and friends.)

Many fundamentalist sects have leaned towards socialism and William Jennings Bryan populism, but Armstrong's group (Herbert W. is an ex-advertising executive) have a strong capitalist bias. Tithing is frequently mentioned as a way to earthly wealth; members are addressed as 'co-worker'; and one article emphasizes that Christ owned his home, paid his taxes, obeyed the law and, especially, *wore his hair short*.

One of Armstrong's prized discoveries is the '19-year time cycle'.

We started on the air on the little station in Eugene, Oregon the first Sunday in January 1934. That first Sunday was January 7.

The number of stations they were using multiplied, until by the 1950s they planned to broadcast to Europe. The first broadcast took place on Wednesday, 7 January 1953,

on the exact SAME DATE – 19 years TO THE VERY DAY! That seemed SIGNIFICANT, to say the least![15]

The significance of it is the astronomical Metonic cycle: every nineteen years the phases of the moon coincide with the calendar date. This message from the Mover of the sun and the moon was too plain to ignore. Armstrong and co-workers looked forward to 7 January 1972, the completion of the next cycle. The first had enabled their message to be brought to the Lost Tribes of America; the second, to the Lost Tribes of

Europe. Would the third mean the completion of the harvest?

The article from which I'm quoting is an explanation, after 7 January 1972, of why nothing happened (except that the group took an ad in *Reader's Digest*). Herbert W. explains that, first, he'd never *positively* said that the world would end; and second, 'Moses made mistakes, Abraham made mistakes, David made mistakes, Elijah made mistakes ...'[16] The messianic tone should leave little doubt as to how Armstrong sees himself: 'I am reminded of the time Jesus was criticized, persecuted, misrepresented by His enemies.'[17]

There is of course nothing especially significant about the Metonic cycle; it is one of many possibilities (the Leap Year cycle; the *Saros*, or eclipse cycle; numerous planetary and cometary cycles, etc.). Armstrong could likewise have fixed on any number of important Biblical durations, and he could have matched any of these with any of the important dates in the history of his magazine-radio-television work.

But, having settled for the 19-year cycle, Armstrong began finding it in the Bible. Jeremiah spent 19 years preaching before Nebuchadnezzar beseiged Jerusalem and 19 years preaching after it (a finding unconfirmed by any other Bible historian). In the prophet's third cycle of 19 years, says Herbert W., he migrated to North Ireland with one of King Zedekiah's daughters, and there founded the Irish race.

Another great reader of the Bible for hidden messages was Charles Manson, but this was only part of his complex of occult beliefs. Manson's hate-fear-death commune has been well documented by Ed Sanders;[18] their religion seems to be a collage of myths derived from Scientology, the Process, the Solar Lodge of the O.·.T.·.O, Beatlemania and elsewhere.

Manson had studied Scientology in prison, and continued to use Hubbard jargon: 'mocking up', 'cease to exist', 'to come to now' and 'putting up pictures'. The Process (The Process Church of the Final Judgement) may have given him ideas through their books (*Satan on War*, *Jehovah on War* and *Lucifer on War*) and magazine issues devoted to *Death* and *Fear*. The leader of this cult claims to be a reincarnation of Christ (so did Manson), his wife claims to be reincarnate of Hecate and Goebbels. Their followers run around in black capes (so did Manson's) and they, too, seem to have borrowed from Scientology.

The Solar Lodge of the O∴T∴O (Ordo Templi Orientalis) was another desert commune, Crowleyites who

> would hold magic meetings where they would try to summon and radiate hate-vibrations into the Watts ghetto in order to start riots. The Solar Lodge believed that a heavy race war ... was imminent.[19]

They drank animal blood, tortured one of their children (see page 337) and hated Negroes. Manson's bunch hated Negroes, drank animal blood, and believed in a race Armageddon in 1969. Both groups worked on converts by

> tearing down the mind through pain, persuasion, drugs and repetitive weirdness – just like a magnet erases recording tape – and rebuilding the mind according to the desires of the cult.[20]

Manson believed in an underground paradise, into which he meant his group to flee when they had touched off the race Armageddon by committing murders they hoped would be blamed on Negroes. This interior land would be entered by means of The Hole, an idea borrowed from Hopi legends, which Manson believed to be somewhere in the desert near his camp. The Family would be lowered into it by means of a golden rope. (To pay for the rope, Manson put three of his girls on the streets in Los Angeles.)

He also began reading messages into Beatles' songs. When their white album came out, he saw it as a personal warning to him of the coming war between white and black. The four Beatles were the four angels of the Apocalypse. Negroes would win the final war, but then Manson would return to earth from The Hole and take power. 'Rocky Racoon' and 'Blackbird' were seen as clear racial references, 'Helter-Skelter' was Armageddon, 'Revolution 9' could only refer to Chapter IX of Revelations, and 'Happiness is a Warm Gun' was taken literally. The song 'Piggies' seems to have actually inspired one of his sect's murders, of a plump middle-aged couple with a carving knife and fork. It seems that not all madmen are holy.

The occult believer or pseudo-scientist often asks his antagonist, 'What would convince you, anyway? How much evidence does it take to prove that UFOs land/ghosts walk/dowsers find water/etc.?' The question is beside the point, for the two factions can never agree on a definition of 'evidence'. There is ample evidence (of a kind) that the sun is a flaming chariot driven across the sky.

In order to arrive at the scientific and the magical definitions of evidence, it's necessary to sketch answers to two questions: How do we use our senses to collect evidence? Why do we believe in what we have collected?

Seeing
Everyone probably hears unidentifiable creaks in the night, sees faces in clouds, or dreams events that can't possibly happen in waking life. Vision (or any of the other senses) is dazzled by simple illusions. From such occurrences, some philosophers were led to conclude that we never really perceive anything at all.

Their argument is that a man cannot see a red table; he only sees the 'appearances' (or 'accidents' or 'sense-data') of a red table. He could be looking at a stereoscopic slide, for example, or at a white table under red light, or at an hallucination.

The usual answer to this is that of course our senses fool us, *but we can only know this through the use of our senses.* A man can test a table's solidity by knocking on it or lifting it; he can test its redness by looking at it in daylight, and so on. Even if he feels that the table is a private hallucination, he can ask others to look at it. We know that there are *some* illusions because we know that there are some genuine perceptions.

One fact, an obvious one, ought to make this clear: Those who cannot use a sense properly cannot experience all sensory illusions. For most of us, a grey area placed next to a red area looks greenish; next to a green area, the same grey looks reddish. For someone with red/green colour blindness this clearly cannot apply. And although vivid visual pictures can be produced as hallucinations in most people – through drugs, extreme pain, isolation or direct electrical stimulation of the brain – they do not occur in people blind from birth.

But even the possession of the equipment for seeing does not automatically guarantee sight. People blind from birth, when an operation suddenly makes it possible for them to see, simply can't. They must still discover objects by touch. The world for them is not as we experience it, but a confusion of colours, shapes and movements without meaning.

Gradually they learn to sort out some of it, but many important factors, such as depth, can remain mysterious for a longer time. R. L. Gregory[1] relates how one such man thought that he could safely lower himself from his hospital window and touch the ground, which was some thirty feet below. Another experiment has shown that babies at the crawling stage have already acquired this kind of depth perception,[2] indicating that it is something that must be learned or developed.

This same man drew pictures of double-decker buses at various times up to a year after his operation. Each showed many new details, but even the last picture lacked a front to the bus. The man simply could not visualize the front of a bus, any more than Dr Watson could visualize, at Sherlock Holmes's request, the number of steps leading to his own rooms.

Seeing seems to be a filtering process. We see the name on a street sign without making a mental note of the style of lettering; we glance at a clock without caring if it has roman or arabic numerals or blobs. Watson no doubt filtered out the, for him, trivial 'observation' of the number of steps. This filtering process seems to apply to hearing also. Colin Cherry[3] speaks of the 'cocktail party problem': How is it that, with a jumble of different voices rattling on in the same room, a person is able to pick out one conversation to listen to? He suggests that a person uses three kinds of filters:

1 Separating voices (by accent, speed, pitch).

2 Identifying what the desired speech is about, and then listening for key phrases, jargon, special syntax, etc. (e.g., a person may prick up his ears at the line 'Have you heard the

one about ... ?' or he may edge away and tune to another conversation).

3 Filling in details not actually· heard – parts of words or even whole phrases. An exmpl mght b wrttn lk ths & stll rmn prfctly intllgbl. Wha★ w★ hea★, se★ & rea★ mus★ depen★ t★ som★ exten★ o★ pas★ experienc★.

If seeing is therefore a filtering process, it must be learned. One's past visual experience determines what one sees. One man. sees a red rose. A horticulturist sees that it is 'really' a Fotheringale's Glory. An artist notices that it isn't red, but a, complex pattern of colours from dark purple to pale pink. Each man's experience has enabled him to build up a different set of categories, making up a different mental model (rose; type of rose; composition) with which he compares the reality.

We all use many types of mental models in this way. They inform our vision that railroad tracks don't actually meet at the horizon; that a man six feet tall doesn't shrink to a midget as he walks into the distance; that shadows fall away from a source of light. (which is usually above. the lighted object); that when an object moves out of sight, behind something else, it doesn't leave the universe; that the nearest corner of a cube looks like this $\updownarrow$ while the farthest corner of a room looks like this $\curlyvee$; that if. the nearest of a row of similar objects is a tree, we can assume that the farthest is also equipped with leaves and branches.

Optical illusions and visual paradoxes exploit the expectations built into these visual models. Our experience tells us that neither of the 'impossible' objects in Figure 26–1 can

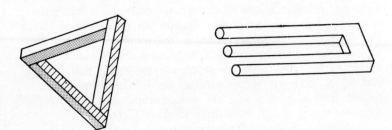

Fig. 26–1   Two 'impossible' figures

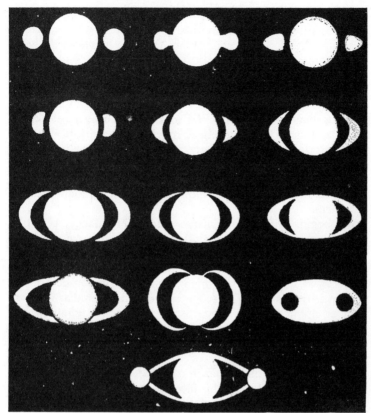

Fig. 26-2 Huygens's drawing of Saturn (Source: R. L.
Gregory, *The Intelligent Eye* (4))

be real.* The first can't be resolved in terms of what we know
about perspective. If you cover any vertex of the triangle, the
other two make sense, but the three are incongruous. Likewise
the second figure makes sense if you cover either end of it.

Whenever we run across a new sight, we try to 'explain' it
in terms of what we know about the visual world – to incor-
porate it into our model. When the astronomer Christiaan

---

* But both can actually be built. The first can be made from
three solid wooden beams (see R. L. Gregory, *The Intelligent Eye*,
pp. 54-7) and the second can be constructed of plastic or glass,
provided that it can be enclosed in a glass box.

Huygens first laid eye on the planet Saturn, he was expecting to see a sphere. Figure 26-2 shows the best he could do with his first glimpse of Saturn and its rings.[4]

After the fact, it's easy to see where Huygens went wrong. But if Saturn had exploded immediately he'd made his drawings, we might be stuck with supposing that it was a sphere with jug handles. Similarly, if I look up at an overcast sky at night, and see a glowing ellipse moving about erratically, my later description of it is likely to depend on whether I expected to see a UFO or a searchlight beam playing upon clouds. It is significant that, in the years when a great many people looked at the sky expecting UFOs, a great many people saw them.

We begin building our visual models in infancy, possibly with faces. One experiment[5] demonstrated that very young babies gaze for longer times at mock faces with properly disposed features, than at similar dummies with the features scattered at random. That this strong model never deserts us is shown by our ability to see faces (and other familiar objects, such as animals, human figures, even assassins gunning for Kennedy) in foliage, clouds or glowing coals. This ability is considerably improved by hallucinogens, again indicating that it is a brain mechanism.

A book by Johann Plesch, mentioned by E. H. Gombrich[6] gives an unusual effect of this face-seeing ability. Plesch peered into the rough brushwork of Rembrandt's paintings and saw 'farmyard animals and grinning faces' upside down in the shadows and folds of garments, which he calls 'Rembrandts within Rembrandts'.

Gregory shows the use we make of this ability, by means of a real object camouflaged by dappled shadow. As you look into the spots, one blob which might be a penguin's bill becomes a dog's ear. Then a nearby crescent becomes a collar, and suddenly the entire dalmatian fills out – though its outline is almost totally invisible. 'We can clearly distinguish the spots making up the dog from similar spots of the background,' says Gregory. 'To make this possible there must be stored information in the brain, of dogs and thousands of other objects.'[7] Gombrich calls the game we play ('penguin bill – no, dog ear') applying a 'test of consistency – the possibility of classifying the whole of an image within a possible range of experience.'[8]

That these tests can lead to false conclusions is evident from any of life's surprises. Almost everyone has had the experience of calling out to a friend in a crowd, only to have the friend turn around and show a stranger's face. When I went from Austria to Italy, I retained a false linguistic model that no longer applied: In Austria faucets are marked *Heiss* (hot) and *Kalt* (cold). In Italy I turned a faucet marked *Caldo*, foolishly expecting cold water.

Less trivial problems beset every translator, and indeed, every user of language. If *index→indices*, why doesn't *kleenex →kleenices*? We seem to learn to use language much as we learn to see objects, so that the paradoxical readings of a sentence like 'What upset Bill was looking at Mary' are not unlike those of Figures 26–1. These can only be resolved by further tests of consistency – the sentence can be read in context to see if Bill or some thing was looking at Mary; objects could be viewed from another angle.

If we see a face in the clouds, we look around for its hair, neck, ears, etc. Not finding them, we can safely conclude that the cloud is not intended to be a sculpture. On the other hand, if we see the cloud letters D-R-I, soon followed by N-K P-E-P-S-I, we are justified in seeing it as human intelligence at work. The failure to apply such tests of consistency, or the application of the wrong tests, has given us most of our Bacon ciphers, coded messages in pulsars, prophecies from the Bible, and certainly lawnmower parts identified as flying saucer litter.

Believing

The sceptic can argue that, no matter how many apples he sees falling, the next apple could remain suspended in mid-air, and gravity is therefore an unprovable assumption. But the naïve realist, advocating 'common sense', sees no reason to fool around with laws at all: Apples just fall because they fall, period. The sceptic has all the logic on his side, but no empirical handle with which to grasp reality. His judgement about any fact must remain forever suspended (like his hypothetical apple. The naïve realist has plenty of empirical handles, but no logical leverage. It couldn't possibly occur to him to get an apple by shaking the tree, since that would involve cause-and-effect logic. The sceptic wouldn't shake the tree either, because it might not work.

If there ever were any real-life sceptics or naïve realists, they've probably starved to death; most people, including mystics and scientists, are far from either extreme. Yet, if a scientist should subject an occult belief to a critical examination, he is almost sure to be accused of 'scepticism', by believers.

Scientists cannot be sceptics, of course. They must take the same risk in believing in their theories that occultists take. They too go out on limbs frequently, and the limbs are frequently sawn off.

The difference between a scientific theory and an occult belief lies in testing. Consider the following statements:

1   The moon orbits the earth.
2   The moon is made of green cheese.
3   The moon has a melancholy soul.

Nos 1 and 2 are scientific theories, but No. 3 is something else. We know how to test the first two, but no imaginable test could show us whether or not the moon had a melancholy soul.

Scientific theories may be tested in four ways: [9]

1   *Do the theory's various conclusions contradict one another?* If someone watching cars pass decides that every second car will be a Ford, and every third car a Volkswagen, it's easy to see that his theory will fail for the sixth car that passes him. So it is with occultists who offer what they call 'explanations of the unexplainable'. So it was when Wilbur Voliva (See page 19) changed the subject.

2   *Is the theory logically meaningful?* That ESP exists, but cannot be tested (because it vanishes just when we seriously look for it) is one of the 'less meaningful' type, and representative of a genre of occult theories. UFO occupants, according to Keel, are actively working to prevent our knowing of their existence. Past civilizations have 'repressed' the memory of Velikovsky's comet collision. Yeti and Loch Nessie are shy to the point of invisibility. Clarion keeps just out of sight behind the sun. The theories always involve explanations of why evidence is not forthcoming to support the theories.

3   *Does the new theory compare favourably with existing theories in explaining facts?* The theory that planets run on railroad tracks goes some way towards explaining their regular movements. That light *comes out of the eye* fits many optical laws perfectly. That germs are the product, not cause, of

disease would explain their simultaneity. Yet, compared with conventional theories, each of these leaves much unexplained. (How can railed planets perturb each other's orbits? How does an image get into the eye? How does disease spread?)

4 *Could the new theory's conclusions be disproved?* It's essential for a scientific theory to be, at least in principle, *disprovable*. The Egyptian priest who perhaps believed that his prayers made the sun rise could have tested his theory only one way – by not praying. The most prominent feature of good scientific theories is that they openly risk testing and disproof. On the other hand, occult and pseudo-scientific theories seldom take this risk. The theory that there is a ghost in Borley Rectory could never be disproved, even if every single ghostly effect were explained as natural. It cannot be shown how Borley Rectory would be any different if its ghosts took a short leave of absence.

Science is not, as people often imagine, a heaping-up of facts or observations. It is the making and testing of theories. In this it resembles seeing, as the following experiment, reported by Thomas S. Kuhn, shows:

Pictures of playing cards were flashed on a screen for brief controlled periods, and subjects were asked to identify them. Among the normal cards were a few anomalies, such as a red six of spades or a black four of hearts. When the exposure was very short, subjects unhesitatingly identified all cards including the anomalies, as normal cards. But when forced to look at them for longer periods, subjects became increasingly confused.

Exposed, for example, to the red six of spades, some would say: That's the six of spades, but there's something wrong with it – the black has a red border.[10]

Longer exposures increased their confusion until, suddenly, they saw the anomaly for what it was. Once they had identified one anomaly, they had no trouble with the others.

A few subjects, however, were never able to make the requisite adjustment of their categories.... And the subjects who then failed often experienced acute personal distress. One of them exclaimed: 'I can't make the suit out, whatever it is. I don't know what colour it is now or whether it's a

spade or a heart. I'm not even sure now what a spade looks
like. My God!'[11]

'Impossible objects' again. Kuhn sees an analogy between this
behaviour and the making of (or failure to make) scientific
discoveries. The scientist begins by trying to apply his experience to a new situation. When his mental model fails to fit
the new situation, he must either give up or adjust the model
and try again. Roentgen's discovery of X-rays began when he
noticed an accidental effect from a cathode-tube experiment.
He did not simply shout 'Eureka! The X-ray'; he began a
series of experiments, during which he was forced to change
many of his notions about radiation. His noticing the glowing
screen effect did not automatically guarantee the discovery, for
others had already noticed it. Rather, his discovery may be
seen as a thorough criticism of his own mental model, leading
to an entirely new model in which radiation could be invisible,
yet still subject to many optical laws.

Contrast this with ghostly investigations. Occultists' discoveries are always Eurekas, confirmations of the beliefs
they've held all along. These firm believers seldom allow their
theories to be criticized or their arguments tentative. No
Theosophist is on record as having disagreed with Madame
Blavatsky on the number of Root Races. Researchers like
Michel Gauquelin, who question some of the tenets of astrology, are forced to work entirely outside that field. Where such
enormous pressures to conform exist, objectivity and discovery
are unlikely to arise.

There are conformist pressures in science, too. Kuhn points
out that science advances not by a progressive accumulation
of discoveries, nor by the complete overthrow of previous
theories (e.g., Einstein has not 'done away with' Newton's
ideas, but subsumed them) but by trying to fit new discoveries
into the existing framework. Arthur Koestler calls this conservatism 'saving the appearances'. Briefly it means not changing a mental model more than absolutely necessary in order to
accommodate some new experience.

This again seems analogous to our perceptual and linguistic
behaviour. Psychologists have found that subjects reading
print that is upside-down, mirrored, or put through some other
bizarre transformation, tend to make certain kinds of mistakes.

About 82 per cent of the errors were substitutions of a recognizable English word for what was actually printed ... in misreading a word the students usually substituted for it a word of approximately the same length.... When the students misread a noun, they tended to substitute a noun; a misread verb was supplanted by a verb, and so on.[12]

This suggests that readers generate a model for the sentence they are reading, and test hypothetical words against this model. It further suggests a tendency to preserve the model, or 'save the appearances'; presumably subjects would have great difficulty in mirror-reading unconventional prose, or poetry.

Koestler rails at scientists for not accepting the reality of UFO phenomena. They are, he says, behaving exactly like former scientists who refused to accept that Jupiter has moons, or that stones fall from the sky. Yet these seem to be typical human reactions to novel situations on many levels.

In occult science it's easy enough to see 'saving the appearances' at work. Gustav Jahoda[13] describes several demonstrations where mental models seem to have dominated the beliefs of people in seance conditions. In one experiment a psychologist 'produced' writing on one of two slates through an ordinary conjuring trick. Most of the audience were afterwards convinced that both slates had first been passed around for inspection. In fact, only one slate had been passed around. In another experiment

subjects were asked to select a line in a book unknown to Lehman [the psychologist] who had arranged to have an unintelligible scribble appear on the blackboard. When this was suddenly presented, some of the subjects were astonished to 'read' what they thought was the correct answer.[14]

Jahoda also mentions the 'investigations' of Borley Rectory's presumed paranormal phenomena by a league of credulous volunteers led by Harry Price. Price more or less set up their expectations by giving them a printed history of the Rectory's hauntings and a list of sights and sounds to watch for. This document appeared under an impressive letterhead mentioning the University of London, but not naming its author (Harry

Price). Jahoda says that the group found ample evidence for the supernatural in the waving of a window blind before an open window, in pencil scribblings on a wall, in an old coat hanging behind a door, and in the discovery that possibly a coal sack in the cellar had been moved. The manner in which the 'investigations' were conducted made it possible for misreadings of these events to occur, and the volunteer force, primed to see ghosts, saw them.

Once, Jahoda and a few friends held their own table-rapping session, the spirits being asked to rap once for yes, twice for no.

> The first question was asked, but nothing happened. We sat for several minutes in the semidarkness, with tension rising. Getting rather stiff, I shifted in my chair, accidentally knocking the table, and was staggered to find that this was taken as the expected answer.[15]

He couldn't resist carrying on the deception for half an hour. Before he could explain things, someone asked the spirit to materialize. It duly appeared to one observer, quickly seconded by two others. Jahoda could see nothing but a shadow, but others were firmly convinced, one so firmly that, when Jahoda tried to explain the trick to him later, he refused to believe him.

This particular man claimed that, prior to that seance, he'd been sceptical about the supernatural. Converts do frequently become as fanatical in their new faith as they were in their old unbelief. Hitler tried to become a Communist; 'queerbashers' are latent homosexuals; Henry VIII was ruthless against Roman Catholics as soon as he stopped being one; and every Saul seems to be a potential Paul.

Conversion

An interesting analysis of the fanatic (of whatever faith or ideology) is given in Eric Hoffer's *The True Believer*.[16] Perhaps it can shed little light on the conversion of the above sceptic, but it does seem to show the psychological and sociological background of many, as he calls them, 'potential converts' including:

1 The poor, especially those who have come down in the world recently, or up from recent slavery, as well as the abject poor, those whose creative abilities are frustrated by poverty, and those who belong to no cohesive religion, clan or tribe.

2 The social misfits who, for one reason or another, find themselves in an alien, hostile world.

3 The inordinately selfish.

4 The ambitious facing unlimited opportunities. 'The attitude is: "All that I am doing or possibly can do is chicken feed compared with what is left undone." '[17] Thus adolescents.

5 Minorities.

6 The bored.

Boredom accounts for the almost invariable presence of spinsters and middle-aged women at the birth of mass movements. Even in the case of Islam and the Nazi movement, which frowned upon feminine activity outside the home, we find women of a certain type playing an important role in the early stages of their development.[18]

7 The sinners.

Self-surrender, which is ... the source of a mass movement's unity and vigour, is a sacrifice, an act of atonement, and clearly no atonement is called for unless there is a poignant sense of sin.[19]

Of conversion, Hoffer says:

The fanatic cannot be weaned away from his cause by an appeal to his reason or moral sense. He fears compromise and cannot be persuaded to qualify the certitude and righteousness of his holy cause. But he finds no difficulty in swinging suddenly and wildly from one holy cause to another. *He cannot be convinced but only converted.*[20] (My italics.)

Similarly believers in one supernatural may earlier or later be the promoters of another. But has the occult believer anything else in common with the ideological fanatic?

They may indeed be the same person. In a study previously cited,[21] potential fascists, who showed strong authoritarian beliefs, ultrapatriotism and race prejudice, also showed a tendency to agree with statements like these:

Science has its place, but there are many important things that can never be understood by the human mind.

Every person should have a complete faith in some supernatural power whose decisions he obeys without question.
Some people are born with an urge to jump from high
places.
Some day it will probably be shown that astrology can
explain a lot of things.
Wars and social troubles may someday be ended by an
earthquake or flood that will destroy the world.[22]

Conversion to occult beliefs may depend upon social, as well
as internal, pressures. A few of these might be: the possession
by the group of a coherent, apparently consistent doctrine
explaining some urgent problem (life after death, reading
thoughts, finding gold); prestige attached to a group or its
leader; the handing over of responsibility, hence guilt, to a
higher power; the ability of the individual to use his creative
potential in an effective and socially rewarding way (the frustrated physicist, cosmologist, mathematician, composer, psychologist, poet and painter can be clearly recognized in (respec-
tively) Reich, Velikovsky, Vincent Lopez, Rosemary Brown, Dr
Rhine, Madame Blavatsky, and Johann Plesch).

In that they pursue a social activity, scientists too are subject
to many social pressures. Science is, as its accusers say, an
orthodoxy, with its own party line, popular opinions and forms
of social brain-washing. In this it resembles almost every other
human group activity, and it is a mistake for scientists to
pretend that, because their *methods* are objective, their *profession* is free from human frailty. This pretence must leave
them open to the criticisms of Theodore Roszak, who calls
attention to the 'myth of objective consciousness' and the
'arrogance' of scientists.

Such criticisms can range into psychology (science neglects
the soul); into space research (millions starve while astronauts
picnic on the moon); into nuclear physics (real Armageddon
becomes a possibility) and so on. But they must be seen as
legitimate efforts to steer science away from vain dreams of
universe-conquest and a crimeless Vacutopia, towards less
hypocritical, more humane goals; not as attempts to destroy
science. I am afraid that anti-scientists will seize these criticisms
eagerly, and apply them with the discrimination of Luddite
axes.

Appendix

Theodore Roszak finishes a brilliant attack on the smug 'objectivity' of the technocrats by, unfortunately, descending to a tabloid level, with disclosures of wicked experiments. He gives as examples of the scientists' Frankensteinism items like these:

1 An 1874 experiment in which painful electrical currents were passed through the brain of a perhaps feeble-minded woman.

2 A World War II test of poison gas, where

> The experimenter has forced a large dose of Lewisite gas into the eye of a rabbit and is recording over the next two weeks precisely how the animal's eye rots away.[1]

Horrible, inhumane ... adjectives fail us in trying to comprehend this kind of brutality. Roszak ascribes it to the takeover of objective consciousness:

> Science deracinates the experience of sacredness wherever it abides, and does so unapologetically, if not with fanatic fervour. And lacking a warm and lively sense of the sacred, there can be no ethical commitment that is anything more than superficial humanist rhetoric.[2]

Very well then, let us descend to the same level, and see what the occult has to offer. The Solar Lodge of the O∴T∴O, mentioned earlier, operated a desert commune where the experience of sacredness never ran dry. Holy it must have been to behold their collection of the magical apparatus of Aleister Crowley, obtained at great expense and venerated as relics of the Master. In June, 1969, a six-year-old boy in the commune set fire to the house, burning up some of the Crowley books and manuscripts. To punish him, cult leader Jean Brayton first tried applying matches to the boy's fingers. He seemed still unrepentant, so another punishment was devised.

The boy was locked in a packing case, set out in the desert sun for fifty-six days. He was chained by one ankle to the ground, fed at intervals, and isolated from human company. Mrs Brayton further suggested to the child that she might burn down his packing case prison. The desert temperatures during this time ran to 110° F. The point that all this was not a scientific experiment, but a lesson in ethics, was probably lost on the boy, who suffered terribly until passing strangers found him.[3]

The depressing truth is, there are sadists living all styles of life, including those of scientist, pseudo-scientist and cult shaman. If the scientific sadist can appeal to 'objectivity', the Auschwitz pseudo-scientist can call upon his theories to show how his victims are subhuman, and the Aztec priest can demonstrate the working of his gods' will through human sacrifice. The sick minded man owes his allegiance to no particular cause. When the wind blows West, he appears as the scientist with his white jacket and scalpel; when, as now, it blows East, he appears as Charles Manson, wearing buckskin and chanting mantras. To blame 'objectivity' for nerve gas experiments is more reasonable than blaming Beatlemania for Mansonism.

Manson may be seen as no more than a fleck in the otherwise clear river of religious feeling, but where in the mainstream do we find a more humane vision? From the ritual murders of the Greeks, through Savonarola and Matthew Hopkins, through Eastern Thuggee and kamikaze, down to today's religious wars in Ireland and the Middle East, that stream flows red. If hundreds of millennia of fervour haven't cleansed the human soul of blood-lust, how is it expected that three centuries of science should have managed the job?

Reference Notes

SCIENCE AS ESAU

1 Theodore Roszak, *The Making of a Counter-Culture* (London: Faber, 1970), pp. 7-8.
2 Gladys I. Spearman-Cook, 'The Focalisation of the Yods as the Divine Stream of Tympanic Royalty,' *Occult Gazette*, May 1971.

WATCH THIS SPACE

Chapter 1: *Before the Invasion*
1 L. Sprague de Camp and Willy Ley, *Lands Beyond*, p. 296.
2 Ibid., p. 310.
3 Peter Goldreich, 'Tides and the Earth-Moon System,' *Scientific American*, April 1972, p. 51.
4 Immanuel Velikovsky, *Worlds in Collision* (New York: Dell, 1967), p. 112.
5 Ibid., p. 73.
6 Damon Knight, *Charles Fort, Prophet of the Unexplained* (London: Gollancz, 1971), pp. 133-7.
7 George Bernard Shaw, *Everybody's Political What's What* (London: Constable, 1945), pp. 360-1.
8 Velikovsky, p. 6.
9 Sir Edwin Bullard, 'The Origin of the Oceans,' *Scientific American*, September 1969, p. 73.
10 H. W. Menard, 'The Deep Ocean Floor,' *Scientific American*, September 1969, pp. 130-1.
11 Bullard, p. 69.
12 Velikovsky, p. 37.
13 Ibid., p. 368.
14 Knight, p. vi.
15 Ibid., p. 108.
16 Charles Fort, *New Lands* (New York: Ace Books, n.d.), p. 9.
17 Knight, p. vii.
18 Fort, p. 209.

Chapter 2: *Will U Kindly F O?*
1 C. G. Jung, *Flying Saucers, a Modern Myth of Things Seen in the Sky* (New York: New American Library, 1969), pp. 102-4.

2 E. J. Ruppelt, 'The Florida Scoutmaster,' in *The Flying Saucer Reader*, ed. Jay David (New York: New American Library, 1967), pp. 247-8.

3 Ibid., p. 251.

4 Donald E. Keyhoe, *Flying Saucers from Outer Space* (London: Tandem, 1970).

5 Ibid., p. 244.

6 Ibid., p. 40.

7 Brad Steiger and Joan Whritenour, *New UFO Breakthrough* (London: Tandem, 1968), p. 14.

8 Gerald Heard, *Is Another World Watching?* (New York: Harper, 1951).

9 George Adamski and Desmond Leslie, 'Visitor from Venus,' in *Flying Saucer Reader*, pp. 61-80.

10 George Hunt Williamson, 'Contact by Automatic Writing,' in *Flying Saucer Reader*, p. 83.

11 Albert K. Bender, 'By Mental Telepathy,' in *Flying Saucer Reader*, p. 90.

12 Ibid., p. 91.

13 W. Gordon Allen, *Spacecraft from Beyond Three Dimensions* (New York: Exposition Press, 1959), illus. opposite p. 98.

14 Coral E. Lorenzen, *Flying Saucers: Startling Evidence of the Invasion from Outer Space* (New York: New American Library, 1966 (Original title: *The Great Flying Saucer Hoax*, 1962), p. 70.

Chapter 3: *The Condon Report*

1 Edward U. Condon, *Final Report of the Scientific Study of Unidentified Flying Objects* ... [Condon Report].

2 Condon Report, p. 290.

3 Ibid., pp. 324-6.

4 Ibid., pp. 287-8.

5 Ibid., pp. 418-26.

6 Ibid., pp. 396-407.

7 Ibid., pp. 407-15.

8 Frank Edwards, *Flying Saucers, Serious Business* (New York: Bantam Books, 1966), p. 41 ff.

9 Condon Report, p. 925.

10 Lorenzen, p. 128.

11 Coral and Jim Lorenzen, *UFOs, the Whole Story* (New York: New American Library, 1969), p. 215.

12 Condon Report, p. 923.

13 John G. Fuller, ' "The Blackout" and the UFOs,' in *Flying Saucer Reader*, pp. 174-5.

Chapter 4: *Reflections on an Astronaut God*
 1 Steiger and Whritenour, p. 144.
 2 Ibid., p. 63.
 3 Ibid., p. 64.
 4 Ibid., pp. 64-5.
 5 Ibid., p. 61.
 6 Lobsang Rampa, *Chapters of Life* (London: Transworld Publishers, 1967), p. 54.
 7 Lobsang Rampa, *The Rampa Story* (London: Transworld Publishers), p. 222.
 8 Ibid., p. 10.
 9 Rampa, *Chapters*, p. 54.
10 Ibid., p. 221.
11 Ibid., p. 77.
12 Ibid., p. 41.
13 Madge Brosius Allyn, 'The Flying Cucumber of 1903,' *Fate* 201, July 1971, pp. 19-21.
14 John A. Keel, 'Mystery Airplanes of the 1930s,' *Flying Saucer Review*, May–June 1970; Carl Grove, 'The Airship Wave of 1909,' *Flying Saucer Review*, Nov.–Dec. 1970 and Jan.–Feb. 1971.
15 John A. Keel, 'The "Flap" Phenomenon in the U.S.A.,' *Flying Saucer Review* Special Issue No. 2, June 1969, p. 26.
16 Erich von Däniken, *Chariots of the Gods?* (London: Souvenir Press, 1969); this was followed up with his *Return to the Stars* (London: Souvenir Press, 1970), more of the same.
17 von Däniken, *Chariots*, p. 56.
18 Ibid., p. 57.
19 Ibid., p. 84.
20 Condon Report, p. 27.
21 Ibid., p. 493.
22 Ibid., p. 493.
23 Peter Kolosimo, *Not of this World* (London: Sphere, 1971), p. 240.

LOST AND PROFOUND

Chapter 5: *Paradise Sunk*
 1 Ignatius Donnelly, *Atlantis* (New York: 1882; and many subsequent editions, the latest being London: Neville Spearman, 1970, ed. Egerton Sykes).
 2 Egerton Sykes, 'Lemuria Reconsidered,' *The Atlantean*, March–April 1971.
 3 de Camp and Ley, *Lands Beyond*, p. 22.
 4 de Camp and de Camp, *Citadels*, pp. 13-14.

5 Ibid., pp. 7-10.
6 Ibid., p. 10.
7 H. S. Bellamy, *Moons, Myths and Man*.
8 H. P. Blavatsky, *The Secret Doctrine* (Adyar, India: Theosophical Publishing House, 1888, six vols).
9 von Däniken, *Return to the Stars*, pp. 149-54.
10 Frank Edwards, *Flying Saucers – Serious Business* (New York: Lyle Stuart, 1966); quoted in Condon Report, p. 495.
11 von Däniken, *Return to the Stars*, p. 151.
12 de Camp and de Camp, *Citadels*, p. 231.
13 Gardner, *Fads and Fallacies*, p. 327.
14 Condon Report, pp. 853-4.

Chapter 6: *Secrets of the Ancients Revealed*
1 von Däniken, *Chariots*, p. 105.
2 I. E. S. Edwards, *The Pyramids of Egypt* (Harmondsworth: Penguin, 1947, 1961), p. 127, says that Davison found the sarcophagus in 1765.
3 Ibid., p. 127; Edwards says that Vyse and Pering in 1838 found quarry markings on the interior surfaces of stones: ochre daubs crediting various work gangs with cutting or moving them. These frequently invoked blessings on the name of Cheops (Khufu).
4 John Taylor, *The Great Pyramid: Why Was It Built? And Who Built It?* (London, 1859).
5 Charles Piazzi Smyth, *Our Inheritance in the Great Pyramid* (London: Daldy & Isbiter, 1877, rev. edn 1890).
6 Richard A. Proctor, *Myths and Marvels of Astronomy* (London: Longmans Green, 1896), p. 56.
7 Gardner, *Fads and Fallacies*, p. 179, gives an amusing demonstration of Great Pyramid mathematics, applying them to the Great Washington Monument.
8 Ibid., p. 178.
9 David Davidson and Herbert Aldersmith, *The Great Pyramid: Its Divine Message* (London: Williams & Norgate, 1924, rev. edn 1940).
10 von Däniken, *Chariots*, p. 97.
11 Ibid., p. 97.
12 Ibid., p 98.
13 Kolosimo, p. 240.
14 Ibid., p. 240.
15 von Däniken, *Chariots*, p. 99.
16 William Kingland, *The Great Pyramid in Fact and Theory* (London: Theosophical Publishing House, 1932-35, 2 vols).
17 This account is derived from Edwards, *Pyramids*; L. Sprague

de Camp, *The Ancient Engineers* (London: Souvenir Press, 1963); and René Poirer, *Fifteen Wonders of the World* (London: Gollancz, 1966).

18 Kolosimo, p. 238.
19 von Däniken, *Chariots*, pp. 48-9.
20 Andrew Tomas, *We Are Not the First* (London: Souvenir Press, 1971).
21 von Däniken, *Chariots*, p. 43.
22 Knight, *Fort*, p. 104.
23 Theodosius Dobzhansky, *Evolution, Genetics and Man* (New York: John Wiley, 1955), p. 305.
24 H. S. Bellamy and P. Allan, *The Calendar of Tiahuanaco* (London: Faber, 1961).
25 von Däniken, *Chariots*, pp. 48-9.
26 Ibid., p. 112.
27 de Camp and de Camp, *Citadels*, p. 257.
28 Gerald S. Hawkins, *Stonehenge Decoded* (London: Fontana, 1970).
29 Ibid., pp. 143, 169.
30 John Michell, 'Glastonbury Abbey: A solar instrument of former science,' *Glastonbury, a Study in Patterns* (London: Research into Lost Knowledge Organization, 1969), p. 32.

Chapter 7: *Lost Pets*

1 Richard Carrington, *Mermaids and Mastodons* (London: Chatto & Windus, 1957), p. 40.
2 Condon Report, p. 572. The italicized portions are direct quotations from UFO observers.
3 Rupert T. Gould, *The Loch Ness Monster and Others* (London: Geoffrey Bles, 1934).
4 Carrington, pp. 41-2.
5 Ibid., p. 42.
6 Constance Whyte, *More than a Legend* (London: Hamish Hamilton, 1957).
7 Tim Dinsdale, *Loch Ness Monster* (London: Routledge & Kegan Paul, 1961), p. 73.
8 *Encyclopaedia Britannica*, 11th edn, s.v. 'Lemmings'.
9 Knight, *Fort*, pp. 122-3.
10 Bergen Evans, *The Natural History of Nonsense* (London: Michael Joseph, 1947), p. 73.
11 Paul Kroll, 'Evolution Gets the Horse Laugh!', *The Plain Truth*, November 1969.
12 Dobzhansky, p. 302.
13 Egerton Sykes, in Donnelly, *Atlantis* (Introduction), p. 67.
14 John E. Portune, 'How Did Noah's Ark Hold All Those

Animals?', *The Plain Truth*, May 1970, p. 23.

15 Frank W. Cousins, *Fossil Man* (Emsworth, Hampshire: The Evolution Protest Movement, 1966, rev. edn 1971), p. 31.
16 Robert Charroux, *The Mysterious Unknown* (London: Neville Spearman, 1970).
17 G. G. Simpson, 'The Case History of a Scientific News Story,' *Science* 92; also quoted in Allport and Postman, *The Psychology of Rumor.*
18 Ibid.
19 Curtis D. MacDougall, *Hoaxes* (New York: Dover Publications, 1958), pp. 208-9.
20 Odette Tchernine, *The Yeti* (London: Neville Spearman, 1970).
21 Ibid., p. 108.
22 Ibid.
23 Bergen Evans, *Nonsense*, p. 97.
24 Tchernine, p. 110.

OF THE FLESH

Chapter 8: *Crank Cures*

1 Gardner, *Fads and Fallacies*, pp. 186-7.
2 Maurice Ernest, *Everyday Chronic Maladies* (London: Adam & Co, n.d.), p. 24.
3 Gardner, *Fads and Fallacies*, p. 188.
4 James Frazer, *The Golden Bough*, abridged (London: Macmillan, 1967), pp. 20-1.
5 Gardner, *Fads and Fallacies*, pp. 195-6.
6 Barbara Cartland, *The Youth Secret* (London: Transworld Publishers, 1968), pp. 37-8.
7 Bergen Evans, *Nonsense*, p. 157.
8 Stanley Davidson and R. Passmore, *Human Nutrition and Dietetics* (London: E. & S. Livingstone, 4th edn, 1969), p. 528.
9 Ibid., p. 527.
10 J-K. Huysmans, *Against Nature*, trans. R. Baldick (Harmondsworth: Penguin, 1959), p. 208.
11 Shaw, *Everybody's Political What's What?*, p. 240.
12 Lionel Dole, *The Blood Poisoners* (Croydon: Gateway Book Co., 1965), p. 8.
13 Ibid., p. 72.
14 *A Dictionary of Biology* (Harmondsworth: Penguin, 1961), s.v. 'Accommodation'.
15 Gayelord Hauser, *Look Younger, Live Longer* (London: Faber, 1969), p. 124.
16 Harry Benjamin, *Better Sight without Glasses* (London: Health for All, 1929, 1941), p. 61.
17 Ibid., pp. 111-12.

18 Ibid., p. 103.
19 Gardner, *Fads and Fallacies*, p. 241.
20 Ibid., p. 194.
21 Sakurasawa Nyoiti, *You Are All Sanpaku* (New York: Dell, 1970), cover blurb.
22 Brian Inglis, *Fringe Medicine* (London: Faber, 1964), p. 124.
23 Pat Wall, 'An Eye on the Needle,' *New Scientist*, 20 July 1972, p. 130.
24 Inglis, *Fringe Medicine*, p. 101.

Chapter 9: *Medicinal Spirits*
 1 Edgar Cayce, *123 Questions and Answers from the Edgar Cayce Clairvoyant Readings* (Virginia Beach, Va.: A.R.E. Press, 1966), p. 9.
 2 Ibid., p. 12.
 3 Ibid., p. 14.
 4 Louis Rose, *Faith Healing* (Harmondsworth: Penguin, 1971).
 5 Ibid., p. 138.
 6 Ibid., p. 145.
 7 Ibid., p. 160.
 8 Ibid., p. 111.
 9 Gardner *Fads and Fallacies*, p. 241.

Chapter 10: *Food Stuff*
 1 Gardner, *Fads and Fallacies*, p. 222.
 2 *TV Times*, 8-15 October 1971, p. 15.
 3 Davidson and Passmore, p. 258.
 4 *TV Times*, 8-15 October 1971, p. 14.
 5 Davidson and Passmore, p. 609.
 6 Ibid., p. 105.
 7 Ibid., p. 105.
 8 Edgar Cayce, *123 Questions*, p. 13.
 9 Gardner, *Fads and Fallacies*, p. 341.
 10 Joseph D. Hollo, *Snap Back from Your Heart Attack* (North Hollywood: Brandon House, 1967), p. 151.
 11 Jerome Irving Rodale, *Natural Health, Sugar and the Criminal Mind* (New York: Pyramid Publications, 1968), p. 15.
 12 Ibid., p. 100.
 13 Eric F. W. Powell, *Kelp* (Rustington, Sussex: Health Science Press, 1968), p. 7.
 14 Ibid., p. 13.
 15 Cecil Tonsley, *Honey for Health* (London: Tandem, 1969), p. 100.
 16 Gayelord Hauser, *Look Younger, Live Longer*, p. 66.
 17 Advertising pamphlet (Locking, Weston-super-Mare, Somerset: Life & Beauty Ltd, n.d.).

18 Hauser, *Look Younger*, p. 35.
19 Gardner, *Fads and Fallacies*, p. 341.
20 George Ohsawa, *Zen Macrobiotics* (Los Angeles: Ohsawa Foundation, 1965), p. 22.
21 Ibid., p. 53.

Chapter 11: *Inside Dope*
 1 Bergen Evans, *The Spoor of Spooks* (London: Michael Joseph, 1955, p. 218.
 2 *Daily Mirror* (London), 24 July 1939; quoted in Michael Schofield, *The Strange Case of Pot* (Harmondsworth: Penguin, 1971), p. 65.
 3 Griffith Edwards, 'Psychoactive Substances,' *Listener*, 23 March 1972, p. 361.
 4 *New Facts about Marijuana* (Pasadena: Ambassador College Press, 1970), pp. 20-1. (Ambassador College Press publishes *The Plain Truth*.)
 5 William F. Dankenbring, 'Marijuana on Trial – New Evidence,' *The Plain Truth*, June 1971, p. 23.
 6 *Sunday Times* (London), 13 June 1971.
 7 *New Facts about Marijuana*, p. 32.
 8 Schofield, p. 180.
 9 Bulletin of Narcotics 24(3) 1970, p. 13.
 10 R. Blum, *The Utopiates* (London: Tavistock, 1970).
 11 I. James, in *British Journal of Criminology*, vol. 9, no. 2, 1969.
 12 Roger Lewin, 'Marijuana on Trial,' *New Scientist*, 8 June 1972.
 13 'Monitor,' *New Scientist*, 13 May 1971.
 14 Leslie L. McCullough and others, 'LSD, the Whole Story,' *The Plain Truth*, May 1969, p. 13.
 15 Schofield, p. 65.
 16 Griffith Edwards, p. 363.
 17 H. B. Huges, *Trepanation* (Amsterdam: Foundation for Independent Thinking, 1971), p. 26.
 18 Ibid., p. 26.
 19 Ibid., p. 10.
 20 Ibid., p. 42.

OF THE HEAD

Chapter 12: *Character Clues*
 1 *Encyclopedia Americana*, s.v. 'Phrenology'.
 2 Sibyl, *The Popular Fortune Teller* (London: W. Foulsham, n.d.).
 3 John Brophy, *The Human Face Reconsidered* (London: Harrap, 1962), p. 183.

4 Noel Jaquin, *The Hand of Man* (London: Faber, 1933), pp. 12-13.
5 Ibid., p. 14.
6 Ibid., p. 17.
7 Cheiro (Count-Louis Hamon), *Cheiro's Language of the Hand* (London: Herbert Jenkins, 1958), pp. 27-8.
8 Jaquin, p. 19.
9 Klara G. Roman, *Handwriting: A Key to Personality* (London: Routledge & Kegan Paul, 1961).

Chapter 13: *Star Attractions*
1 'Astrology is the Bunk, Isn't It?', a radio discussion between Derek Parker and Jonathan Miller, BBC Radio 4, 14 September 1971.
2 Herman Kahn and Anthony J. Wiener, *The Year 2000: A Framework for Speculation* (New York: Macmillan, 1967).
3 P. B. Medawar, *The Art of the Soluble* (Harmondsworth: Penguin, 1967), p. 128.
4 E. H. Gombrich, *Art and Illusion* (London: Phaidon, 1968), p. 90.
5 Ellic Howe, *Urania's Children* (London: William Kimber, 1967), p. 171.
6 Michel Gauquelin, *Astrology and Science* (London: Peter Davies, 1970).
7 Ibid., p. 167.
8 John Anthony West and Jan Gerhard Toonder, *The Case for Astrology* (London: Macdonald, 1970).
9 Ibid., pp. 170-2.
10 Ibid., p. 173.
11 Ibid., pp. 174-6.
12 Ibid., pp. 178-80.
13 Ibid., p. 180.
14 Joseph A. Goodavage, *Write Your Own Horoscope* (New York: New American Library, 1968), pp. 278-88.

Chapter 14: *ESP and Dr Rhine*
1 J. B. Rhine, *Extra-Sensory Perception* (London: Faber, 1935).
2 C. E. M. Hansel, *ESP: A Critical Evaluation*, pp. 162-5.
3 J. B. Rhine and J. G. Pratt, article in *Journal of Parapsychology*, 1954; quoted in Hansel, p. 165.
4 Hansel, pp. 99-100.
5 Rhine, p. 142.
6 J. L. Kennedy, article in *Psychology Bulletin*; quoted in Hansel, p. 100.

7 John Scarne and Clayton Rawson, *Scarne on Dice*, 1945; quoted in Gardner, *Fads and Fallacies*, p. 307.
8 Gardner, *Fads and Fallacies*, p. 307.

Chapter 15: *Other Brain Waves*
1 Arthur Koestler, *The Roots of Coincidence* (London: Hutchinson, 1972), pp. 38-41.
2 M. G. Kendall and B. Babington Smith, *Tracts for Computers No. XXIV* (Cambridge: University Press, 1960).
3 G. R. Price, 'Science and the Supernatural,' *Science* 122, no. 3165, 26 August 1965.
4 S. G. Soal and H. T. Bowden, *The Mind Readers* (London: Faber, 1959).
5 Hansel, p. 148.
6 Koestler, *Roots*, pp. 50-81; Sir Cyril Burt, 'Psychology and Parapsychology,' in *Science and ESP*, pp. 76-141.
7 M. Guthrie and J. Birchall, *Journal of the Society for Psychical Research*, vol. 2, pp. 24-42 and vol. 3, pp. 424-52.
8 René Warcollier, *Hand to Mind* (New York: Collier Books, 1963), p. 64.
9 Upton Sinclair, *Mental Radio* (Pasadena: Upton Sinclair, 1930).
10 Koestler, *Roots*, p. 35.
11 Hansel, p. 37.

OF THE SPIRIT

Chapter 16: *Early Ectoplasms*
1 Simeon Edmunds ed., *Spiritualism: A Critical Survey* (London: Aquarian Press, 1966), p. 2.
2 George Trobridge, *Swedenborg, Life and Teaching* (London: Swedenborg Society, 1945), p. 46.
3 Ibid., p. 125.
4 Edmunds, p. 7.
5 Viscount Adare, *Experiences in Spiritualism* (London, privately printed, 1869): a more accessible source is T. H. Hall, *New Light on Old Ghosts* (London: Gerald Duckworth, 1965), pp. 93-4.
6 Hall, pp. 68-9.
7 Ibid., p. 70.
8 Annie Besant, H. P. Blavatsky and the *Masters of Wisdom* (London: Theosophical Publishing House, 1907).
9 Hansel, p. 214.
10 P. Pickering, 'Scouring the Supernatural,' *Nova*, August 1972.
11 Archie Jarman, 'High Jinks on a Low Level,' in Edmunds, pp. 195-204.

12 Ibid., p. 200.
13 H. Curtis, 'The Houdini Testament,' in Martin Ebon ed., *The Psychic Reader* (New York: New American Library, 1970), p. 154.
14 Ibid., p. 155.
15 Ibid., p. 156.
16 *Psychic News*, 20 February 1971.

Chapter 17: *Late Arrivals*
 1 *Psychic News*, 20 February 1971.
 2 Jess Stearn, 'Crime Busters with a Sixth Sense,' in Brant House ed., *Strange Powers of Unusual People* (New York: Ace Books, 1963), pp. 44-63.
 3 Ed Sanders, *The Family* (London: Rupert Hart-Davis, 1972), pp. 332-3.
 4 Jess Stearn, p. 46.
 5 Hansel, pp. 197-200.
 6 Carl Hertz, *A Modern Mystery Merchant* (London: Hutchinson, 1924), p. 280.
 7 H. J. Eysenck, *Sense and Nonsense in Psychology* (Harmondsworth: Penguin, 1958), pp. 115-17.
 8 Ibid., pp. 116-17.
 9 Hudson Hoagland, article in *Atlantic Monthly*, November 1925.
10 S. Ralph Harlow, 'The Woman Who Could Put Objects into Motion,' in Brant House ed., *Strange Powers of Unusual People*, pp. 158-75.
11 S. Ralph Harlow, 'The Man Who Transported Objects Through Space Without Ever Leaving the Room,' in House, *Strange Powers*, pp. 176-89.
12 Bishop James A. Pike, *The Other Side* (London: W. H. Allen, 1969).

Chapter 18: *Hocus Focus*
 1 Hansel, p. 209.
 2 *International Herald Tribune*, 23 August 1971.
 3 Ibid.
 4 Carl Hertz, p. 282.
 5 Edmunds, p. 114.
 6 Major Tom Patterson, *100 Years of Spirit Photography* (London: Regency Press, 1965).
 7 Ibid., p. 48.
 8 Jule Eisenbud, *The World of Ted Serios* (London: Jonathan Cape, 1968).
 9 Ibid., pp. 29-30.
10 Ibid., p. 309.

11 W. A. H. Rushton, 'Serios-Photos: If Contrary to Natural Law, Which Law?', *Journal of the Society for Psychical Research*, vol. 44, no. 736, June 1968, pp. 289-93.
12 Ibid.

CLAY FEET

Chapter 19: *The Emperor's New Lab Coat*
1 William Gaddis, *The Recognitions* (London: MacGibbon & Kee, 1955), p. 64.
2 Alfred Russel Wallace, as quoted in Edmunds.
3 Herbert Wendt, *After the Deluge* (London: Paladin, 1970), p. 53.
4 Arthur Koestler, *The Sleepwalkers* (Harmondsworth: Penguin, 1968), pp. 374-5.
5 Arthur Koestler, *The Roots of Coincidence* (London: Hutchinson, 1972), p. 11.
6 Gerald Wick, 'In Search of a More Viable Science,' *New Scientist*, 30 September 1971.
7 Arthur Jensen, 'Environment, Heredity and Intellegience,' *Harvard Educational Review*, vol. 39, 1969.
8 Samuel Goudsmit, *ALSOS* (London: Sigma Books, 1947), p. 212; Goudsmit is quoting *Captain von Stepanitz, The German Shepherd Dog in Words and Pictures*, first published in 1901.
9 Adolf Hitler, *Mein Kampf*, trans. Ralph Manheim (London: Hutchinson, 1969), p. 279.
10 *Protocols of the Elders of Zion*, as quoted in Curtis D. MacDougall, *Hoaxes* (New York: Dover Publications, 1958), p. 201.
11 Walter R. Fuchs, *Computers, Information Theory and Cybernetics*, trans. K. Kellner (London: Rupert Hart-Davis, 1971), p. 53; part of a brief, but comprehensive description of 'German science'. See also the following reference.
12 William L. Shirer, *The Rise and Fall of the Third Reich* (New York: Fawcett Publications, 1962), p. 345.
13 Goudsmit, p. 150.
14 Ellic Howe, *Urania's Children*, p. 111.
15 Ibid., pp. 90-1.
16 Quoted in Gardner, *Fads and Fallacies*, p. 163.

Chapter 20: *Cult Figures*
1 Marshall McLuhan, *The Gutenberg Galaxy* (London: Routledge & Kegan Paul, 1962), p. 17.
2 Jonathan Miller, *McLuhan* (London: Fontana, 1971), p. 107.
3 Marshall McLuhan, *Understanding Media* (London: Sphere, 1967), p. 26.

4 Cyrus Teed as quoted in Gardner, *Fads and Fallacies*, p. 24.
5 Marshall McLuhan, *The Mechanical Bride* (London: Routledge & Kegan Paul, 1951), p. 87.
6 Billy Graham, *Peace with God* (Kingswood, Surrey: World's Work Ltd, 1966), p. 13.
7 Pierre Teilhard de Chardin, *The Phenomenon of Man* (London: Collins, 1959).
8 P. B. Medawar, *The Art of the Soluble* (Harmondsworth: Penguin, 1967), p. 91.
9 Ibid., p. 88.
10 Teilhard de Chardin as quoted in Medawar, p. 87.
11 R. Buckminster Fuller, *Nine Chains to the Moon* (Carbondale & Edwardsville, Ill.: Southern Illinois U.P., 1963), p. 132.
12 Ibid., p. 131.
13 Ibid., p. 370.
14 R. Buckminster Fuller, *No More Secondhand God* (Carbondale & Edwardsville, Ill.: Southern Illinois U.P., 1967), p. 121.
15 Ibid., p. 163.
16 H. Hartley, 'Shearer and His Rays,' *New Scientist*, 22 January 1970, p. 151.
17 Ilse Ollendorf Reich, *Wilhelm Reich, a Personal Biography* (New York: Avon, 1969), p. 133.
18 Gardner, *Fads and Fallacies*, p. 267.
19 Ibid., pp. 267-8.
20 Pauline Cooper, 'The Tragi-Farce of Scientology,' *Queen*.
21 Ibid.

EUREKA!

Chapter 21: *Cranks in Perpetual Motion*
1 These examples are drawn from Gardner, *Fads and Fallacies*; John Phin, *The Seven Follies of Science* (London: Archibald Constable, 1906); and Augustus de Morgan, *A Budget of Paradoxes* (London: Longmans Green, 1872).
2 Gardner, *Fads and Fallacies*, p. 326.
3 de Morgan, *Paradoxes*, p. 186.
4 Gillette, quoted in Gardner, *Fads and Fallacies*, p. 87.
5 Ibid., p. 87.
6 John Fenn Smith, *The Laser* (London: privately printed, 1971).
7 Phin, *Seven Follies*, p. 41.
8 W. Ehrenberg, 'Maxwell's Demon,' *Scientific American*, November 1967; also *Sci.Amer.* Offprint No. 317.
9 John E. W. Keely, quoted in Curtis D. MacDougall, *Hoaxes*, p. 71.
10 Frank Edwards, *Stranger Than Science* (London: Pan, 1959).

11 A. S. E. Ackermann, *Popular Fallacies* (London: Old Westminster Press, 1950), p. 708.

12 Peter Lennon in *Sunday Times* (London), 7 February 1971.

13 Ackermann, p. 586.

14 Ibid., p. 586.

15 Ibid., p. 586.

16 Ibid., pp. 586-7.

17 Kenneth Roberts, *Henry Gross and His Dowsing Rod* (1951) is reviewed at length in Gardner, *Fads and Fallacies*, pp. 106-13.

18 Joseph Jastrow, *Error and Eccentricity in Human Belief* (New York: Dover Publications, 1935), pp. 128-9, summarizes several investigations of the ouija board, pendulum, and related devices.

19 D. H. Rawcliffe, *Illusions and Delusions of the Supernatural* (New York: Dover Publications, 1959), pp. 359-60.

20 Ibid., pp. 338-48.

21 Jastrow, *Error*, p. 139.

22 Gardner, *Fads and Fallacies*, p. 205.

23 Ibid., pp. 210-11.

24 Brian Inglis, *Fringe Medicine* (London: Faber, 1964), p. 257.

25 Louis Rose, *Faith Healing* (Harmondsworth: Penguin, 1971), p. 167.

26 Gardner, *Fads and Fallacies*, p. 347.

27 John W. Campbell, editorial, *Astounding Science Fiction*, November 1956, p. 91.

28 John W. Campbell, *Astounding Science Fiction*, June 1957, p. 53.

29 Adrian Hope, *Why Didn't I Think of It First?* (London: David & Charles, 1972), p. 86.

30 Campbell's *Astounding* (now called *Analog* and edited by Ben Bova) is still at it. The December 1972 issue features an article by astrologer Joseph A. Goodavage ('Magic: Science of the Future') which revives the Hieronymous machine yet again. Goodavage sees links between the machine and other occult stuff: Drown therapy, Ted Serios, mesmerism, Odyle, dowsing and ESP. Hieronymous is current killing insect pests by elopting photos of infested crops, and working with another old friend, Henry Gross. Hieronymous also has a warning for astronauts: There is a 'lethal belt of radiation on the Moon' about fifteen feet under the surface (p. 31, my roman type).

31 John W. Campbell, *Astounding Science Fiction*, October 1960, p. 77.

32 Ibid., November 1956, p. 3.

Chapter 22: *Irrational Numbers*

1 Martin Gardner, 'Mathematical Games,' *Scientific American*, October 1972, p. 111.
2 Vincent Lopez, *Numerology* (New York: New American Library, 1969), p. 101.
3 de Morgan, *Paradoxes*, p. 179.
4 See Martin Gardner, 'Mathematical Games,' *Scientific American*, April 1971, p. 115, for a trick 'proof' to end all *pi* discussions, showing that *pi* is equal to 2. The fallacy involved is explained in the following month's issue, p. 116.
5 Martin Gardner, *More Puzzles and Mathematical Diversions* (Harmondsworth: Penguin, 1966), p. 179.
6 Le Corbusier, *Modulor*, trans. P. de Francia and A. Bostock (London: Faber, 1961), p. 56.
7 Benedetto Croce quoted in Jonathan Miller, *McLuhan*, p. 129.
8 Oswald Spengler, in J. R. Newman ed., *The World of Mathematics* (New York: Simon & Schuster, 1956, 4 vols paperback), p. 2,347.
9 Edward R. Dewey, *Cycles: Mysterious Forces that Trigger Events* (New York: Hawthorne, 1971).
10 Earth (cold-dry), air (warm-wet), fire (warm-dry) and water (cold-wet).
11 Condon Report, p. 534.
12 Aimé Michel, in David, *Flying Saucer Reader*, p. 188.
13. Condon Report, p. 535.
14 John A. Keel, in *Flying Saucer Review* Special No. 2, June 1969 pp. 14-18.
15 Knight, *Fort*, pp. 95-8 and pp. 114-17.
16 The key positions named are *opposition* (Mars and Earth aligned on opposite sides of the sun); *conjunction* (aligned on the same side of the sun); and *quadrature* (Mars and Earth forming a right angle, with the sun at its corner).
17 Knight, *Fort*, p. 115.
18 The 'sixteen hundred years' is an overestimate. Since the claim is to compare cycles, every possible stretch of 16 years in the 130 years of data is relevant. There are 115 of these, or more than enough for Knight's purposes.
19 Arthur Waley, 'The Book of Changes,' *Bulletin of the Museum of Far Eastern Antiquities, Stockholm* No. 5, 1934, pp. 121-2.
20 Ibid, p. 122.
21 Ibid., p. 112.
22 Is, for instance, prophecy No. 25 about the theft of a cow and misfortune, as Wilhelm claims? Or is it about a scapegoat ritual to drive off pestilence, as Waley claims? Compare these, and a third version, in Waley, pp. 132-3, and Richard Wilhelm,

The I Ching or Book of Changes, trans. C. F. Baynes (London: Routledge & Kegan Paul, 1968), pp. 102-3.

23 C. G. Jung, Foreword to R. Wilhelm, *I Ching*, p. xxiv.
24 Ibid., p. xxxix.
25 C. Sklaire, broadsheet, n.d.
26 Ibid.
27 Ibid.
28 Ibid.
29 Ibid.

Chapter 23: *Head Codes*
 1 David Kahn, *The Codebreakers* (New York: Macmillan, 1968), p. 875.
 2 Ibid., p. 877.
 3 Ibid.
 4 L. Sprague de Camp and Catherine de Camp, *Citadels of Mystery* (London: Fontana, 1972), p. 11.
 5 Kahn, *Codebreakers*, p. 879.
 6 Ray Nunn, 'Queen of Drag,' *The People* (London), 12 September 1971.
 7 W. F. Friedman and E. S. Friedman, *The Shakespeare Ciphers Examined* (Cambridge: C.U.P., 1957).
 8 Kahn, *Codebreakers*, p. 880.
 9 Jonathan Swift, *Travels by Lemuel Gulliver*, Part III, Chap. VI.
10 See Kahn, *Codebreakers*, pp. 880-8 for many other strange decipherments of Shakespeare's plays and tombstone, all demolished by the Friedmans.
11 Kahn, *Codebreakers*, p. 917.
12 This idea seems to come from Auguste le Plongeon (1826-1908), who worked from Bishop Land's Mayan 'alphabet' (see p. 65 above) to prove that both Mayans and Egyptians came from Mu. No one else ever succeeded in reading Mayan or Egyptian using his methods.
13 I. J. Gelb, *A Study in Writing* (Chicago: U. of C.P., 1963), p. 56.
14 H. S. Bellamy, *Moons, Myths and Man* (London: Faber, 1939), p. 180.
15 Kahn, *Codebreakers*, p. 869.
16 Ibid., p. 870.

THE END

Chapter 24: *Advance Warnings*
 1 J. P. Chaplin, *Rumor, Fear and the Madness of Crowds* (New York: Ballantine, 1959), p. 121.

2 G. W. Allport and L. Postman, *The Psychology of Rumor* (New York: Russell & Russell, 1965).

3 Izola Forrester, mentioned in C. D. MacDougall, *Hoaxes*, p. 165.

4 Finis Bates, mentioned in MacDougall, *Hoaxes*, p. 165.

5 Lawrence Schiller, *The Scavengers and Critics of the Warren Report* (New York: Dell, 1967).

6 Ibid., p. 105.

7 Len Deighton, *The Assassination of President Kennedy* (London: Jonathan Cape, unbound 'Jackdaw', 1967).

8 Schiller, *Scavengers*, p. 192.

9 MacDougall, *Hoaxes*, p. 93.

10 E. H. Gombrich, *Myth and Reality in German War-time Broadcasts* (London: University of London Athlone Press, 1970).

11 Ibid., p. 5.

12 T. W. Adorno, E. Frenkel-Brunswik, D. J. Levinson and R. N. Sanford, *The Authoritarian Personality* (New York: Harper & Row, 1950).

13 Ibid., p. 66.

14 Joel Sayre, 'Berlin Letter,' *New Yorker*, 20 July 1946; also quoted in Allport and Postman, *Psychology of Rumor*.

15 Chaplin, *Rumor, Fear*, p. 104.

Chapter 25: *The Last Trumpet*

1 J. L. Borges, 'Time and J. W. Dunne,' *Other Inquisitions 1937–1952*, trans. R. L. C. Simms (New York: Washington Square Press, 1966), p. 21.

2 *The Life and Prophecies of Ursula Sontheil, Better Known as Mother Shipton* (Knaresborough, Yorkshire: Dropping Well Estate Ltd, ca. 1900).

3 Bergen Evans, *The Spoor of Spooks*, p. 15.

4 Ellic Howe, *Urania's Children*, pp. 161-3.

5 Stewart Robb, *Prophecies on World Events by Nostradamus* (New York: Liveright, 1961), p. 133.

6 Ibid., p. 133.

7 Ibid., p. 42.

8 Ibid., p. 40.

9 Ellic Howe, *Urania's Children*, p. 217n.

10 Ibid., p. 186.

11 Broadsheet (Bedford, Bedfordshire: The Panacea Society, n.d.).

12 Robert Coover, *The Origin of the Brunists* (London: Panther, 1968); a sensitive exploration in fiction of a modern cult very like the Millerites.

13 Leon Festinger, Henry W. Riecken and Stanley Schachter,

When Prophecy Fails (New York: Harper & Row, 1956).
14 Herbert W. Armstrong, 'Bible Prophecy Foretells a Strong United Europe,' *Tomorrow's World*, February 1970, p. 6.
15 Ibid., p. 4.
16 Ibid., p. 32.
17 Ibid., p. 33.
18 Ed Sanders, *The Family* (London: Rupert Hart-Davis, 1972).
19 Ibid., p. 162.
20 Ibid., p. 162.

Chapter 26: *Believing Is Seeing*
1 R. L. Gregory, *Eye and Brain* (London: Weidenfeld & Nicolson, 1966), p. 195.
2 Ibid., pp. 201-2.
3 Colin Cherry, *On Human Communication* (Cambridge, Mass.: MIT Press, 1966), p. 280.
4 R. L. Gregory, *The Intelligent Eye* (London: Weidenfeld & Nicolson, 1970), p. 120.
5 Gregory, *Eye and Brain*, pp. 198-201.
6 Gombrich, *Art and Illusion*, pp. 193-4.
7 Gregory, *Intelligent Eye*, p. 15.
8 Gombrich, *Art and Illusion*, p. 200.
9 Karl R. Popper, *The Logic of Scientific Discovery* (London: Hutchinson, rev. edn 1968), pp. 27-48.
10 T. S. Kuhn, *The Structure of Scientific Revolutions* (Chicago: U. of C.P., 1970), p. 63.
11 Ibid., pp. 63-4.
12 Paul A. Kolers, 'Experiments in Reading,' *Scientific American*, July 1972, p. 88.
13 Gustav Jahoda, *The Psychology of Superstition* (Harmondsworth: Penguin, 1970).
14 Ibid., p. 38.
15 Ibid., pp. 50-1.
16 Eric Hoffer, *The True Believer* (New York: Harper & Row, 1951).
17 Ibid., p. 48.
18 Ibid., p. 51.
19 Ibid., pp. 52-3.
20 Ibid., p. 84.
21 Adorno *et al.*, *The Authoritarian Personality*.
22 Ibid., p. 256.

Appendix
1 Theodore Roszak, *The Making of a Counter-Culture*, p. 276.
2 Ibid., p. 273.
3 Ed Sanders, *The Family*, pp. 165-6.

Bibliography

The Life and Prophecies of Ursula Sontheil, better known as Mother Shipton. Knaresborough, Yorkshire: Dropping Well Estate Ltd, n.d.

New Facts about Marijuana. Pasadena: Ambassador College Press, 1970.

Ackermann, A. S. E. *Popular Fallacies.* London: Old Westminster Press, 1950.

Adorno, T. W.; Frenkel-Brunswik, Else; Levinson, Daniel J.; and Sanford, R. Nevitt. *The Authoritarian Personality.* New York: Harper & Row, 1950.

Alexander, Rolf. *The Power of the Mind.* London: Werner Laurie, 1956.

Allport, Gordon W., and Postman, Leo. *The Psychology of Rumor.* New York: Russell & Russell, 1965.

Allyn, Madge Brosius. 'The Flying Cucumber of 1903.' *Fate*, July 1971, pp. 19-21.

Armstrong, Herbert W. 'The 19-Year Time Cycles – What Happened January 7 – What My Commission Is!' *Tomorrow's World*, February 1972, pp. 1-4, 30-3.

Bellamy, H. S. *Moons, Myths and Man.* London: Faber, 1939 (revised edn).

Bellamy, H. S., and Allan, P. *The Calendar of Tiahuanaco.* London: Faber, 1961.

Benjamin, Harry. *Better Sight without Glasses.* London: Health for All Publishing Co., 1929, 1941.

Besant, Annie. *H. P. Blavatsky and the Masters of Wisdom.* London: Theosophical Society Publishing House, 1907.

Blavatsky, Helena Petrovna. *The Secret Doctrine.* Adyar, India: Theosophical Society Publishing House, 1888. 6 vols.

Borges, Jorge Luis. *Other Inquisitions 1937–1952*, trans. R. L. C. Simms. New York: Washington Square Press, 1966.

Brophy, John. *The Human Face Reconsidered.* London: Harrap, 1962.

Campbell, John W. Editorial, *Astounding Science Fiction*, November 1956.

——. Editorial, *Astounding Science Fiction*, June 1957.

——. Editorial, *Astounding Science Fiction*, October 1960.

Carrington, Richard. *Mermaids and Mastodons.* London: Chatto Windus, 1957.

Cartland, Barbara. *The Youth Secret.* London: Corgi, 1968.

Cayce, Edgar. *123 Questions and Answers from the Edgar Cayce Clairvoyant Readings.* Virginia Beach, Virginia: A.R.E. Press, 1966.

Cayce, Edgar Evans. *Atlantis – Fact or Fiction?* Virginia Beach, Virginia: A.R.E. Press, 1962.

Chaplin, J. P. *Rumor, Fear, and the Madness of Crowds.* New York: Ballantine, 1959.

Charroux, Robert. *The Mysterious Unknown.* London: Neville Spearman, 1970.

'Cheiro' (Count-Louis Hamon). *Cheiro's Language of the Hand,* 27th edn. London: Herbert Jenkins, 1958.

Cherry, Colin. *On Human Communication.* Cambridge, Mass.: M.I.T. Press, 1966.

Churchward, Col. James. *The Lost Continent of Mu.* New York: Ives Washburn, 1933.

Condon Edward U. (project director). *Final Report of the Scientific Study of Unidentified Flying Objects Conducted by the University of Colorado under Contract to the United States Air Force.* New York: Bantam, 1969.

Coover, Robert. *The Origin of the Brunists.* London: Panther, 1968.

Cousins, Frank W. *Fossil Man.* Emsworth, Hampshire: A. E. Norris, 1966, rev. edn 1971.

Däniken, Erich von. *Chariots of the Gods?* London: Souvenir Press, 1969.

——. *Return to the Stars.* London: Souvenir Press, 1970.

Dankenbring, William F. 'Marijuana on Trial – New Evidence.' *The Plain Truth,* June 1971.

David, Jay, ed. *The Flying Saucer Reader.* New York: New American Library, 1967.

Davidson, David, and Aldersmith, Herbert. *The Great Pyramid: Its Divine Message.* London: Williams & Norgate, 1924, rev. edn 1940.

de Camp, L. Sprague, and de Camp, Catherine. *Citadels of Mystery.* London: Fontana, 1972.

de Camp, L. Sprague, and Ley, Willy. *Lands Beyond.* New York: Rinehart, 1952.

de Morgan, Augustus. *A Budget of Paradoxes.* London: Longmans Green, 1872.

Dewey, Edward R. *Cycles: Mysterious Forces that Trigger Events.* New York: Hawthorne, 1971.

Dinsdale, Tim. *Loch Ness Monster.* London: Routledge & Kegan Paul, 1961.

Dobzhansky, Theodosius. *Evolution, Genetics and Man.* New

York: John Wiley, 1955.

Dole, Lionel. *The Blood Poisoners.* Croydon, Sussex: Gateway Books, 1965.

Donnelly, Ignatius. *Atlantis: The Antediluvian World.* London: Neville Spearman, rev. edn 1970. Introduction by Egerton Sykes.

Ebon, Martin, ed. *The Psychic Reader.* New York: New American Library, 1970.

Edmunds, Simeon. *Spiritualism: A Critical Survey.* London: Aquarian Press, 1966.

Edwards, Griffith. 'Psychoactive Substances.' *The Listener,* 23 March 1972.

Edwards, I. E. S. *The Pyramids of Egypt.* Harmondsworth: Penguin, 1961.

Ehrenburg, W. 'Maxwell's Demon.' *Scientific American,* November 1967. Also *Scientific American* Offprint No. 317.

Eisenbud, Jule. *The World of Ted Serios.* London: Jonathan Cape, 1968.

Ernest, Maurice. *Everyday Chronic Maladies.* London: Adam & Co., 24th edn, n.d.

Evans, Bergen. *The Natural History of Nonsense.* London: Michael Joseph, 1947.

——. *The Spoor of Spooks.* London: Michael Joseph, 1955.

Eysenck, H. J. *Sense and Nonsense in Psychology.* Harmondsworth: Penguin, 1958.

Festinger, Leon. 'Cognitive Dissonance.' *Scientific American,* October 1962. Also *Scientific American* Offprint No. 472.

Festinger, Leon; Riecken, Henry W.; and Schachter, Stanley. *When Prophecy Fails.* New York: Harper & Row, 1964.

Freud, Sigmund. *Studies in Parapsychology.* New York: Collier Books, 1963.

Friedman, William F., and Friedman, Elizabeth S. *The Shakespeare Ciphers Examined.* Cambridge: C.U.P., 1957.

Fuller, R. Buckminster. *Nine Chains to the Moon.* Carbondale and Edwardsville, Illinois: Southern Illinois University Press, 1963.

——. *No More Secondhand God.* Carbondale and Edwardsville, Illinois: Southern Illinois University Press, 1967.

Gardner, Martin. *Fads and Fallacies in the Name of Science.* New York: Dover Publications, 2nd edn, 1957.

——. *More Puzzles and Mathematical Diversions.* Harmondsworth: Penguin, 1966.

——. 'Mathematical Games.' *Scientific American,* October 1972.

——. 'Mathematical Games.' *Scientific American,* November 1972.

Garrett, Eileen J. *Many Voices.* New York: Dell Publishing Co., 1968.

Gauquelin, Michel. *Astrology and Science*. London: Peter Davies, 1970.

Gelb, I. J. *A Study in Writing*. Chicago: U. of C.P., 1963.

Gombrich, E. H. *Art and Illusion*. London: Phaidon, 1968.

——. *Myth and Reality in German War-Time Broadcasts*. London: U. of L. Athlone Press, 1970.

Goodavage, Joseph A. 'Magic: Science of the Future.' *Analog Science Fact/Science Fiction*, December 1972, pp. 23-37.

——. *Write Your Own Horoscope*. New York: New American Library, 1968.

Gould, R. T. *The Loch Ness Monster and Others*. London: Geoffrey Bles, 1934.

Gregory, R. L. *Eye and Brain*. London: Weidenfeld & Nicolson, 1966.

——. *The Intelligent Eye*. London: Weidenfeld and Nicolson, 1970.

Hall, T. H. *New Light on Old Ghosts*. London: Gerald Duckworth, 1965.

Hansel, C. E. M. *ESP, A Scientific Evaluation*. London: MacGibbon & Kee, 1966.

Hartley, H. 'Shearer and His Rays.' *New Scientist*, 22 January 1970.

Hauser, Gayelord. *Look Younger, Live Longer*. London: Faber, 1951, 1969.

Hawkins, Gerald S. *Stonehenge Decoded*. London: Fontana, 1970.

Hoffer, Eric. *The True Believer*. New York: Harper & Row, 1951.

Hollo, Joseph D. *Snap Back from Your Heart Attack*. North Hollywood: Brandon House, 1967.

Holt, Michael. *Mathematics in Art*. London: Studio Vista, 1971.

House, Brant, ed. *Strange Powers of Unusual People*. New York: Ace Books, 1963.

Howe, Ellic. *Urania's Children*. London: William Kimber, 1967.

Hubbard, L. Ron. *The Creation of Human Ability*. East Grinstead, Sussex: The Department of Publications Worldwide, 1954.

——. *Scientology, the Fundamentals of Thought*. London: The Department of Publications Worldwide, 1967.

Huges, H. B. *Trepanation*. Amsterdam: Foundation for Independent Thinking, 1971.

Inglis, Brian. *Fringe Medicine*. London: Faber, 1964.

Jahoda, Gustav. *The Psychology of Superstition*. Harmondsworth: Penguin, 1970.

Jaquin, Noel. *The Hand of Man*. London: Faber, 1933.

Jastrow, Joseph. *Error and Eccentricity in Human Belief*. New York: Dover Publications, 1935.

Kahn, David. *The Code Breakers*. New York: Macmillan, 1968.

Keyhoe, Donald E. *Flying Saucers from Outer Space*. London: Tandem, 1970.

Knight, Damon. *Charles Fort, Prophet of the Unexplained*. London: Gollancz, 1971.

Koestler, Arthur. *The Roots of Coincidence*. London: Hutchinson, 1972.

Kolers, Paul A. 'Experiments in Reading.' *Scientific American*, July 1972.

Kolosimo, Peter. *Not of This World*. London: Sphere, 1970.

Kroll, Paul. 'Evolution Gets the Horse Laugh!' *The Plain Truth*, November 1969.

Kuhn, Thomas S. *The Structure of Scientific Revolutions*. Chicago: U. of C.P., 1970.

Le Corbusier. *Modulor*. London: Faber, 1961.

Lewin, Roger, 'Marijuana on Trial.' *New Scientist*, 8 June 1972.

Lopez, Vincent. *Numerology*. New York: New American Library, 1969.

Lorenzen, Coral. *Flying Saucers: The Startling Evidence of the Invasion from Outer Space*. New York: New American Library, 1962, 1966. Original title: *The Great Flying Saucer Hoax*.

Lorenzen, Coral, and Lorenzen, Jim. *UFOs: The Whole Story*. New York: New American Library, 1969.

MacDougall, Curtis D. *Hoaxes*. New York: Dover Publications, 1958.

Medawar, P. P. *The Art of the Soluble*. Harmondsworth: Penguin, 1967.

Michell, John. 'Glastonbury Abbey: A Solar Instrument of Former Science.' *Glastonbury, a Study in Patterns*. London: Research into Lost Knowledge Organisation, 1969, pp. 31-5.

Ohsawa, George. *Zen Macrobiotics*. Los Angles: The Ohsawa Foundation, 1965.

Patterson, Tom. *100 Years of Spirit Photography*. London: Regency Press, 1965.

Phin, John. *The Seven Follies of Science*. London: Archibald & Constable, 1906.

Pike, Bishop James A. *The Other Side*. London: W. H. Allen, 1969.

Portune, John E. 'How Did the Ark Hold "All Those Animals?" ' *Tomorrow's World*, May 1971.

Powell, Eric F. W. *Kelp*. Rustington, Sussex: Health Science Press, 1968.

Proctor, Richard A. *Myths and Marvels of Astronomy*. London: Longmans Green, 1896.

Rampa, Lobsang. *Chapters of Life*. London: Corgi, 1967.

——. *The Rampa Story*. London: Corgi, 1966.

Rawcliffe, D. H. *Illusions and Delusions of the Supernatural.* New York: Dover Publications, 1959.

Reich, Ilse Ollendorf. *Wilhelm Reich: A Personal Biography.* New York: Avon, 1969.

Reich, Wilhelm. *The Function of the Orgasm.* London: Panther, 1970.

Rhine, J. B. *Extra-Sensory Perception.* London: Faber, 1935.

Robb, Stewart. *Prophecies on World Events by Nostradamus.* New York: Liveright, 1961.

Rodale, Jerome Irving. *Natural Health, Sugar and the Criminal Mind.* New York: Pyramid, 1968.

Roman, Klara G. *Handwriting: A Key to Personality.* London: Routledge & Kegan Paul, 1961.

Rose, Louis. *Faith Healing.* Harmondsworth: Penguin, 1971.

Roszak, Theodore. *The Making of a Counter-Culture.* London: Faber, 1970.

Rushton, W. A. H. 'Serios-Photos: If Contrary to Natural Law, Which Law?' *Journal of the Society for Psychical Research*, vol. 44 no. 736, June 1968, pp. 289-93.

Rycroft, Charles. *Reich.* London: Fontana, 1971.

Sanders, Ed. *The Family.* London: Rupert Hart-Davis, 1972.

Schiller, Lawrence. *The Scavengers and Critics of the Warren Report.*

Schofield, Michael. *The Strange Case of Pot.* Harmondsworth: Penguin, 1971.

Shaw, George Bernard. *Everybody's Political What's What?* London: Constable, 1945.

'Sibyl.' *The Popular Fortune Teller.* London: W. Foulsham, n.d.

Sinclair, Upton. *Mental Radio.* Pasadena: Upton Sinclair, 1930.

Smyth, Charles Piazzi. *Our Inheritance in the Great Pyramid.* London: Daldy, Isbiter, 1877.

Smythies, J. R. ed. *Science and ESP.* London: Routledge & Kegan Paul, 1967.

Soal, S. G., and Bowden, H. T. *The Mind Readers.* London: Faber, 1959.

Steiger, Brad. *Real Ghosts, Restless Spirits and Haunted Minds.* London: Tandem, 1968.

Steiger, Brad, and Whritenour, Joan. *New UFO Breakthrough.* London: Tandem, 1968.

Taylor, John. *The Great Pyramid: Why Was It Built? And Who Built It?* London: 1859.

Tchernine, Odette. *The Yeti.* London: Neville Spearman, 1970.

Teilhard de Chardin, Pierre. *The Phenomenon of Man.* London: Collins, 1959.

Tomas, Andrew. *We Are Not the First*. London: Souvenir Press, 1971.

Tonsley, Cecil. *Honey for Health*. London: Tandem, 1969.

Trobridge, George. *Swedenborg, Life and Teaching*. London: Swedenborg Society, 1945.

Velikovsky, Immanuel. *Worlds in Collision*. New York: Dell, 1967.

Wall, Pat. 'An Eye on the Needle.' *New Scientist*, 20 July 1972.

Wendt, Herbert. *After the Deluge*. London: Paladin, 1970.

West, John Anthony, and Toonden, Jan Gerhard. *The Case for Astrology*. London: Macdonald, 1970.

Wilhelm, Richard, trans. *The I Ching or Book of Changes*. Rendered into English by Cary F. Baynes. London: Routledge & Kegan Paul, 1968. Foreword by C. G. Jung.

Index